GLIMPSES of
GLORY

From the Garden of Eden to Jesus' Glorious Return,
A Cosmic Collision of Biblical Truth, Exploding to Life
Upon the Tapestry of the Mind and Soul

GLIMPSES *of*
GLORY

CARL GALLUPS
Critically Acclaimed Bestselling Author

Foreword by Derek Gilbert
Host of Skywatch TV and Bestselling Author

DEFENDER

CRANE, MO

Glimpses of Glory
By Carl Gallups

Defender Publishing
Crane, MO 65633
© 2021 Thomas Horn

All Rights Reserved. Published 2021.
Printed in the United States of America.

ISBN: 9781948014526

A CIP catalog record of this book is available from the Library of Congress.

Cover design by Jeffrey Mardis.

~⁀

For my dad, Dr. Bill Gallups. One of the greatest fans of my books, and a consistent source of resolve that this one should be written.

Also for my two beloved sisters, Beth and Brenda, as well as our baby brother and precious mom—Paul and Holly—who have both now passed "beyond the veil."

ACKNOWLEDGMENTS

"Thank you!" to my precious wife, Pam. She is my rock, my reason for getting up each morning, the fresh breath of each new day, and God's most precious gift to me in this earthly life. She is also the first reviewer, advisor, and critic of all my books. I am, indeed, a blessed man to have you by my side as we walk through this journey of life together.

My sincere appreciation is given to my editor, Angie Peters. Through her amazing skills and gifts she always manages to turn my initially cluttered labor of love into books that so many seem to enjoy. Thank you, Angie. You are amazing. You make me look far better than I deserve.

I cannot say enough about the talent of Jeffrey Mardis. Every cover he has designed for my Defender Publishing books has garnered consistently high praise from readers. The outpouring of accolades concerning his work on those covers are often the very first compliments I receive. Thanks Jeffrey. Your talent is God-given, and stunning.

To Tom and Nita Horn of Defender Publishing, and the entire Defender and Skywatch TV staff. You took a chance on me years ago.

Not only do we still work together, but now, I truly consider you and your family to be among the dearest friends in my life! What a blessing of the Lord you are to me and my family.

I also extend a word of my deepest gratitude to my treasured and precious friend, Messianic Rabbi Zev Porat (www.messiahofisraelministries.com). The story of how we met is an amazing and remarkably supernatural one. You can read that account for yourself in a previous Defender book that we coauthored, titled *The Rabbi, the Secret Message, and the Identity of Messiah*. Without his graciously shared insight into several of his deepest biblical revelations—from the mind of one who was born steeped in Orthodox traditions and speaking Hebrew as his first language—I might not have been able to bring several relatively hidden biblical truths to explosive life within the pages of *Glimpses of Glory*. Thank you Zev!

CONTENTS

Part Seventeen: Final Glimpse

FOREWORD

If you've ever had the pleasure of hearing Carl Gallups speak, you already know that he's been blessed with a gift. Words are tools for communicating ideas and emotions, and Carl wields language with the skill of an artisan.

This is true of his writing as well. In his previous books, Carl illustrated biblical truths with vignettes that bring readers into the scene, helping us better appreciate the wonder of God's plan to restore humankind to His family.

It seems backward, but concepts like sin, salvation, and redemption seem more real when they're conveyed through stories. In his new book, *Glimpses of Glory*, Carl takes readers on a journey into the past, spotlighting key inflection points in history so that we can better understand our future.

From Eden to John's visions of the end times, Carl Gallups paints images of God's handiwork on the canvas of human history—pictures of glory, but also of the human failings and frailty that make His ultimate victory all the more powerful.

Through his gift, Carl takes you into the Garden, where Adam and Eve encountered the *nachash*, an enchantingly beautiful, serpentine being who schemed to establish his own kingdom above that of the Creator's. He places you inside the ark, describing the horror of Noah's family at the agonized cries of their neighbors struggling in vain to survive the deluge by clinging to the boat. And he shares with you the anguish of our Savior as He struggled with His human emotions—and the goading of the tempter—on the night He was betrayed.

> He looks back over His shoulder at His slumbering disciples, far away in the shadows, nestled under the mammoth olive trees. They are sleeping like children, without a care in the world. His lips begin to tremble as He fights back more tears. The spectacle of His sleeping companions reminds Him.… He is still alone. So very, very alone.

We've heard and read these stories before. As powerful as the biblical accounts are, however, they are brief, mainly intended to convey historical truth. Carl has added color and dimension to the details recorded by the prophets and apostles, careful not to stray from the facts while bringing the scenes into focus.

Storytelling is a wonderful tool for conveying spiritual truths. Again, that may seem counterintuitive. As the author of two novels, I can attest that some object to the use of fiction to share the hope we have in Christ. *Glimpses of Glory* is not fiction, but the artful use of imagination and language to bring the Bible to life.

This is, after all, why Jesus used parables to illustrate the spiritual truths He taught during His ministry. He wired us from the beginning to understand and appreciate the world around us through the art and beauty of stories.

It's a beautiful tactic, really. The enemy has weaponized Hollywood against us. But unlike mainstream depictions of Bible stories that twist events to serve politically correct, twenty-first-century environmental or social-justice narratives, Carl has turned the enemy's stratagem around. *Glimpses of Glory* shows you biblically accurate portrayals of the actors, both human and divine, through whom God has worked since He placed Adam in the Garden.

As a man with a pastor's heart, Carl's calling is to use every tool at his disposal so the gospel message isn't just delivered, it's *received. Glimpses of Glory* makes God's love for us, even in our rebellion, come alive.

—Derek Gilbert, host of SkywatchTV and best-selling author

GLIMPSES *of* GLORY

This…was the first sign Jesus gave, the first **glimpse
of his glory**. And his disciples believed in him.
JOHN 2:11, *THE MESSAGE*; EMPHASIS ADDED

For presently we see through a glass in obscurity;
but then, face to face. Presently, I know in part;
but then I will know fully, even as I have been fully known.
1 CORINTHIANS 13:14, BEREAN'S LITERAL BIBLE; EMPHASIS ADDED

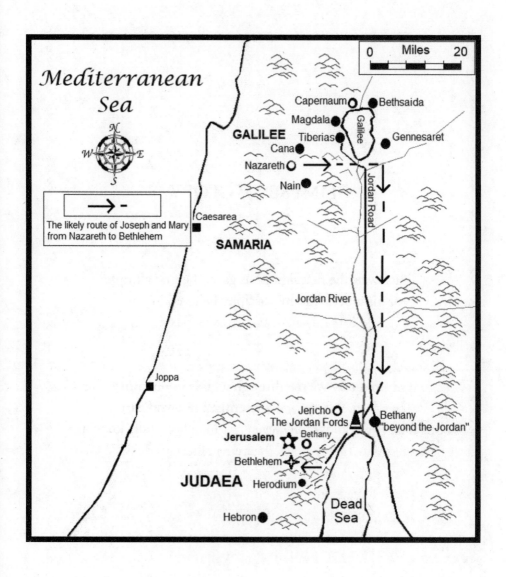

Mediterranean
Sea

The likely route of Joseph and Mary
from Nazareth to Bethlehem

GALILEE

SAMARIA

JUDAEA

Mediterranean
Sea

Capernaum
Bethsaida
Magdala
Galilee
Tiberias
Gennesaret
Cana
Nazareth
Nain

Caesarea

Joppa

Jordan River

Jordan Road

Jericho
The Jordan Fords
Bethany
"beyond the Jordan"
Jerusalem
Bethany
Bethlehem
Herodium

Hebron

Dead
Sea

Miles
0   20

PROLOGUE

A WORD FROM THE AUTHOR

Over the years, a good number of readers from around the world have indicated that they particularly enjoyed the portions of my past books in which I inserted them—*in the theater of the mind*—directly into various biblical encounters through an immersive-narrative style of writing.

At the same time, a sizeable portion of them also asked me to revisit the topic of multiple dimensions. They were especially interested in how that subject relates to the perspective it brings to the quickly changing prophetic world in which we're currently living.

Those two requests sparked a new idea: Why not emphasize the pervasive biblical truth of multidimensional realities by weaving it together with a narrative-styled presentation of the Scriptures that would be similar to reading a novel? After giving the idea considerable reflection, I came to believe a book of that nature might actually give depth to the central story of the Word of God beyond almost anything most students of the Bible might have imagined. I finally developed a clear picture of where I wanted to go with the idea. With the Lord's help, that's what I've tried to accomplish here.

I assure you, this is not just another book about the life of Jesus. It is much more. It focuses on key sections of the Bible that summarize its entire message, from Genesis to Revelation...with its central focus upon Jesus and His absolute command over the multiple dimensions.

Glimpses of Glory is based upon the true and contextually interpreted Word of God. In the narrative sections that follow, I have endeavored to stay in line with the biblical text, as well as the foundational truths that the Bible declares. I've also attempted to connect the fundamental dots of Scripture that tell the whole story of the Word, *in a nutshell*...all the way through to the last pages of Revelation, and even beyond.

Some readers might recognize certain parts of this book as being similar to what you've seen in several of my previous works. While it's true that I have indeed drawn upon select material from the preceding eleven books I've written, I've also greatly enhanced those passages, as well as arranged them in chronological order. Additionally, I've included a large portion of brand-new material in order to properly tie together the bigger picture.

In several selections of the narrative, I've filled in the details of important backstories by adding a few invented characters, as well as a smorgasbord of fictional—but contextually plausible—dialogues that keep the story moving forward, and engaging. However, nothing has been added or enhanced that maligns the doctrinal truths of the Bible. Any artistic license I've employed was designed only to augment what I believe to be the clear intent of the overall scriptural message.

In short, I'm asking you to simply enjoy the adventure and trust that it will all come together into several powerful explosions of biblical revelation as you follow the path of the saga all the way to the end.

All I know is *this*—practically every time I've presented the various truths that follow, lives have been dramatically changed for the glory of the Lord Jesus Christ. It is my earnest prayer that the perspectives you'll uncover through the following pages will accomplish that same kind of outcome in your own life.

I am honored that you've chosen to take this journey with me. In light of the startling and unprecedentedly prophetic days in which we are currently living, I'm convinced the adventure that awaits will be one you'll not regret taking.

Neither, I believe, will it be one you'll soon forget.

What no eye has seen, what no ear has heard, and what no human mind has conceived—the things God has prepared for those who love him—**these are the things God has revealed to us by his Spirit.** (1 Corinthians 2:9–10; emphasis added)

PART ONE

Before the Foundation of the World

Scriptural Backdrop:

He is the Lamb who was slain from the creation of the world. (Revelation 13:8)

He was chosen before the creation of the world, but was revealed in these last times for your sake. (1 Peter 1:20)

1

FIRST KINGDOM

Bethlehem, about 4 BC

The first cry of a newborn baby boy has just shattered the tranquility of another Bethlehem night.

Normally, this wouldn't be an unusual occurrence. Many baby boys have been born in Bethlehem before this night. At this moment, though, there are only two people on the planet who truly understand why this particular child is so inexpressibly different from all those who came before Him, or from any who will come after.

Of course, at this point, there are still things about Him that even they can't fathom. Most of those details will be revealed decades from now. Tonight, however, the first natal tones of the newborn have fallen upon their ears alone…and that's all that matters. He has entered their arms safely, and Mom is fine.

Also, at this very moment—unbeknownst to them—a company of Bethlehem's shepherds are running across the fields…headed their way. Until that magnificent surprise arrives at their door, the young parents are immersing themselves in the majesty of these private moments with their son.

As they stand, hands joined, gazing into His tiny, searching eyes, they're overwhelmed by what they *are* privy to—what this occasion *really* means within the scope of all eternity. They alone possess the foundational answer to the mystery of His presence among them. A divine messenger who entered their realm from *behind the veil* told them that much a little over nine months ago.

God's cosmic plan of humanity's salvation had begun, and they were both to become a pivotal part of it.

However, neither the reprobate kingdoms of humanity nor the dark domain of the fallen ones comprehend the significance of what has transpired on this holy night. The arrival of this child has been flawlessly hidden from them. He is nestled away in the obscurity of a seven-hundred-year-old prophecy—lying in this uniquely dedicated manger and guarded by unseen warrior angels.[1]

Thirty-three years from now, the "rulers of this age" will be consumed by an unquenchable rage when they come to recognize that the entire ordeal will have been pulled off without their ability to thwart its coming. It will have been concealed from them! By then, they will understand more fully what actually happened…but, *by then*, it will be far too late to do anything about it.[2]

In the years to come, in the midst of Satan's ever-growing awareness that his stolen domain is, in fact, being targeted by the Creator of the universe, he'll realize that his time is rapidly diminishing with every turn of the calendar's pages. So he'll steel himself and cobble together one vicious attack after another, hoping to somehow derail Heaven's battle plan amidst the chaos of it all. That brand of unmitigated conceit will prove to be the dangling, loose thread of his eventual undoing.

Following is the account of when the saga first commenced…and why this specific Bethlehem night is necessary.

PART TWO

Restoration

Scriptural Backdrop:

Then Jesus went with his disciples to a place called Gethsemane, and he said to them, "Sit here while I go over there and pray." (Matthew 26:36; emphasis added)

But this is how God fulfilled what he had foretold through all the prophets, saying that his Messiah would suffer.... Heaven must receive Him **until the time comes for God to restore everything,** as He promised long ago through His holy prophets. (Acts 3:18–21; emphasis added)

2

TIME AND PLACE

Garden of Gethsemane, Jerusalem, circa AD 30–33

As the nighttime deepens somewhere near the outer walls of Jerusalem, a distraught donkey bellows out a disharmony of mournful protests. Its obnoxious braying is downright bone-jarring. Digging its hooves into the earth, the animal comes to a jolting halt and looks as if it's staring in horror at some ghastly sight right in front of him. In the human realm, there appears to be absolutely nothing there—certainly nothing that should invoke *this* response. Nevertheless, the poor creature seems to be inconsolable.[3]

After several choice words—and a whip—the master gets the animal's begrudging attention. Minutes later, its cantankerous grievances begin to wane. A few more moments pass, and the commotion finally folds into the mixture of all the other sounds of the night.

The crickets once again resume their soothing night songs, having been stunned into silence by the sudden burst of the ruckus. Now Jerusalem's serenity, at last, slips back to a more normal level.

But even while the brief disturbance ensues, most of the city's residents sleep through it. They have no idea of the cosmic clash of kingdoms that's coming to a vicious conjunction…on this very night. That battle is about to commence in a normally serene grove of olive trees.

The grove is located only a short walk across the Kidron Valley just outside the city's East Gate. To get there, one has to first cross over the brook Kidron—an ancient tributary that eventually winds its way down to the Dead Sea. The garden, located immediately across the stream, is known by the locals as Gethsemane.

Right now, the man widely identified as Jesus of Nazareth is in that garden.

He is here in order to recover what is rightfully His.[4]

As He kneels to pray, He knows He has only a little less than a day to live. From this point forward, every moment will prove to be eternally significant.

As far as the *divine reclamation process* goes, the exact location and the precise timing of each subsequent event is vital. Every detail is now in the course of completing its appointed convergence.

This night has been planned from the beginning of time itself.[5] And this spot is not an accidental one. It is here, in Gethsemane, where the defilement began. And it is here, in this garden, where it will begin to come to an end.[6] This is also where the cosmic personage of evil will appear, one last time, to torment Him and again attempt to turn Him from His divine mission.

This prescient evening is a huge part of the reason Jesus covertly entered earth's domain in the first place—through the womb of a woman, and through Bethlehem's obscure corridors—three decades ago.

So, He waits…

Just now, an owl hoots out its ominous drawling tones somewhere nearby, adding to the bleakness of the evening. It's as though the creature is stoically announcing the cosmic duel—shouting its arrival to the world….

The battle for restoration of all things is now underway!

3

THE GARDEN OF AGONY

He tears at the earth as He agonizes, filling His hands with great scoops of dirt.

The evening has finally melted into the depths of an eerie oblivion.

It's that time of the approaching morning when almost nothing virtuous lurks in the shadows. The Passover moon melted behind the hills hours ago. Like a primeval mist, the fog has slipped into the stillness of the night as if it were a serpent easing upon its prey, having first fallen from the canopies above, then slowly gliding through the tall grass, unnoticed…until it's suddenly there.

It will still be another handful of hours before the aureate splashes of the rising sun will spill out across the eastern horizon and bathe the jagged peaks of the surrounding mountains in its sparkling glory. But the arrival of that magnificent exhibition will contradict the treachery that will eventually engulf the day it's announcing.

However, at this moment, in the depths of the garden's eerie darkness, *Heaven's Trap*—in the flesh of a mortal man—is sitting cross-legged beside a massive boulder. He is burdened with an unspeakable grief. With His face buried in his hands, He groans aloud. But no human ear pays attention to the guttural utterance He makes. For now, He's hidden to the earthy world to which He has come, cloaked in the night's shadows.

Jesus eventually unfolds His legs and arranges Himself so He can kneel beside the rock, laying both hands upon it for support. He bows His head in prayer. That singular boulder—now His altar of supplication—is located in the midst of the grove of huge olive trees. It is a well-known place, located at the base of the highest mountain in Jerusalem proper— the Mount of Olives.[7] Oddly, the rock where He now prays looks like an ancient boundary stone of sorts—some kind of signal for all who see it…a sign that this spot might actually be important to Heaven itself.[8]

The Mount of Olives towers over the city below it—appearing as a faithful sentinel—with a perfect view of its legendary Temple Mount. But, that same lofty hill is also infamously known for some of the vilest sacrileges that have ever occurred in the annals of Israel's storied history. It's as though Satan has, over the centuries, turned this place into a monument of mockery—perpetually declaring the dark realm's contempt for Heaven's throne. Tonight, still another abominable chapter is about to be added to its saga.[9]

Jesus shudders as He contemplates the horrors that await Him.

Under normal circumstances, He shouldn't feel so alone…so utterly isolated. After all, He's accompanied by almost a dozen of His closest friends. *But not really.*

Oh, they're here, to be sure—but, at this moment, they're spread out on the ground, heads pillowed by rolled-up garments. They've been asleep for a while—off in the distance, hidden in the shadows of the fog-laden garden. They had promised to stay awake with Him throughout the night, and to pray. They're keeping neither of those promises. They had started well. But that was the end of it…after the first hour, they had fallen into a deep sleep.

It seems His closest friends still don't understand the gravity of the events that will soon unfold before them. However, three days from today, they will see it more clearly. But, because of their lack of resolve tonight, they will later have to nurse immense regrets and haunting memories. They will then remember that they actually *slept*—during the most important moments of prayer in the entire saga of fallen humanity's sorry history.

The loneliness of Jesus' grief has grown increasingly unbearable. A thick heaviness settles throughout the garden. The enormity of the moment has taken on a life of its own—becoming almost palpable. He lets out another groan under the burden of it. The weight of thousands of years of humanity's rebellious degradation has been strapped to His shoulders. If there was ever a moment when He might truly be tempted to give up the ordeal...it is this one.

Jesus knows what awaits Him over the course of the coming day. The divine plan was ordained before Adam sucked in his first breath of life. Soon, within the next few hours, all the horrors of the dark kingdom will be unleashed upon Him with a voracious and intensely personal fury. But He *has* to submit to it, every last humiliating and excruciating bit of it, if the trap is to work.

But...maybe there's still some other way to accomplish the plan?

He already knows the answer to this flesh-darkened temptation. But the question races through His mind anyway. It has been doing so for days, pounding away at Him, like a mallet's strike upon the steely heads of iron spikes. *Pa-pinggg! Pa-pinggg! Pa-pinggg!*

That's when He hears the vile, serpent-like seduction again:

"Deliver yourself from here! You have the power to do so...just *sss*ay the word! Bow to me, and I can give you the kingdom*sss* of thi*ss* world! There's no need for you to suffer like thi*ss*!"

Jesus shakes His head in an attempt to dispel the abominable enticements. They slash and claw at His soul, as if a ravenous lion has just begun tearing away at its newly captured prey.

Father, give me your strength...give me courage to complete the plan, to take this to the very end!

So far, the divine strategy of redemption's plan has worked. There have been a few close calls over the last three years, to be sure. But everything has flowed right into the filthy mire of this particularly necessary moment. This is the point of no return—for Him, as well as for *Nachash*.[10]

That old serpent[11] is mere moments away from being entangled in the secreted snare that has been laid for him. His dripping arrogance has brought him right up to the point of sealing his ultimate demise. He just doesn't know it yet. Oh, how far Nachash has plunged! How unspeakably and desperately wicked he has grown! The original guardian cherub of Eden's Garden is now the despicable *fallen one.*[12]

The night shift of the Sanhedrin's Temple guard will be arriving soon. It shouldn't be much longer now…

The next words Jesus hears slip upon Him as slight undertones of carefully crafted enticements. They originate from deep within the recesses of His own mind. But He knows the voice is real. The words are spoken from a certain cosmic being, one that possesses interdimensional vocal chords, with murmurs that are able to penetrate the mind of a mortal and even interrupt the prayers of the righteous. They are genuinely seductive words—sodden with repulsive condescension, laden with diabolic power.

"You don't have to do thi*sss*!" the voice whispers. "You *don't!*"

There it is again!

He falls back to His face and prays. He claws at the earth as He agonizes, filling His hands with great scoops of dirt slowly sifting through His fingers.

Father, please give me more strength! My soul is overwhelmed with sorrow!

His closest friends are about a stone's throw away, oblivious to everything that's happening to Him. Even now, He can hear their wheezing breaths and rattled snorting.

You couldn't stay awake with me to watch, and pray? Just for a while?

4

THE SLUMBERING ONES

He knows the words are true.... But to live them out—*in human flesh*—
that is a different matter altogether.

Only a handful of hours earlier, Yeshua[13] and His disciples had eaten their fill. They were in a privately secured upper room in downtown Jerusalem. It was another Passover...another joyous feast. How He loved to partake with them in those ancient meals of remembrance.

But this Passover had been different from all the others before it, vitally so. He had explained to them what this evening's celebration truly meant, its deepest meanings—how it had always pointed to Him and what He was getting ready to do, and also what the lessons of it would mean to them in the years to come. But, had they really understood the depth of the explanation? *No. Not entirely.* It was obvious they hadn't. That understanding would come later.

~

Warm tears spill from His eyes. The overflow of His grief streams down His cheeks and splatters into the soil beneath Him. Once again, He leans heavily against the huge rock.

He sucks in a deep breath, letting it out in a long, husky moan, as He looks up into the star-splashed heavens. Its canopy of countless glittering pinpoints looks like sparkling diamonds spilled out upon a sheet of glass. The beauty of what He beholds is breathtaking. But what He sees through His human eyes is nothing compared to what, one day in the future, will be revealed—after the rolling up of the dimensional scrolls... the final unveiling of what was there all along! It lay just behind the cosmic curtain that had been lowered in Eden eons ago.[14]

No human eye has ever seen the glory that is to come. No mortal mind has even come close to conceiving its majesty. *But He knows*. He alone spoke the entirety of it into existence in the very beginning. Oh, how He longs to show His dearest friends just a glimpse of the splendor that is to come! And that time *will* come—but today isn't the day.

⤚⤙

Right now, He aches for the luxury of a little rest. It's been more than twenty-four hours since He last enjoyed that sweet release. And, it's been weeks since He's had a good night's sleep. From this point forward, He won't taste of that pleasure again. His eyelids grow heavy with grief, weighted down with a cosmic burden that no human has ever carried or could even comprehend.

Can He allow Himself the treat of a short nap...even for only a moment? *Surely a little innocent rest would do no harm.* Just then, His eyes slam shut, startling Him. His neck quickly stiffens. He catches His head, at the last instant, as it almost drops to His chest.

So...here is yet another enticement? Even the modest thought of the delightful bliss of a little respite—only the simple resting of His eyes and soul—have now become an unrelenting fleshly allurement. But, He *must* not. He must stay awake. He must stay alert.

He looks back over His shoulder at His slumbering disciples a good distance away, in the shadows, nestled under the mammoth olive trees. They are sleeping like children, without a care in the world. His lips begin to tremble as He fights back more tears. The spectacle of His sleeping companions reminds Him…He is still alone. So very, very alone.

If they only knew what is just down the road for them and their families. *How I love them, Father! I know that you will not yet remove them from the tribulation of this world, but, please…Father…protect them in the midst of the coming evil.*

With the back of His hand, He wipes more sweat from His forehead as He continues to agonize. It is a form of grief that ruthlessly rips at His soul, torturing His mind beyond any hope of immediate relief. In this body of earthly human flesh, He has never felt anything like this before. But, He knows there is more to come. Much more.

He looks down at His hand, having just pulled it away from His face. The dampness is bright red. Under the traumatic stress of what He knows awaits Him, tiny capillaries in His temples have burst open. Now, as a result, great drops of bloody sweat continue to trickle down His face. [15]

Where are His dearest friends when He needs them—especially now! *Couldn't you stay awake with me?* He utters the question aloud, knowing that no one actually hears His words. They're still snoring.

He struggles for a proper breath…and again bellows out an unearthly sound of agonized grief. But, He presses on, remembering how far He's journeyed to get here. *The strong man's house will soon be plundered. Paradise will be restored, and Satan and his emissaries will be banished forever.*

He allows Himself a brief moment of inward celebration at the thought of the reclamation of Paradise. This, in spite of the fact that the terrorizing flashes of what is just around the corner of this day continue to pummel His thoughts.

If I can only hold out. Help me Father! Strengthen me…so that I am able to accomplish the task for which I've come!

⁓◦

The atmosphere around Him sparks. He knows what it is, and He knows *who* it is. In that instant, He feels a hand upon His shoulder. It's a familiar touch. A loving hand—bringing with it a divinely comforting grip.

He turns and looks. One of His own, created before the foundation of the earth, a true and obedient *bene elohim*, stands at His side.[16] He has come in response to Yeshua's agonizing prayers. This messenger of Heaven has slipped, undetected, into earth's domain, from just behind the separating veil.[17]

Jesus beams through watery eyes. *Here is a friendly face! A friend who is not asleep!* The two grasp each other by the hand. The angel returns His greeting. "Your prayers are heard. You are not alone," he assures the Suffering One.

When Jesus doesn't answer in words, the angel continues. "Give the command and this ordeal will be over. If it is your will, we'll strike down those who are coming for you, every single one of them! I have more than twelve legions of your *holy ones* at my side. Just behind the veil. Just in case! Simply provide the order…"[18]

Jesus firms His grip on the angel's hand. That grasp, and the look upon His face, tells the heavenly servant: *That will not be necessary. This mission must be carried through…to the end.* As a loyal subject before his beloved King, the divine being lowers his head in obedience, understanding the unspoken signal he has just received. His tears splat into the dirt as he bows.

The angel speaks again. "Then I must leave," he says. "The prince of this world approaches. He must not know that I was here."

And then…*he's gone.* In a mere twinkling, Jesus is alone again—His hand still outstretched where it once held the hand of His servant.

Yeshua looks up towards the sparkling heavens and whispers, "I am now ready, Father. This must be done."

Those words had been the heartfelt focus of Jesus' prayers throughout the night. But to actually live out the supplications—*in human flesh*—that is a different matter altogether. Those utterances, that goal, no matter how beautiful—or how necessary—will also come with an enormously agonizing price.[19]

What is waiting just ahead will necessitate the spilling of blood.

Lots of blood. And not just *any* blood.

5

THE GRAND ENTRANCE

There is a directness and firmness in the intonation
of His voice that is uncharacteristic.

The serpent's appearance in Gethsemane's garden is first accompanied by
an atmospheric flash of light and then a sharp, popping noise. It sounds
like the soft crack of a small whip.[20]

A slight, eerie breeze glides through the treetops, lightly swirling the
leaves. Nachash has just entered earth's domain. He has come from the
other side, from another realm…unseen by the eyes of mortal men.[21]

The foreboding presence is now somewhere behind Yeshua, in the
murky shadows. He has known the *prince of vileness and filth* would show
up. In fact, He has been counting on it. This is all a part of the trap.

The sulfuric odor of Nachash's depravity permeates the night air—as
a suffocating presence begins to envelope Jesus. At this moment—as He
still kneels at the rock—He hears the familiar voice.

"*Hmm.*" Nachash clucks his tongue as he approaches from behind,
his arrogance dripping with every word that slithers from his lips. "So,
we're together again…*one more time*? Just like I thought it would be. Just
as I told you! Isn't that right…*Son of God?*"

Jesus offers no reply.

"I promised I would see you again. Didn't I? And, I always keep my promises…"

The words are silky. They are hypnotizing and musical. Almost irresistible.

"Didn't I try to warn you? I figured it would eventually come to *this*."

He spreads his arms open wide as if indicating that the agony of "this" is actually Jesus' own fault. He clucks his tongue several more times, then shakes his head with closed eyes, feigning empathy. But the look on his face betrays the underlying masquerade. Everything is always a dramatic ruse with this one.

A slight groan is Jesus' only response.

Nachash continues, "You have to admit, though, I actually gave you the opportunity to skip all thi*ss*…did I not? Don't you remember?" The serpent waits for an answer. Jesus offers none.

"Of course you remember!" Satan grins, answering for Him. "But you wouldn't listen, would you? You could have saved yourself from thi*ss* dreadful me*ss*. But…*no…*"

Jesus leans heavier into the rock as the ground beneath Him trembles slightly. Even creation itself groans as it struggles to bear up under the burden of the serpent's ancient perversion.

Jesus lowers His head again.

Nachash continues his taunt. *"Instead,* you just had to make your point…didn't you? Well, you've certainly taken your stand now! You've had your say for three full years. Yes—ye*sss*, your power is from Heaven's throne. Okay then. Have it your way. Everyone know*sss* what you're claiming now. Everyone has seen your wondrous display*sss* of heavenly might, and your uncanny wizardry. I must say, even I've been jealous of it, from time to time. Everybody's talking about it!"

Nachash persists, "But, if that's all the validation you require, *the acclaim of the people*—well…I can easily arrange it for you. In fact, that's one of my most cherished specialties!"

Satan cocks his head as he continues with his alluring offers. "Why, I'll have everyone bowing and scraping at your feet in no time…if that's what you *really* desire. It's quite simple to manipulate them. They're like naïve little sheep. I can show you how to do it, if you want. It's really not all that difficult. What *sssay* you?" The serpent sneers, waiting for a response.

Just like in the Judean wilderness three years back, Jesus refuses to acknowledge Satan's presence. Those earlier challenges had been equally vile. They deserved no response then, and there will be no banter with this profanely rebellious cherub[22] on this occasion either.

Jesus doesn't turn to look—even though He can feel, down the back of His neck, the heat of Nachash's presence. The fallen one is standing right over Him, just behind Him. The vileness of his rancid breath reeks of the stench of death.

"I'll make this offer just once more, but thi*ss* is the last time I'll do it," Nachash hisses. "*Here*—I'll hold out my offer of indulgence. *Take it!* Then all of your suffering will be over!"

Jesus sees the hand.

"*There*…you see?" Nachash unfurls his gnarly appendage, dangling it across His shoulder. "Am I not merciful? Ye*sss*?" the serpent smugly hisses. There is even something serpent-like about the movement of his hand and arm.

Jesus turns His head away from it.

Father! If it is possible! Please…take this cup from me!

"Oh, come now! Don't be ridiculou*sss*! You won't even take my hand? That's a bit rude, wouldn't you say?"

Jesus kneels there, silently.

"*Who* are you anyway?" Nachash seductively whispers, while scanning Jesus up and down with his penetrating gaze. "*What* are you? And, where is your *Father* now? He appears to be awkwardly silent, don't you think? I've not heard Him answer your pleas yet. *Have you?*"

Jesus looks straight ahead. He still has not uttered a word to Nachash.

"Okay, okay," the serpent persists. "I'll make my offer just one more time. Simply bow to me as the prince of this world and I'll give you all the kingdoms of the earth! After all, they are *mine* to give. Isn't that ultimately what you want, anyway? A kingdom of your own? We can rule together! At no cossst to you! No ludicrousss price to pay. No 'cup' to drink. No one has to 'lay down their life' for anything—or for *anyone*.[23]

"What is your answer?

"What will it be?"

6

REVERSING THE CURSE

His heart is steeled for the gruesome mission ahead.

Jesus knows the precise moment has finally arrived.

It's time to reverse the original blasphemy of Eden's Garden.[24] On that fateful primordial day, in dark ages past, Satan, in his insolent rebellion, had effectively declared—along with Adam and Eve at his side, "*Not your will, but ours!*" In that moment of ancient debauchery, they had plunged themselves into a cesspool of despicable disobedience. It was there where Jesus' heart had first been crushed…and betrayed.

Here He is once more.[25] In just a few more moments, He will again suffer heartrending disloyalty…by Satan, who has entered the body of a man[26] and even now is on his way to the Garden of Gethsemane to kiss Him on the cheek—and to gloat.

Jesus once again speaks. This time, however, there is a resolve in His voice that will unnerve the evil one. But, like before, His words are not spoken to Satan.

Nevertheless, Father…not my will, but yours.

Streams of sweat pool together into larger rivulets, spilling down His face, dripping off the tip of His nose, and splattering into the dirt. It is

25

sweat that is still mixed with His blood. Yeshua knows that, with those words, He has sealed His own fate. There will be no turning back.

Satan snarls in a cavernously derisive tone, "*You fool!* Have it your way then! You have no idea what you've just forfeited!"

As Satan levels those words of threat, Jesus thinks: *And you have no idea what you've just stepped into.*

Satan positions himself in front of Jesus, glaring at Him through slatted, serpent-like pupils—His face just inches away from the Suffering One—slowly swaying from side to side, like a cobra ready to strike. The foggy mist envelops his repulsive countenance, settling upon him like an aberrant kingly robe...his breath sour and revolting.

"Look at you! Look what you've become! You claim to be able to save others, but you can't even save yourself from what's coming now, I promise you *that*! You'll *not* 'save' yourself!"

Jesus still doesn't acknowledge his presence.

"Well then!" Satan continues. "If this is the road you insist on traveling, then I *do* have a very special cup prepared for you, at the end of it—and you *will* drink from it, deeply! I'll personally see to it. I'll be there the whole time. *Watching. Enjoying.* Relishing each long and dreadful moment of it! If you will not join me...then you most assuredly will be destroyed!"

His threats persist. "The whole thing has already been arranged, just in case you are insolent enough to refuse my compassionate offer. But I can assure you of this, you'll lament this moment—the night you declined my hand." He pauses again, and glares—but only for a moment, then he continues the pummeling.

"I promise! Before this new day is over, there'll be a multitude of times when your indescribable suffering will bring back memories of this very moment, and these very words, and the horrendous mistake you're making! Then you'll wish you had been more gracious to me, and *grateful* for the offer I've held out to you!"

Jesus raises His head and looks directly into the serpent's eyes. Nachash slowly turns away, unable to meet the challenge of holding this first experience of a soul-penetrating gaze from the Suffering One.

With his eyes still directed away from Yeshua, he spits his words into the air, "*Pffft!* I've had enough of this!" Satan expels the declaration like a defeated bully on a schoolyard playground. He moves toward Jesus, glaring at Him, then raises his hand over his head.

When he does, the air *pops*. The ground rumbles again. There is a slight folding of the atmosphere—barely discernible to the human eye. Sparkles of a glitter-like substance fall in front of Jesus and melt into the ground.

The rumbling stops. Nachash is gone—but only temporarily. Jesus knows the serpent will be back to taunt Him again before the day is over.

⁓

This is it. No turning back. No more struggling. No more doubt.

Jesus wipes His brow again, His sweat bloodier than ever.

He stands from His place of torment and makes His way back to the sleeping disciples, His heart steeled for the gruesome mission ahead. There are still convergences that need to take place, more meetings to be endured.

Jesus slips through the shadows like a whisper and stands directly over John. After a few brief moments, He stoops and eases His hand down upon the beloved disciple's shoulder. He nudges the young man—just a couple of gentle prods—until he stirs. John opens his eyes as though he is awakening from an all-night drinking binge, both fists twisting in his eye sockets, trying to clear the haze of deep sleep.

"John, why do you sleep? And why *now*, of all times?"

Jesus' countenance startles him. There is a firmness in the intonation of His voice that is uncharacteristic. His face glistens with a reddish hue. What happened while Jesus was praying? *What has He seen? Has someone attacked Him? Why is blood on His face, and hands?* John is suddenly embarrassed. And…afraid.

"Get up, John. Wake the others, and pray—so that you won't fall into temptation."

"What do you mean, Lord? What happened to you? What *temptation*? Why are you bleeding? *Who*—" He was cut off midsentence by Jesus' sudden uplifted hand of warning.

Yeshua nods toward Jerusalem. "Never mind that now," He says. "The betrayer draws near. Satan approaches—and he's inside the body of a man."

John turns around to look, afraid of what he might see.

What he beholds are the approaching torches. The flames bob about in the darkness like a swarm of gigantic fireflies flittering in the night. And he can also, just now, begin to make out the forms of the Temple guards who are carrying the fiery harbingers.

The guards draw ever closer, picking up their cadence as they come; their conglomerated footsteps are sounding more like a rushing military troop.

It's obvious that this looming horde is headed straight for *them*!

There are dozens of them—and Judas is leading the way.

THE SIXTH HOUR

It has been three torturous hours since the first spikes
slammed into their hands and feet.

The sunrise has, indeed, brought forth a splendid day. But it's going to eventually become a dreadfully sweltering one. There's not a cloud to be seen, only crystal blue sky and an orange fireball in the heavens blasting down its heating rays upon the earth below.

Hours ago, another bustling crowd of curious onlookers scrambled through the narrow streets of Jerusalem, then darted outside the city gate, following the throng that was already ahead of them. Jerusalem was alive with swarms of people, visitors from all over the Roman Empire. They were of every shape, dress, skin color, and language. It was the week of the Feast of Unleavened Bread, commencing with the Passover meal at the sunset of this day.

But this morning, a tantalizing report had spread throughout the city like an out-of-control wildfire. That vigor had been set ablaze by the Sanhedrin's lackeys. Another Roman spectacle of gore was soon to unfold. This one had been rumored to be like no other before it.

Something had been whispered about a famous rabbi being crucified today. He had been arrested deep in the darkness of last night, and
had apparently been tried and convicted in today's early-morning hours at
Caiaphas' home office. Governor Pilate had even become involved, along
with the entire Sanhedrin Council of Jewish elders. The gossiping pilgrims murmured amongst themselves: *Whoever that poor rabbi is, this can't
bode well for him!*

So the curious hordes scurried toward Golgotha, a place familiar to
practically everyone in that region. Horrible things had happened there,
all the way back to the days of King David and Solomon. The people, for
ages, had nicknamed it the *Place of the Skull.*[27]

A young man named Jacob was among those in the crowd. He had
traveled for several days to be a part of the Jerusalem Passover celebration.[28] He unexpectedly became caught up in the conglomerated spirit of
morbid fascination and bloodlust. Later, he would be overwhelmed with
guilt—laden with an unshakable indignity—for having so easily rushed
to the scene. *Why had he felt such a drawing to something so despicable?*

Crucifixions were certainly not uncommon, particularly around Jerusalem and throughout the surrounding countryside—and especially not
with the Romans in charge. After all, they were the imperial overlords of
the region. But this execution was different. This one involved three men:
two common thieves and, of all things, a beloved rabbi. Or at least that's
what some called Him. Others among the throngs called Him *Yeshua Ha
Mashiach*—Jesus, the Messiah.

The *Messiah*? Really? If so, why would they so easily acquiesce to the
demand for crucifying their Messiah? Little about this day made much
sense.

Jacob had arrived, ascending the famous trail that led to the site just
as the soldiers were pounding in the first spikes and the initial panicked
cries of agony had been let loose from the first two victims. They were
convicted thieves.

With the slamming of the big hammers, their pitiful squeals and animal-like grunts had reverberated across the hills and bounced off the walls

of the great city. What Jacob eventually witnessed that day shook him to the core of his soul…and would haunt him for the rest of his life.

⤳

But right now…it is the sixth hour.[29] It has been three torturous hours since the first spikes smashed into their hands and feet. At this very moment, an eerie and thick darkness is falling over the land. This event is so seemingly unnatural that the crowd is becoming unnerved by it; they murmur amongst themselves and point toward the heavens.[30]

Up and down. Up and down, the three helpless men on the hillside crosses pump for each life-sustaining breath. They pitifully strain against the spikes that are buried deep within the sinews and muscles of their feet and hands. They have no choice. They are slowly suffocating. They have to push up to get a quick breath of air into their burning, screaming lungs. There will be no mercy—no relief—for them on this day, only a wickedly humiliating and asphyxiating death. Slowly, *very slowly*, they will miserably suffocate, and die.

A small group shuffles their way forward from the crowd; they attempt to gather just below the one in the middle—but are forced back by the Roman soldiers. For now, only a few women and a couple of men are allowed to be in that spot. They presently stand right under the feet of *that one*. They sob as they stand there.

Then, the one they call Yeshua speaks up. Faintly, and agonizingly, He mumbles the words: "Woman—behold your son."

Moans of inconsolable grief pour from the women in the group beneath Him as He utters the words—words that are guttural, rattling with the amalgamated fluids rising from His tortured throat and lungs. The men in the group hang their heads—cupping their faces in their hands, hiding their quivering lips and pushing back their cascading tears with the folds of their already-dampened sleeves…their beards soaked with their grief.

Mary, the mother of Jesus, reaches up and attempts to caress His feet as one might comfort an infant son—but failing to reach Him, to actually touch Him, her hands shaking uncontrollably as she stretches towards her son, she faints into the dust. She is gently revived by her entourage and is escorted back among the front edges of the throng of onlookers.

Some claim this Yeshua actually predicted—even longed for—this moment. *Ridiculous!* How could anyone desire such a death? And in the presence of His own mother and closest friends? A madman? *Surely!* What purpose would a "predicted" and unspeakably gruesome death serve, anyway?

Others say He had entered the city only a few days earlier in a boisterous procession. The multitudes had lined the streets that day shouting that He was their Messiah, the divine Son of God...the son of David. He had arrived through the East Gate, riding on the back of a donkey. His entrance was befitting of a king. The people lined the road in front of Him with their cloaks and palm branches.[31]

The divine Son of God? The Messiah? Apparently tens of thousands had thought so. *Silly zealots. I wonder what they're thinking now.*

Fanatics? *Yes.* And probably just a bunch of simpletons. Someone was constantly looking for a messiah. But their so-called messiahs never came. They never would. The Romans would simply eliminate them—one by one. *When would these simple, obstinate people learn the Roman lesson?*

The cries continue to emanate from amongst the gathering crowd. Taunting. Cajoling. "Come down *now*, if you can—*if you dare*—if you really are the Messiah!"

The Messiah? Surely not! Save Himself? Doubtful!

Jacob has never heard of anyone coming down off a Roman cross. Not a single person! That feat is, of course, an impossibility. It isn't going to happen this time, either. He is certain of it. Not this day. *Not ever.* The deed has gone much too far for anyone to be "saved" now.

The audience still grows. They have been attracted to this spot by the occasional roars of the people and their reverberating echoes that consistently flow to the crowds below.

Two thieves and an infamous religious personality. Those are the ones hanging on the crosses before them on this day. But—why such a crowd?

Especially for *these* three pitiful ones? Or, has the throng actually gathered…just for *the one?* The one in the middle?

This *Jesus of Nazareth* had come very close to bringing the wrath of Rome down upon all their heads—at least, that's what their religious rulers had told them. What a horror that consequence could prove to be! If the threat had come to pass, then that might very well be some of *them* up there, nailed to a cross—or it could even be members of their own families! Even the thought of it was unthinkable, unbearable.

Jacob had seen the unspeakable results of those kinds of spectacles on full display, lining the Roman roads—sometimes by the scores. Roman cruelty knows no boundaries for those who challenge the power and reign of Tiberius Caesar—*the Divine Son of God.*[32]

Oh well, maybe our rabbis have been right after all, Jacob thinks. *Better that one should die instead of the many.*[33] At least that's the way the religious elite convinced most of the crowd to accept the "necessary execution" of the trouble-making teacher. After all, He is only the son of a mere carpenter from Nazareth. And, as everybody knows, "*Nothing good* ever came out of Nazareth."[34]

Then…through the agony of the horror, one of the whimpering thieves mumbles out unbelievable words.

He is holding out a seemingly impossible request.

A PROMISE OF PARADISE

"Adonai, remember me when you come into your kingdom."

What's *this?* An argument among the dying?

Jacob sees that the two on either side are in a dispute over the one hanging between them. He can hear them talking to each other! One is saying something about the Teacher being a fraud. The other is defending Him.

"This man has done no wrong. We deserve what *we're* getting. This man is innocent! Leave Him alone! Your accusations are simply not true!"

Well—would you listen to this! Out of the mouth of a thief! A declaration of innocence on behalf of *someone else.* This is probably a first... especially coming from a crucified criminal!

The repentant thief turns to Yeshua and mournfully admits his fate. Yet, he also asks Him for a favor.

"*Adonai,*[35] remember me when you come into your kingdom." His eyes fill with water as he speaks. His lips tremble with each word.

The man in the middle slowly turns His head, looking deep into the eyes of the dying thief with an expression of loving tenderness.

35

"I tell you the truth, today you will be with me in Paradise. This very day, we will be in the Garden of Eden together—just like it was in the beginning."[36]

Yeshua looks down again. His eyes scan the crowd.

Then…He appears to look straight at Jacob, whose eyes are still riveted on the astonishing scene before him.

The young man feels as though Jesus is saying to each person in the crowd: "And this offer is for you as well…if you will only believe."

Jacob clenches his eyes shut and shakes his head in disbelief. Is he going mad? Only *thinking* that Jesus has looked at him? *As though He knows him?* But, how can this be? He's never met Jesus before…*ever*!

Had he only imagined that Jesus spoke of Paradise and that, on this exact day, Jesus and the repentant thief would somehow be there…in Eden? How can Jesus possess the power to offer *anyone* the Garden of Eden—especially in such an immediate sense?[37]

Several in the crowd are also speaking of some sort of a coming *resurrection.* They claim Yeshua has promised He will rise from the grave after His crucifixion. Others say He even claimed it would happen within three days!

Another impossibility! How can such an incredible thing be accomplished—and by a Galilean carpenter-turned-preacher? Yet…He *has* managed to get Himself crucified, just like He said He would. So…*maybe*…?

Jacob shakes his head again, as though trying to clear such thoughts from his mind. Oh well. Getting crucified in this day and age is not such a difficult thing to do. But, rising again—from the dead? That miracle just isn't going to happen. How could it?

⟿

Yeshua gasps for another tortured breath and pushes His slumping body upwards, trying to fill His aching, burning lungs again.

What a difference only a dozen hours make! Yeshua thinks. *Not long ago, I was in the Garden at Gethsemane, surrounded by sleeping disciples and visited by an angel of mercy.*

Father, forgive them, He prays. *They couldn't even stay awake to pray with me. But…they were there. At least they were there near me, in my time of deepest agony.* He pauses as He contemplates their slumbering presence in the Garden.

Now, most of them are gone again! But John is here. Jesus looks down at the youngest of His disciples. He is standing next to Mary, His mother. Oh, how Jesus loves John!

His head drops back to His chest.

His lungs scream for another breath of air. But the ability to fill them is getting harder by the moment.

Soon it will be over.

He simply doesn't have the strength to do this many more times…

He knows, however, that He *has* to hold out. The very second of His last breath has to happen at one precise moment in time.[38]

It is an hour, a minute, and a uniquely designated second—a mere instant on the entire timeline of humanity's existence. But this, too, is a part of *the plan.* It has to be precise.

Because that singular moment will forever change history and the eternity to come…long after history is done.

Part Three
Dimensional Perspectives

Scriptural Backdrop:

Jesus

One of the criminals who hung there hurled insults at him: "Aren't you the Messiah? Save yourself and us!" But the other criminal rebuked him. "Don't you fear God," he said, "since you are under the same sentence? We are punished justly, for we are getting what our deeds deserve. But this man has done nothing wrong." Then he said, "Jesus, **remember me when you come into your kingdom.**" Jesus answered him, "Truly I tell you, **today**[39] **you will be with me in paradise.**"[40] (Luke 23:39–43; emphasis added)

Stephen

When the members of the Sanhedrin heard this, they were furious and gnashed their teeth at him. But Stephen, full of the Holy Spirit, looked up to heaven and saw the glory of God, and Jesus standing at the right hand of God. **"Look,"** he said, **"I see heaven open** and the Son of Man standing at the right hand of God." (Acts 7:54–58; emphasis added)

Paul

As [Saul—later called Paul] neared Damascus on his journey, **suddenly a light from heaven** flashed around him. He fell to the ground and **heard a voice say to him,** "Saul, Saul, why do you persecute me?"

"Who are you, Lord?" Saul asked.

"I am Jesus, whom you are persecuting," he replied….

Saul got up from the ground, **but when he opened his eyes he could see nothing.** So they led him by the hand into Damascus. (Acts 9:3–8; emphasis added)

I know a man in Christ who fourteen years ago was **caught up to the third heaven.** Whether it was **in the body or out of the body I do not know**—God knows. And I know that this man—whether in the body or apart from the body I do not know, but God knows—**was caught up to paradise and heard inexpressible things,** things that no one is permitted to tell. (2 Corinthians 12:2–4; emphasis added)

John

After this I looked, and there before me was a door standing open in heaven. And the voice I had first heard speaking to me like a trumpet said, "Come up here, and I will show you what must take place after this." **At once I was in the Spirit, and there before me was a throne in heaven** with someone sitting on it. (Revelation 4:1–6; emphasis added)

9

EYES TO SEE

Different dimensions of physical realities that are yet unseen by us actually exist in the same physical space...and they can even overlap one another.

I hope I have your attention by now!

Believe me...we've only just begun our "theater-of-the-mind" journey. But, before we get back to that immersive narrative, let's pause for a few pages of important consideration. If you've never before seen the following truths, prepare to be stunned. But, even if you have, I pray your understanding will be further illuminated beyond what you already know.

At this point in our expedition, you might want to ask: What's all this talk about "other dimensions," especially as they were creatively presented in the last few chapters? Actually, it's not as strange an idea as you might think. The concept is certainly not foreign to the Word of God.

Think of it. In the opening pages of Genesis, we are introduced to a multidimensional reality. God is outside of our reality, and then He speaks...and our dimension of a created universe and everything that makes it up is presented to us without explanation of multidimensional truth. We are simply invited to accept it—by faith.

Now faith is confidence in what we hope for and assurance about **what we do not see.** This is what the ancients were commended for. By faith we understand that **the universe was formed** at God's command, so that **what is seen was not made out of what was visible.** (Hebrews 11:1–3; emphasis added)

By the time we get to the end of the third chapter of Genesis, a veil has been dropped between God's domain of existence and the earth's—the portal to which is guarded by cherubim.

And then, in the very first pages of the New Testament, Mary, the soon-to-be mother of Jesus, receives an angelic visit from God's throne. Gabriel has come through a dimensional portal, if you will, and suddenly appears in Mary's presence. By the time we reach the last pages of God's Word, we are introduced to the last-days "rolling up of the sky," and a New Heaven and New Earth are presented to us as "coming down" from Heaven. The fact is, the Bible is saturated with this truth, from first to last and practically every page in between. And, as you'll soon see, the understanding of these dimensional barriers is not foreign to modern scientific knowledge either.

Once we wrap our minds around this fact, we are well on our way to acquiring an eye-opening load of stunning insight into the living Word of God. And that particular insight better equips us to more fully understand what God's really up to. It speaks of what life is truly all about—what the concept of "eternity" means—and what our divinely appointed purpose is as we are living in the midst of it all.

The Science

Let's begin with what the world of science is currently realizing regarding these truths. They are revelations that many of today's physicists apparently don't know have existed within the pages of God's Word for many thousands of years, long before they were "discovered" by "modern science."

A *Phys.org* article explains some of the most recent scientific understanding:

> The **existence of parallel universes** may seem like something cooked up by science fiction writers, with little relevance to modern theoretical physics. **But the idea** that **we live in a "multiverse" made up of an infinite number of parallel universes has long been considered a scientific possibility**.... It is important to keep in mind that the multiverse view **is not actually a theory**, it is **rather a consequence** of our **current understanding of theoretical physics**. This distinction **is crucial.**
>
> We have not waved our hands and said: "**Let there be a** multiverse." Instead the idea that the universe is perhaps **one of infinitely many** is derived **from current theories** like quantum mechanics and string theory.[41] (Emphasis added)

That same article goes on to describe how the various "universes" that are scientifically predicted by string field theory[42] and "inflation" theory[43] actually exist in the same physical space—and can even overlap one another. (I'll give a powerful physical illustration of that potential in chapter 11, "Up Periscope.")

Have a look at a couple more scientific assertions. A *Discover Magazine* article, "Three Totally Mind-bending Implications of a Multidimensional Universe," reveals the following:

> Nearly a century ago, Edwin Hubble's discovery of red-shifting of light from galaxies in all directions from our own suggested that space itself was getting bigger.... Hubble's discovery implied that **the cosmos exists in more than the three dimensions we're familiar with** in everyday life.... **We don't see or feel more dimensions;** nevertheless, **theoretical physics predicts that they should exist.**[44] (Emphasis added)

Interesting, isn't it? Now, let's go just a bit further.

Dr. Michio Kaku is a world-renowned theoretical physicist.[45] He is the cofounder of *string field theory*—the scientific theory asserting that multiple universes and dimensions truly exist—and continues Einstein's search to unite the four fundamental forces of nature into one unified theory.[46]

Dr. Kaku writes:

> It sounds preposterous that electrons and atoms can be in **many states at the same time**, but this is **the foundation** of modern civilizations. [The theory] **has been tested** to 1 part in 100 billion in accuracy, making it **the most successful physical theory of all time**.... The idea that **you can be in many places at the same time can be proven** indirectly, by looking at the properties of many atoms, but testing it on single atoms and single photons was beyond reach. **Until now.**[47] (Emphasis added)

The following excerpt is from yet another article at the quantum physics site *Phys.org*. The article is titled "A Universe of 10 Dimensions."

> When someone mentions "different dimensions," we tend to think of things like parallel universes—alternate realities that exist parallel to our own.... However, the reality of dimensions and how they play a role in the ordering of our Universe is really quite different from this popular characterization....
>
> **We are immediately aware of the three dimensions that surround us on a daily basis**—those that define the length, width, and depth of all objects in our universes.
>
> Beyond these three **visible** dimensions, **scientists believe that there may be many more.** In fact, the theoretical framework of Superstring Theory posits **that the universe exists in ten different dimensions.**[48] (Emphasis added)

Something Evil This Way Comes

Let me offer even more information concerning all this talk about "extra dimensions" of physical reality. This info specifically illuminates the stunning claims that concern the internationally acclaimed CERN[49] Hadron Collider located in Switzerland.

The excerpt that follows was written by Adam Milton-Barker, a network engineer and intel software innovator in the fields of artificial intelligence, the internet of things, and virtual reality. Milton-Barker asserts:

> **The Large Hadron Collider or LHC is the world's most powerful particle accelerator,** [located] 300 ft. below the ground at the CERN Control Centre in Geneva, Switzerland.[50] The machine is the result of thousands of scientists and engineers planning and building over the last few decades. **To explain simply what the machine does, it sends sub-atomic particles at the speed of light** hurtling around the loop in opposite directions and then **smashes them into each other.**
>
> CERN wants to use the LHC to find out the fundamentals of our universe and **how it was created.** [They are also] **expecting to find other dimensions** and [then] **open portals** to these dimensions.[51] (Emphasis added)

And then there's this. Another leading global online tech publication, with more than nine million monthly unique browsers worldwide, reported this mind-boggling quote from Sergio Bertolucci, CERN's director of research and scientific computing:

> A top [scientific researcher] at the Large Hadron Collider (LHC) says that the titanic machine **may possibly create or discover** previously unimagined scientific phenomena, or "unknown unknowns"—for instance "**an extra dimension.**"

"Out of this door might come something, or we might send something through it," said Sergio Bertolucci.[52] (Emphasis added)

Are you convinced yet? More than that, do you think there's any coincidence between the ominous prophetic events of our own times and humanity's fascination with attempting to "go through the doors" of other dimensions of reality? These are dimensions, by the way, that we *know* are there. Imagine the unmitigated power that would belong to the people who might first discover the "portals." Or, imagine the unmitigated *evil* that might accompany that discovery.

In no uncertain terms, the Bible warns us about these "unseen realms," or other dimensions. Scripture informs us that some of them are populated with beings of unmitigated evil, and they interact with our own daily existence within this earthly realm. These are interdimensional beings. They are able to travel through interdimensional portals and are not human. Humanity has known this truth from the earliest of days, thus the First Commandment: "Thou shalt have no other gods [fallen *elohim*—demons[53]] before me."

Also consider what the Apostle Paul stated regarding this matter:

For our wrestling is not against flesh and blood, but against the principalities, against the powers, against the world-rulers of this darkness, against the spiritual hosts of wickedness in the heavenly places. (Ephesians 6:12, ASV)

Gee. Who do you think might be behind all of this modern, technologically motivated allurement to "peer into the other side"?

10

ENTANGLEMENT

These are just a few divinely wonderful things to ponder as
they relate to the scientific discoveries of our own times.

Following is yet another striking assertion from the realm of quantum science. This one, like the revelations we saw in the last chapter, adds even more insight to several of the deepest declarations and eternal truths found in God's Word.

Two Places at One Time

Following are the opening paragraphs from another *Phys.org* article titled, "Record Quantum Entanglement of Multiple Dimensions":

An international team [of quantum physicists] has managed to create an entanglement[54] of **103 dimensions** with only two photons. The record had been established at **11 dimensions**.

The states in which elementary particles, such as photons, can be found have **properties which are beyond common sense.** Superpositions are produced, such as **the possibility of being in**

47

two places at once, which defies intuition. In addition, **when two
particles are entangled a connection is generated: measuring the
state of one affects the state of the other particle instantly, no
matter how far away from each other they are.**[55] (Emphasis added)

Dr. Michio Kaku further explains the scientifically proven phenomenon of *quantum entanglement* in this easy-to-grasp manner:

If I have two electrons close together, they can vibrate in unison…
Now, separate those two electrons so that they're hundreds or even
thousands of light years apart, and they will keep this instant communication bridge open. "If I jiggle one electron, the other electron 'senses' this vibration instantly, faster than the speed of light."[56]

Did you catch that? Some of the smallest components of an atom—
i.e., *electrons*—can "communicate" with each other and respond to that
communication *at the speed of light*. Furthermore, this process between
particles occurs whether they are in the same atomic structure or even
if they are separated by any distance imaginable, effectively putting that
particle in a totally different "dimension" of reality altogether!

Biblical Application of the Science

Is all of this perhaps a little mind-blowing? Maybe so, but quantum entanglement is now a scientifically proven fact. It's even used in several of our
own current technologies.[57] And, the knowledge of quantum entanglement might also help explain a few things about certain biblical narratives.

Consider what we've just discovered: *instantaneous communication, at
the speed of light, from one dimension to another dimension.* That sounds
awfully close to the supernatural concept of prayer, doesn't it? Surely
"prayer" is an interdimensional form of communication, right?

And, quantum entanglement comes fairly close to shining a bit of
light on the concept of *God the Father* being located within the dimen-

sion of His own cosmic glory while, at the very same instant, existing in human flesh on earth—even on a cross—as *God the Son.*

Let's have a look at God's own words regarding this interdimensional truth.

The Pierced One

The book of Zechariah was written more than 2,400 years ago, a full four hundred years before Yeshua went to Calvary's cross. Yet God plainly asserted that He would, one day in the future, be in two places at one time! He doesn't *explain* it—there are no scientific arguments or long dissertations made concerning the matter. We are simply called upon to believe by faith what He declares in His Word.[58] Make sure you have a look at my notes in the bracketed sections within the following Scripture passage.

The Lord, who stretches out the heavens, who lays the foundation of the earth, and who forms the human spirit within a person, *declares*:

> **And I will pour out** on the house of David and the inhabitants of Jerusalem **a spirit of grace** [His sacrificial forgiveness of sin for all who will call upon Him] and supplication....
>
> [On that specific day, and in that specific moment,] [t]**hey will look on me, the one they have pierced**, and they will **mourn for him as one mourns for an only child** [all happening at the same time], and grieve bitterly for him **as one grieves for a first-born son.**[59] (Zechariah 12:1, 10; emphasis added)

Observe a representative sample of how several renowned contemporary scholars understand the multidimensional nature of God's declaration in that passage.

Coffman Commentaries on the Bible (1905–2006)[60]

> **Me whom they pierced,** and they shall mourn for "him..." This passage sends the critics into a frenzy.... But, "'They shall look

unto me whom they have pierced' is the authentic reading." Baldwin spoke of **some who were embarrassed** by the "apparent contradiction that God had been put to death." Unregenerate man has difficulty with the proposition that **God indeed died in the person** of his Son **on the Cross.**[61] (Emphasis added)

Expository Notes of Dr. Thomas Constable[62] (contemporary to the writing of this book)

The unusual combination "they will look to me whom they have pierced" and "they will mourn for Him" suggests two different individuals, but the deity of the Messiah solves this problem. **Yahweh Himself would suffer for the people in the person of Messiah.**[63] (Emphasis added)

In the endnotes, I've supplied four additional *classical* commentary entries that attest to the same truths you've just read. Those specific authors wrote their observations well over a hundred years ago! Yet, they too understood something of the dimensional characteristics of God's own declarations in Zechariah.[64]

Wait a minute! Both God *and* man—at the same time? Really? Yes! That's exactly what the Bible declares, from the Old Testament through the New Testament. These are just a few divinely wonderful things to ponder as they relate to the scientific discoveries of our own times.[65]

Imagine that! The fact that God purposely created multiple realms of interdimensional reality is not the stuff of science fiction, it is *science reality*. More importantly, it is biblical reality.[66]

The plain fact is that the Word of God is never "catching up" to "truth." Rather, genuine truth is always catching up to the Word of God!

Is the Word of God beginning to make more sense now, even from a "scientific" point of view? With these facts in mind, and just before we get back to our immersive narrative, let's have a quick look at everyday examples of how multiple dimensions of physical reality actually surround us—*even now*.

11

UP PERISCOPE!

Are we not repeatedly promised in the Word of God that
there are indeed supernatural "portals" to a new life?

One of the most useful ways that I've been able to assist people in conceptualizing the biblical understanding of physically existing multiple dimensions is through the use of real-life examples. Following are a couple of illustrations.

Hydrothermal vents are openings in the earth's surface at the bottom of some of the deepest parts of the oceans. Geothermally heated water gushes from these fissures, many of which are located miles beneath the ocean's surface. The deepest *known* hydrothermal vents exist at a site in the Caribbean three miles beneath the ocean's surface—almost sixteen thousand feet deep.[67]

None of the biological organisms living at such extreme separation from our world "above" has ever witnessed the complexities of human life just on the other side of the surface of the ocean—and they never will. Yet, in those vast depths below the sea's waves, there are, indeed, intricately interconnected societies of life that have no idea that the rest of us, *billions of us,* much less the greater universe around us, even exist.

Imagine if one hydrothermal-vent sea creature said to another, "I know for a fact that no other worlds or realities exist beyond the location of our own realm or beyond our present physical limitations. How could they exist? That notion is preposterous! Absolutely impossible! I mean, all you have to do is *look up*! It's a scientific fact that all you see is blackness, and it *obviously* goes on forever!"

Of course, that unknowing creature would be entirely incorrect in its "scientific" pronouncements, which would be based only upon what it can "see" or "imagine" within its limited scope of knowledge. But, in reality, that creature could have no way of knowing, or even of finding out, if its theory was genuinely correct. That sea dweller simply cannot exist outside of the domain in which it is physically equipped to live. Therefore, it is incapable of imagining that anything else exists beyond its own realm of isolated reality. It is hemmed in from the ultimate truth of its own existence because of its physical limitations.

Everything above the surface of the miles-deep ocean truly does exist, but only in the *unseen realm*. However, what is an unseen realm to that little sea creature is still a very real level of physical reality—and is "seen" by billions of other life forms. In fact, it's where *our own* existence is lived out. And we know the full reality of it. The ocean-bottom sea creatures never will.

A Straight-Line Excursion

What if one of those hydrothermal-vent creatures decided it would "explore" the seemingly eternal reaches of its "universe"? What if it simply started swimming—in a straight line—in a "westerly" direction through the blackness of its "ocean world"? If it could actually swim in that one direction, in a perfectly straight line, and survive, it would eventually wind up right back where it originally started! In so doing, it would have had no sensation whatsoever that it had been traveling in a linear direction that was actually situated upon an unimaginably large globe of a planet. Also, it could never imagine that the globe that held and nurtured its very existence is literally hanging in space—on nothing—and revolving around a sun that is more than ninety-three million miles away. None of these facts would be even knowable to the sea creature.

Think of it! How could that same hydrothermal-vent organism begin to imagine that the globe it swims around, and the sun and planets that surround that globe, all exist in only *one solar system,* within a very large galaxy that is situated within a universe of trillions of other galaxies?

Not only do they not know *we* exist, but they know nothing at all of *anything* within our world or beyond it. Neither do they have any inkling of the microscopic world or the life forms within those dimensions of reality. Nor do they have any comprehension of the subatomic realm of quantum physics, or the particles and cosmic "activity" within them that govern all the laws of the physical universe in which every one of us—including those ocean-bottom creatures—dwells. These really are mind-boggling considerations.

The point of this simple illustration is to attest to an important and scientifically settled fact: Various forms of intelligent physical life can live within a common sphere of existence, yet remain completely unaware that anything similar subsists around them within genuinely physical realms of dimensional separation.

However—and this is a very important consideration—humans are able to penetrate several of the multiple *realms* of life and alternate realities that are known to us! For example, we can accomplish this feat, starting from the earthly surface and going all the way down to the uttermost depths of the ocean floors. We can also reach into certain limits of outer space. And—at the opposite end of the spectrum—ultimately, we can delve into the quantum realm within some of the deepest levels of the submicroscopic worlds! Not only are we able to interact within these other dimensions, but also, we can actually make certain changes within some of those realms. We do it every single day.

Now, reconsider the spiritual implications of these truths. Read again that universally familiar passage of Scripture we saw earlier in this book:

For our struggle **is not against flesh and blood**, but against the rulers, against the authorities, against the powers of this dark world and **against the spiritual forces of evil in the heavenly realms.** (Ephesians 6:10; emphasis added)

It's been right there all along. The Word of God has not hidden the matter from us.

Since before the days of the Garden of Eden, multiple dimensions of physical realities completely outside of our physical grasp have been revealed to us as a certainty. And this is exactly what Jesus came to demonstrate to our time.

Before long, the world will not see me anymore, but you will see me. Because I live, you also will live. (John 14:19)

What If?

Think about this mind-bending proposition. What if the world we are presently living in—the one in which we go about our daily lives, business endeavors, and relationships, is not the truly genuine one? What if this life is only a murky, dirty shadow of the truly ineffable *divine life*—the life that was meant for us from the beginning?

What if another kind of life actually exists just behind an indiscernible veil, on the other side of a dimensional shift in a presently unseen and indescribable realm of physical reality—a physical existence where death is virtually impossible? Where misery and disease are nonexistent? Where there is only *life*, as it was meant to be...from the beginning? What if that were so?

What if, before this moment, you had missed the absolute reality of such a thing? What if you had previously been unwilling to think outside the sphere of *only the known*, refusing to believe in something better and ineffably different?

For presently we see through a glass in obscurity; but then, face to face. Presently, I know in part; but then I will know fully, even as I have been fully known. (1 Corinthians 13:12, Berean's Literal Bible)

Now we understand why the Bible declares that no one will enter the dimension called Heaven, or Paradise, without first going *through* Jesus Christ.[68] He is the only One that is *the way*. He alone is *the door*. No one but Jesus is *the gate*. No one else holds *the keys*! In other words, Jesus is *the only portal* to that, or any other, dimension that exists anywhere in the totality of reality. And only He has the power to physically transform us into a glorified state that is fit for the new life of each and every dimension He has created for us.

Metaphorically, it's as if Jesus transported Himself to the bottom of the "ocean" of mankind in order to swim among us, in the form and in the flesh of a lowly ocean dweller. He did this in order to demonstrate the unbounded magnitude of His love for us. And He did it for the purpose of showing us the way, the truth, and the real life—the alternate, but very physical reality that awaits us in Paradise—the place that is just through a dimensional divide, a realm that exists all around us, a realm to which only He holds the keys.

He came into our world to assure us that something much bigger exists outside our strictly earthbound, temporary reality. He wants us to ultimately live with Him in that dimension of Paradise. He wants to restore us to the glory our primordial ancestors once held in Eden, before its Fall. He reaches down into our lowly and fallen current existence at the bottom of the "ocean" and offers to pull us out and transform us—*into His likeness.*[69]

Because of our Creator's loving activity in our world, occasionally, some of us get to experience a little peek into those divine truths and into those unseen realms. When that happens, our lives are rarely ever the same.

Now…let's rejoin our immersive journey.

12

WHEN ANGELS CRIED

The Place of the Skull, Jerusalem, nearing the ninth hour
3 p.m., circa AD 33

There He hangs—a mere spectacle of morbid entertainment for the masses. He's spiked to a Roman cross, a cruel device meant to inflict maximum pain in the excruciatingly drawn-out process of certain death. That hideous invention is also designed to invoke maximum terror—as well as unquestioned obedience—among the masses who are guaranteed to gather and watch.

The whole thing is animalistic and repulsive. The air is laden with the suffocation of demonic presence.

Yet most can't seem to turn their eyes from the hideous display. Not a soul dares to leave. They were drawn here like moths to a flame, and now their eyes are glued upon the shocking display before them. And, to add to the drama of the spectacle, the victims are actually talking to each other!

Just moments ago, a dying thief was guaranteed immediate entrance into *Paradise*. The promise was made by the one in the middle. What did *this* mean? How could such a thing be assured—especially from one suffering the very same fate?

Within minutes, a foreboding shroud of darkness has unnaturally blanketed the entire land. Those gathered at the foot of the cross grow increasingly unnerved by the seemingly supernatural display. *What does this mean? Has anyone ever seen anything like this before?*

Hanging there in agony, suspended between earth and sky, just moments from His last few breaths, Jesus lowers His head again.

Yeshua's mind goes back to the first fiendish betrayal suffered by Heaven's throne—in Eden's Garden. That was the event that brought Him *here*, to this agonizing set of diabolical circumstances.

That ominous day in Eden had been wrapped in a primordial mist of intrigue, deceit, treasonous infidelity, and unspeakably vile vulgarity. The treachery had been perpetrated by the same *fallen one* who now lurks, unseen to the human eye, around the edges of the onlooking crowd. But Yeshua sees Him, just as He had peered through the dimensions and had seen Nachash hanging behind Peter at Caesarea Philippi, diabolically manipulating Peter's faithless and godless assertions.[70]

The crowd stands gawking at Yeshua. They openly scoff at and mock Him…speaking the words of Nachash as his puppets, but with their own human lips.

The evil one pulls the strings of his marionettes…and again plants it in their hearts to speak his foul taunts. "He saved others! Let Him save Himself! Come down off that cross!" They shake their fists in the face of Heaven's Son. They don't even know what they're doing, and for whom they're really doing it. It was for this reason Jesus had prayed to the Father, "Forgive them. They don't know what they are doing."

Yet, even in these last torturous hours, Satan still does not possess the fullest understanding of who he thinks he has impaled on that middle cross.[71] Nor does he comprehend that Yeshua's presence on Golgotha is actually the commencement of the devastating demise of his own kingdom of darkness.[72]

But, the divine snare has been set. Nachash has stumbled into the depths of it, like an animal falling headfirst into a cleverly concealed pit, a death trap with poisonous spikes implanted in the bottom of it, waiting for its prey. This very day is the integral key of Heaven's setup. The matter is now out of the serpent's control, and he doesn't even realize it. But soon, everything will explode into its divinely appointed finale. And *then* Satan will know.[73]

But, way back in time, in that uniquely hideous Garden ignominy, not long from the beginning of Creation itself—the angels of Heaven had mourned almost inconsolably. And in that moment of an arrogantly attempted *coup d'état*, they had become enraged by what they had witnessed.

After the deed had been done, their continued faithfulness to Heaven's plan had been forever steeled. Whatever it took, the *First Kingdom* would be restored to the state it had once enjoyed, all the way back in the beginning.

That's when the divine attendants of Heaven first understood...what happened that day in Eden would change everything, for all of eternity.

And, without a doubt, they knew what came next. *This was war.* And their valiant Warrior-Creator would lead the way into that cosmic battle.

᠁

Jesus' head falls back to His chest.

Already, He's mustering His strength to push back up again for another breath. One more time, His mind drifts to the ancient outrage of what took place in the Garden of Eden and what it was that had brought Him here in the first place—why He's doing this, why He's agonizing, immersed in this unspeakable horror.

Why He *has* to complete what He has come to accomplish.

PART FOUR

In the Beginning

Scriptural Backdrop:

Eden

The LORD God planted a garden in Eden, toward the east, where he placed the man whom he had formed. The LORD God caused every tree that is both beautiful and suitable for food to spring up out of the ground. The tree of life was also in the middle of the garden, along with the tree of the knowledge of good and evil…. The LORD God took the man and placed him in the Garden of Eden in order to have him work it and guard it. The LORD God commanded the man: "You may freely eat from every tree of the garden, but you are not to eat from the tree of the knowledge of good and evil, because you will certainly die during the day that you eat from it." (Genesis 2: 8–9, 15–17)

Satan's Death Sentence

So the LORD God said to the serpent, "Because you have done this, Cursed are you above all livestock and all wild animals! You will crawl on your belly and you will eat dust all the days of your life. And I will put enmity between you and the woman, and between your offspring and hers; he will crush your head, and you will strike his heel." (Genesis 3:14–15)

13

THE SEDUCTION

About four thousand years before Golgotha's cross

When the young couple first lay their eyes upon him, he has material- ized out of an ethereal mist.

As he approaches, a shimmering vapor encircles him and wisps around his visage as though it were a numinous robe of regality. A slight breeze tiptoes through the treetops, rustling the leaves upon his arrival.

Actually, they heard him meandering in the Garden before they saw him. In fact, they thought they had even *felt* his presence. It was as if he had already been there—among them, watching them—before he became visible to their own eyes.

As the fullness of his form becomes perceptible through the surround- ing fog, his swaggering saunter captivates them. It is as though he slightly floats, rather than walks, toward them.

How can a creature appear to be so breathtakingly beautiful—so stun- ningly lovely—in countenance and deportment? His bodily movements are dance-like. Other than the Creator Himself,[74] nothing they have ever seen is as magnificently divine as this one[75]

They know he has been appointed by the throne of Elohim as the guardian of earth's newly created domain.[76] He is, after all, one of the holy cherubim. He is the royal regent of the Garden of Eden—that's what Creator had called him.[77]

Earth's first husband and wife truly want to feel honored that this regal being from the Divine Council of Elohim[78] has come to them. But, they have also been cautioned about him. Apparently, something is beginning to go askew in their Garden of Paradise. From what they have gathered, it is suspected that this divinely created Mighty One[79] is now the author of a cloud of uneasiness previously foreign to the normal atmosphere of Eden.

Yet, here he is. Right in front of them. Gigantic—and utterly beautiful. What are they to make of his grand entrance?

It is in the first moments of their stunned awe when he speaks.

The Encounter

"Well, well. *Here* you are!" A childlike innocence engulfs his countenance. His voice is deep and rich, saturated with deceitfully contrived compassion.

"I was just taking a stroll," he explains, "roaming to and fro upon this magnificent domain of mine—" He pauses in midsentence, spreading his arms wide, as if everything they now behold ultimately belongs to him. As if somehow it has always belonged to him. As though he had actually created it himself! The morning mist continues to swirl about his head as he speaks, causing the heavy droplets to sparkle like a luminous crown of diamonds.

He tilts his head to one side, seeming to indicate that he has suddenly been struck with a great curiosity. His eyes scan their forms from head to foot. There is something serpentine in his fluid movements, something seditiously licentious in his glances.

"*My*, the two of you certainly *are* very beautiful! I don't think I've ever realized just how amazingly exquisite you are…" His words are smooth and hypnotizing—almost musical, and strangely irresistible.

The couple freezes in their tracks. Eve blushes in the flattery of the moment.

Adam leans in, whispering in her ear. "Eve!" he cautions. "We were warned not to have anything to do with him—*you know this!* In fact, we were specifically instructed by Creator Himself not to partake of the fruit he offers us. We are not even to touch it!"

"I know that," she whispers back. "But he hasn't *offered* anything yet. Let's hear him out. After all, he *is* Elohim's royal regent. In that regard alone, he's certainly deserving of our utmost respect. He's also deserving of our full attention—don't you think?"

Adam eases his head away from her ear and slips back a few feet, still trying to size up the gravity of the meeting. There is no doubt about it: Eve is flatly enthralled by the majesty of the one who now stands before them. In fact, she'll later protest before the Creator that she'd been unfairly *beguiled* by him. But for now, she refocuses her gaze, resting it upon his breathtaking beauty.

"Come now," he purrs. "I'm anxious to introduce you to a multitude of amazing considerations, things that could radically enhance your life and purpose. Also—and please forgive me for not mentioning this before now—but I have stunningly glorious knowledge at my disposal, information you have never imagined." He pauses briefly, as though sizing up their ability to handle what would come next, then he carries on with his seduction.

"Why, I *could* even offer you—"

There it is! He's going to make a proposal, just as they have been warned that he might do!

With an uplifted hand, Eve interrupts him. "But, we are *not* to eat of the fruit you offer us!" She seems to have stepped up to a more sober moment of consideration. Adam's eyes widen at her boldness. The glorious cherub of Heaven looks on in shocked curiosity. For a brief moment, he's actually speechless. *This female species has spunk!* Eve gathers her courage and continues.

"In fact, we are not to even *touch* whatever it is you might offer to us. This is what Creator has commanded."

There. She has said it. Now, in her nervousness, she struggles to catch her breath. Eve drops her head as soon as she utters the words. She's embarrassed that she has spoken so hastily.

Have I done the right thing?

Why didn't Adam defend my position?

Instead, Adam just stands there like a lifeless lump of clay.

The royal keeper of the Garden gently kneels before them, as if Adam and Eve are his very own precious children. They are still standing some distance from him—hesitant to approach.

"Come now," Satan seductively hisses, feigning benevolent intentions. "Come just a little clo*sss*er."

When he sees they are still awash in timidity, he smugly cocks his head again. "Surely, Elohim did not say all of that? Why would He even utter such a charge in the first place? Think about it for a moment—my dear little one*sss*, you don't even know what I'm offering."

He almost whines as he speaks the words. Eve feels her face growing hot with embarrassment. Has she offended him?

Her voice trembles as she defends her memory of Elohim's prior conversation with them. "Yes. *It certainly was* what He told us." She speaks much softer now. She finds it difficult to look directly at him.

Maybe, she thinks…*is it possible?* Perhaps she misunderstood Elohim as she and Adam had walked with Him in the Garden a few evenings back. What if she were falsely accusing the Garden's regent? Would Creator be disappointed in her for showing such disrespect?

She shoots a disapproving glance at Adam, signaling her frustrated thoughts: *Why have you not yet said a word?*

"Well, then, if Elohim really said *that*," he pauses in contemplation, then snaps, "then He *lied!* There! I said it. It's the truth, like it or not. That's all there is to it!"

Eve gasps. Does she actually hear those words coming from his lips? Has he just called Elohim, the Creator of the universe…*a liar?*

None of this makes sense. Her thoughts begin to swirl with confusion. Those utterances of blasphemy and rebelliousness are coming from a *fruit* she has never tasted.

"As a matter of fact," the serpent declares, "the real problem is this*ss*. Elohim knows that in the day you follow me, you'll become like *uss*. You'll even be like Elohim Him*ssss*elf! And…it appear*ss* that He's purposely keeping this*ss* delightful morsel of enjoyment from you." The hissing lisp in his voice heightens a bit as he becomes increasingly frustrated with her.[80]

"That certainly doesn't seem fair now, does it?" the mesmerizing cherub continues his appeal. "Don't you see how perfect this is, how beautiful to the eye?" He points to the forbidden fruit as he speaks. "Look how lovely it is…how *sss*weet to the ta*sss*te."

Eve gazes upon the object of his offer. It *is* beautiful, and almost irresistibly alluring. He has at least spoken the truth in this regard.

Before she can respond to his question, he speaks again. "What harm could come from only *partaking* just one little, tiny nibble? Ponder it for a moment! You'll soon come to understand that I *am* correct in this*ss* matter! *You'll see*… If you don't like it, you can simply stop. No harm done. Come now, give it a try, just a quick taste—see for yourself what He has been keeping from you."

Eve takes a step closer. Adam sheepishly follows.

Aha! The hook is embedded! Here they come!

Nachash has their attention. He's almost accomplished his purpose. The entangling net of their soon-coming captivity draws tighter…and tighter.

14

BEGUILED

He can see her beginning to melt to his will.

Eve and Adam—the still-silent lump of clay—ease a few paces closer to the Mighty One. The three are now just a few feet from each other.

"But...*but*," Eve whimpers as she approaches, "Elohim also said... that if we did this...we would surely invite death upon ourselves.

"In fact," she protests, "He made it very clear that we would be separated from Him, and from His love, forever."

She wipes a tear that slips from her eye. Here is something else she has never tasted—*sorrow*. It is bitter, and salty—and it causes an odd heaviness to bury itself deep within her chest, as if it is a living thing.

"I'll let you in on another little *sssecret*," the creature hisses. "You surely shall *not* die! I am here to straighten all of that out for you. *Trust me!* There's simply been a huge misunderstanding. Besides*s*, it's utterly impossible for you to die! Have a little faith. I wouldn't *lie* to you..."

The distressed couple step back a few feet, considering retreat.

Confusion overwhelms Eve. Sorrow settles into a dreadful heaviness deep within her being. Then fear strikes, and her throat tightens. From where are these emotions flowing? What is this sorcery that dances in the halls of their minds, bodies, and souls? The serpent can see that he might be losing them, as they are cautiously easing away from him.

"Wait! Wait!" the serpent pleads. "Don't leave yet! I assure you—*no, no, no,* I *promise* you—" the serpent pleads, holding up both of his hands as a sign of sincerity, "—if you'll only eat thi*ss* fruit with me, all will be well. You'll *sssee…*"

Why can't they seem to resist him? Where does this gripping power of enthralling persuasion come from? Not to mention…how utterly gorgeous he is!

Once more, an expression of virtuosity overshadows his countenance. "It's such an effortless thing to do. And there are no consequences whatsoever! What do you have to lose? If you don't like it, no big deal. I'll never ask you to do it again. I guarantee it. I simply want you to experience what the rest of *us* get to experience! Just one time…it won't hurt a thing."

They stop their retreat.

"Such a *small* thing to do," he reassures. "Come now…" Eve's countenance changes. She looks as though she might succumb. He can see her beginning to melt to his will. It is also apparent to the serpent that Adam will go wherever Eve leads.

"And, just think, you'll soon be filled with incredible knowledge, *just like* the rest of us, once it's done!"

Here is that wonderful sensation again. It's magical, mystical…his words *feel* so right, so warm—so inviting.

The Fatal Step

Eve reasons: *How can something that feels so good be such a bad thing? Surely, it can't! Surely this gloriously divine cherub is telling us the truth! Elohim has just made a simple mistake. This is all just a big misunderstanding. Maybe it is I who misunderstood Him! In any case, the Mighty One promises he can fix everything… What can it hurt?*

The serpent looks amused as he scrutinizes them. The ambient intoxicating music of his presence inhabits the atmosphere around them.[81] Eve returns the greeting with her own expression of fascination. Adam still hasn't registered a single complaint, an imprudent nonresponse that he will regret for the rest of his life.

So, with Eve leading the way, they once again move closer to the *beguiling one*. As they do, they stretch out their hands like little children, and willingly take his hand. A surge of ecstatic energy sweeps through them as they touch him. They are transfixed by his beauty. Nachash revels in his mesmerizing power over them. He knows he now has them in his hands. He has thoroughly charmed them both.[82]

And so...they eat.

Beautiful to the eye. Sweet to the taste.

But poisonous to their souls.

Death has won.

Descending into Darkness

They had walked, after much cajoling and manipulation, right into his outstretched arms. The great predator had finally bagged his coveted prey. It had taken some doing to bring the thing to completion, requiring much more effort than he had estimated. But, alas, they had eventually fallen for his scam. He prides himself for being such a tenacious hunter.

When the deed is done, Nachash screeches out a fiendish cackle echoing through the Garden, a sound that seems to bounce off every tree and boulder as it goes. The startled young couple frantically bolts from his presence. He has now gone from lovely and unquenchably alluring...to utterly terrifying.

He watches the pair scamper off into the woods like a couple of rabbits, reduced to animal-like instincts, covering their nakedness as they scurry away. Only now are Adam and Eve certain of it: They have been deceived, just as Creator had tried to warn them! But, it's too late now— way too late. The plan of the evil one has been accomplished, and it was done with their direct involvement and ultimate permission. Nachash had never once laid a forceful hand upon them.

The evil one sighs in ecstatic delight as he immerses himself in the self-congratulatory exhilaration of the moment. Satan has pulled off every single thing that Yahweh hates, in one thrashing sweep.[83] And in so doing, he has been stunningly successful in enticing the first humans into the diabolic act of crushing Elohim's heart.[84]

He doesn't relax, however. His complex plan is headed toward ultimate fruition, but he still has a multifaceted agenda to execute if he is to actually possess his own longed-for kingdom. However, of one monumental thing he is absolutely certain: This day will, itself, rearrange the whole of Yahweh's creation. *Soon,* Satan muses, *I'll rule over the whole thing! It will all be mine!*[85]

The coup has begun. This is precisely what Nachash has planned from the moment he laid eyes upon the earthly work of Elohim's hand, when he first beheld the worshipful reaction of the rest of the divine realm.[86] But now, Creator will be forced to turn His back on this newly crafted "Paradise." After all, it has been thoroughly corrupted—*perverted*—and so perfectly and irreversibly profaned.[87]

Satan knows Yahweh's holiness will not abide what has happened here this day. He will have to drop the veil on the whole thing. The result will be two distinctly different dimensions of reality[88]—a complete separation from the throne of God. Elohim can have His own realm of rule, and Satan can have his. Certainly, there will now be a cosmic clash of dimensional empires. But whatever else happens, he, *Nachash*, will be the ruler of *this* one.

This is the moment he has longed for. This is *his* victory—or, so he thinks.

~⌒

But Yahweh has seen it all. Not a moment, or a word, has been indiscernible to Him.

For now, Heaven's throne has yet to speak in the matter.

And it will speak. With a Voice like thunder.

15

INTERCESSION

First, there must be a purging.

The defilement process had begun.

The hideous corruption of Yahweh's Paradise would continue down through the ages, with blinding indignation. The adversary was determined to drive a deepening wedge between humanity and their *Creator*. He had come to kill, steal, and destroy. And, thus far, he had been thoroughly successful in all three of his psychopathic aspirations.

But these were only the opening salvos of his strategy. The ultimate goal was to capture the throne of God itself. He would stop at nothing less. He *would be* worshiped among the humans, as well as among the divine ones. One day, every single one of them would bow to him! He was going to see to it.[89]

However, there was one hugely glaring obstacle. Yahweh had threatened him. In truth, He had more than just threatened. Yahweh had vowed to destroy him for what he had done in the Garden. That declaration of judgment was delivered in the form of a complex riddle:

From the womb of a woman will come forth the Seed that will crush your head.[90]

73

Those were the words Yahweh had used. But what, exactly, did He mean by them? It was clear that somehow a child would be born—in the *human way*. A human child that would destroy his freshly usurped kingdom? But how could that be—a mere child? Really? A *mortal* child, at that? Impossible! Utterly ridiculous!

From where would this child come? Where would he be born? And *to whom* would he be born? *When* would this absurd idea of a cosmic dragon-slayer come into being? And, most important, *exactly how* would this vain imagination of Heaven's throne defeat his divine power, much less *destroy* him?

It was at Yahweh's speaking of those threatening words in the Garden of Eden that Satan knew something must be done. If his kingdom was to prosper—and ultimately be victorious—Heaven's bizarre plan of redemption must be defeated. But there was still so much missing information.

⤳

By the time several generations of humanity had begun to populate the newly created planet, the flesh of both humans and animals had grown increasingly defiled. Satan and his allies from the rebellious angelic realm had seen to it. Gruesome aberrations among all living things had begun to manifest. The indescribable beauty the planet had once enjoyed folded into a process of rapid degeneration.[91] Satan was attempting to recreate as much of the original perfection as possible, but this time, the design was in his own twisted image.

Violence engulfed the corrupted animal kingdom as well as the altered human realm. Terror and dread had become the defining characteristics of daily existence. Gigantic, vicious men, with deepening allegiances to the evil one, brought their unspeakable horrors to every human encampment. An unholy alliance formed between the bulk of humanity and the cloaked demonic realm—the fallen ones who were now masquerading as messengers of light among the populace of earth.[92]

But Yahweh also had a plan, a strategy that was utterly unknown to the evil one. It had been in place since before the foundation of the universe itself.[93] There was no doubt that Yahweh's tactic would succeed. He knew, from the moment He first created the now-fallen cherub, that every bit of this would eventually take place.[94]

First, there must be a purging. Everything would have to be destroyed, especially anything that possessed the debased breath of life in it, both man and beast. The cosmic reset would be activated from Heaven's throne itself. Elohim had declared it, and the Divine Council had aligned themselves with the ominous decree. They would be the celestial witnesses of Elohim's authority and of His holy righteousness—both now and in the final judgment that would eventually result from it all.[95]

However, this particular divine cleansing process had not been designed to immediately "correct" the situation. Rather, it would serve as a heavenly pattern of the ultimate judgment that was yet to come. This is because there would still be scores of new human generations to live upon the earth.[96]

In the midst of those generations, kingdoms would rise and fall and, ultimately, Jerusalem would be established as the very center of the nations—a testament to the coming restitution of the Garden of Eden itself. Not only would it be the epicenter of the earth, but in the very last days, it would once again become the focal point of the abject hatred of the nations and their diabolical, geopolitical wrangling against Heaven's throne.[97]

The Harbinger

To be sure, this primordial global deluge would stand as an eternal harbinger to those future nations. It would be a sign of Elohim's overwhelming power and righteous indignation. But for now, at the decree of Yahweh, the cosmic weeding-out process would commence. And henceforth…the angels of Heaven and the peoples of the earth, along with their kings, would be forced to choose sides. One kingdom or the other. Each to his own desire.

This initial cleansing would be accomplished with water.

Lots of water…

A flood, of epic proportions.

PART FIVE

The Divine Reset

Scriptural Backdrop:

Genesis

Now after the population of human beings had increased throughout the earth, and daughters had been born to them, **some divine beings noticed how attractive human women were,** so they took wives for themselves from a selection that pleased them. So the LORD said, "My Spirit won't remain with human beings forever, because they're truly mortal. Their life span will be 120 years."

The Nephilim were on the earth at that time (and also immediately afterward), **when those divine beings were having sexual relations with those human women,** who gave birth to children for them.[98] These children became the heroes and legendary figures of ancient times.

The LORD saw that human evil was growing more and more throughout the earth, with every inclination of people's thoughts becoming only evil on a continuous basis. Then the LORD regretted that he had made human beings on the earth, and he was deeply grieved about that. So the LORD said, "I will annihilate these human beings whom I've created from the earth, including people, animals, crawling things, and flying creatures, because I'm grieving that I made them." The LORD was pleased with Noah, however. ...

[The LORD said] "For my part, I'm about to flood the earth with water and **destroy every living thing that breathes.** Everything on earth will die. However, I will establish my own covenant with you, and **you are to enter the ark—you, your sons, your wife, and your sons' wives."** (Genesis 6:1–8, 17–18, International Standard Version; emphasis added)

16

THE TORRENT

1,600 years after Eden's Fall, circa 2350 BC[99]

The last nail has just been driven into the frame of the massive wooden door.

As the spike finds its stopping point, it lets out an earsplitting *clang!* Its trilling ring echoes throughout the surrounding terrain, the reverberations racing through a world that will soon be immersed in a watery grave. The sound seems to carry with it a warning that screams, "Judgment is coming soon!"

Listening to the haunting sound ricocheting from tree to tree and rock to rock, the old man shudders. The tenor of the blow has unnerved him. He senses that this very same clank, the precise intonation, will be heard again somewhere in the distant future. He sees a brief "vision" of it as it rings out. Then the numinous image is gone, like a wisp of smoke that's captured by the wind and dissipates.

But Noah knows he has heard it before. The sound is as familiar to him as his own voice. And he knows exactly where he heard it. That's why he's shaking.

Those echoing notes had come to him in the form of several prescient dreams—deep in the silky, dark hours of the night. This particular moment, the one in which he now stands, has awakened him to those memories.

Pa-Pinggg. Pa-Pinggg. Pa-Pinggg!

But there is something else. The ringing from his dreams had also been accompanied by a haunting cry of agony. That plea had burst forth from the tortured lungs of an ethereal figure, a mysterious presence upon which Noah couldn't quite put his finger. The visage he beheld had been impaled through his hands and feet…on what appeared to be some sort of suspended wooden beam. The man had also been surrounded by a vile mob, huddled together under his blood-soaked body. Cursing him, mocking and reviling him.[100]

Noah is certain the nighttime revelations are in some way intertwined with what he is doing this very moment—building a gigantic wooden vessel, a ship of potential salvation being offered to his world…if that world will only listen, and come, and be saved! So far, however, they have not come—they have not heeded his pleas and warnings. They've only ridiculed.

He has erected the multilevel boat in the field beside his house, just as the Lord instructed…to the smallest detail. It is visible for miles around, available for all who care to inquire. It is Noah's divine assignment from Yahweh Himself. Driving the nails, driving the nails, driving the nails… day in and day out. For decades, and decades…*and decades*. Some have come to ask questions. Some have wanted a tour of the gigantic vessel. Others have come to intimidate and revile. But no one, absolutely no one…has believed.

Noah reaches up to where he has driven the final spike. He rubs his hand over the crown, its cap barely protruding from the wood. With his index finger, he encircles the nail's head, tracing its rugged iron edges… slowly…contemplating. Mesmerized by it.

Then the vision is gone, as quickly as it came.

17

THE MANIFESTATION

The family gathers in the center of the ship as it starts to groan
under the strain of its weighty living cargo.

For now, the animals are securely ensconced inside the gigantic vessel.

Each pair is situated in its own specially constructed enclosure. Seven days ago, the dreamlike procession had commenced. The beasts came streaming in from around the countryside, headed straight toward the ark. They came of their own accord, hearkening to a voice apparently heard only by them…the beckoning sound of their Creator.

What a beautiful thing to behold! Here was a virtual parade of created beings coursing to his own front door. It was as if the animals knew. But this spectacle was exactly what Yahweh had told him would happen.[101] Noah had never doubted it would be so, even though from the beginning it had still been a thing hard to imagine. But seeing it with his own eyes—right this moment—this was something else altogether!

Noah and his family stood in awe as the animals entered. From the smallest to the greatest, the creatures moved forward in pairs…each according to its own kind.

So many thoughts had poured through Noah's mind as he watched the animal cavalcade. *Is this really happening? Why don't these hard-hearted people listen? Family, friends, fellow citizens…they have all been warned, and for such a long time! But they refuse to heed the message. Instead, they simply curse us!*

Then Noah had turned to look at his wife, his sons, and their wives. "Take a look around!" he said. "You'll never see anything like this again!"

Noah's sons and daughters-in-law, all with widened eyes, began to circumnavigate their surroundings. Father was right. Everything within their current world would be gone within days. It *would* happen. His family didn't doubt him. Especially now. They continued to gawk at the animal parade, until they finally grasped the reality of the matter that was before them, and went to work. So much had yet to been done before the flood came!

It is at the end of the seven days of receiving the animals and securing them within the ark when it commences.

Noah speaks up as he and his family are finishing the final preparations. "Yahweh has again spoken to my soul…in this very moment!" he says. "Everything is getting ready to burst asunder, my dear family. This is it! It's about to come to pass."

"Don't be frightened!" he continues, surveying the faces of those around him. "God has not given us a spirit of fear. We are to be strong. We're wrapped in His divine protection now. He Himself will carry us along, above the waters of His wrath, as if we are being carried upon the wings of His divine messengers!"

As Noah finishes speaking, the earth begins to roil under their feet as though the fabric of its foundation is beginning to rip apart at the seams. The door to the great vessel snaps loose from its thick mooring ropes, sounding like the crack of a giant's whip. The massive wooden entryway crashes down against the cradle of its frame. At the thundering impact of its closing, they are sealed inside.

At that same moment, an unearthly explosion fills the air, causing their ears to pulsate with maddening thumping sensations. After that, yet another otherworldly sound—a metallic groaning—bursts forth from the heavens. It sounds like ten thousand resounding shofars have unleashed their doleful notes throughout the entire earth.

As the terrain churns and heaves, an instantaneous shaft of brilliant light illuminates the interior of the ark. The animals cower when they see it, and they hush in the wonder of it all. The presence of something holy is among them. They seem to know they are safe—protected inside the ark Noah built…at God's command.

Then, on that very day, in the six hundredth year of Noah's life, on the seventeenth day of the second month—the torrents finally burst forth. The downpour starts with one single, solitary *splat!* Then another *splat!* And then another.

After the first few spatters, vast oceans begin pouring from the sky as if a canopy of previously unseen water has been ripped asunder and released in violent, thunderous torrents. Within moments, the landscape is engulfed in cascading streams. The streams froth into roaring rivers, then the rivers meld into gigantic, bubbling lakes. Soon, the lakes merge their watery arms and blend into a never-ending sea, stretching to every horizon.

The earth is being covered over in water! The white-capped oceans continue to rise, creating violent, foam-covered, blackened depths…a foreboding chasm of watery death. At this rate, the swelling waters will consume the mountains themselves!

Just then, another *cracking* sound rumbles across the surface of the deep. With that last outburst, portions of the earth's depths open up their gigantic, gaping mouths. Yawning fissures burst forth from the secreted pits of the globe's crust. Geysers of water blast miles into the air, intermingling their inundation with the torrential columns of water that continue to empty themselves from the highest heavens.

The ominous crevasses gape open, as far as their eyes can see. Noah and his family stand slack-jawed, peering through the tiny portholes. The blackest clouds they have ever seen canopy the sky like a divine vestment of inky black cloth draped over the tabletop of the entire universe. The middle of the day has become as dark as midnight. The stars are gone. The sun and moon are nowhere in sight, blanketed out of view. Will those glorious heavenly lights ever be seen again?

Their eyes have never beheld, their ears have never heard, their minds have never before contemplated such raw, unmitigated, majestic power. The gigantic boat that once looked so enormous to them now feels small. So very, very tiny.

The family gathers in the center of the ship as the structure starts to groan under the strain of its weighty living cargo. The vessel is moving! They can feel it beginning to float! Their whole world is being covered over in water, even to the tops of the highest mountains. And they are floating on top of it all, on what now feels like a mere stick of wood. They fall to their knees in prayer.

In the next moments, what is left of Elohim's first creation lets forth a long, heaving sound, like that of a grief-stricken mother groaning over her dying child's last breath of life.

The end has come.

So far...they have survived.

What happens next, however, will stun them. And the weight of the jolt will envelope them in unspeakable and suffocating grief.

18

THE AGONY

At times, it is hard to distinguish between the pitiful bellows of the humans and those of the beasts.

Hush!

What's that noise? Noah and his family scramble to peer through the tiny portals. But it's too dark to see anything, so they press their ears against the ship's walls.

In horror, they begin to finally make out the sounds.

Can it really be?

Unthinkable! Must we now be forced to endure this additional sorrow?

All around, they hear the cries. Close by. Even right beneath them.

They realize that gigantic masses of people on the outside of the vessel are clinging to the hull, searching, frantically scratching and clawing, looking for a life-saving crevice they can grasp and cling to. The desperate people scream and plead, their pitiful cries occasionally muffled by the moaning of the wind and the slapping of the angry waves against the ark—and the pounding, beating, drumming, wretched, never-ending rain...

As if this isn't enough, the ark's occupants are hearing the agonizing pleas coming from far off as well. They can make out wailing and cursing, even above the tumult of the geological upheaval. Surely there are tens of thousands, floating in giant masses of panicking humans, mingled with livestock and wild animals, desperately trying to stay afloat in the chaos. Great roars emerge from the perishing swarm—in unison, resembling an explosion of thunder, sounding like a massive crowd that has gathered for a huge sporting event. The planet itself seems to be weeping, grieving from its own heartbreaking depths of anguish.

The wrenching pleas for mercy are shouted over and over again, in the futile hope that the mere repetition will somehow cause the doors of the vessel they had previously ignored to fling open and relent...inviting them all inside, to safety. But the portal will not concede. It has been sealed shut by the divine hand of Yahweh. Noah and his sons could not open the doors at this point even if they wanted to.

The wailing continues in undulating crescendos, but no one is coming to their rescue. Not now. Not ever.

Those inside the heaving ship lament over the outside shrieks, the pleas for help that violate the depths of their hearts. They agonize over those they used to live among, only hours earlier. Many of them they know by name. But Noah and his family are now helpless to save a single person, or to even offer comfort. All of them...are *perishing*...just outside the walls of the ark.

At times, it's difficult to distinguish between the pitiful bellows of the humans and those of the panicked drowning beasts that swim among them. And, every now and then, they think they actually recognize an individual voice. A friend? A family member? A personal acquaintance? A merchant with whom they have done business? The horrors are ceaseless. The ark's inhabitants cover their ears as they weep, praying for the cries just outside the heaving hull of their ship to come to an end.

It has only been a few days ago that some of those were planning huge wedding celebrations. Others had been feasting and drinking at their raucous parties, reveling in their debauchery and insolence...mocking God and reviling His servants. They had been counting their piles of money. Planning their next business ventures. Parading about in their fancy clothes and fine jewelry. Making judgments among themselves, dividing each other into "acceptable" or "unacceptable" classes, according to their perceived stations in life. But now it is too late. None of that matters anymore. As they are gasping for their last breaths of life, none of them thinks of any of those things. Right now, in this moment, as their lungs scream for more air...they are all finally equal as they are sucked under the surface of the churning depths.

For 120 years, the mocking ones had been reasoned with by Noah and his family. At times, they had even been begged. And now, by their own choosing, they are all being wiped out as if they are a mere anthill, destined for annihilation. What a difference just one day can make in the scheme of all things. One moment, it's life as usual. The next moment... it's death, sheer terror, and unspeakable devastation. It didn't have to be this way though. *It didn't.* They could have been saved, too—if they had only believed.

Now, none of their previously presumed legacies will ever again mean a thing...to anyone. Their best-laid plans have come to naught. In their collective greed and fleshly lusts, they had clung to the demonically corrupted world to which they had become so attached, and they had lost their souls...forever.

Vast multitudes are giving up now, too exhausted to struggle any longer. They release what little strength they still have as that one last gasp fills their lungs with a burning gulp of putrid, muck-laden water. The oceans of black swallow them whole, like a gigantic, ravenous beast. They vanish into the darkness as if they have never existed. Some are still shaking their fists toward the heavens and screaming vile words of rebuke at their Creator while they slip out of sight. Their names will never be remembered, or spoken of, again. By anyone.

And slowly, but surely, through the last few hours that have ensued, the screams of agony, the shrieks of unmitigated pride, have all but stopped.

Over the next days and weeks, they will all be gone. Those who have found a semblance of safety by floating on wooden objects and trees will soon die of thirst, starvation, sickness, or exposure. Others will be eaten alive by scavenging sea creatures snatching the weakened ones who slip off their floating islands like limp and worn-out rags. Still others will be consumed by the vicious beasts that swim their way to the floating dinner plates of human victims—a virtual smorgasbord of helpless dead flesh, waiting to be picked off.

But, as time moves on, even those well-fed beasts will begin to die. There is no more drinkable water. There is no more food. No more shelter. And the world is still drowning in water that is filled with decaying, dying filth.

All the evil that has lived in the hearts of the mocking humans and the corrupted beasts has gone down to the depths with them. Mercifully so.

And then, at the end of seven more months…

It. Is. Finished.

19

THE CLEANSING

With the eight of them and Yahweh's hand of mercy, everything will begin again.

For the ark-bound family and their collection of Heaven-selected animals, the only sound that envelopes them now is the storm—and the relentless, crashing waves. And animals in their cages and stalls. Multitudes of animals.

The rocking, creaking, groaning of the boat sets the predominant ambiance of their new home—their fortress of floating safety. That atmosphere is defined by the persistent mooing, moaning, crying, yelping, tweeting, cawing, bellowing, and bleating of the beasts—the sounds that ripple throughout the craft, day in and day out. The animals have survived something unspeakable, and they seem to sense it.

A new beginning is on the way. But, there is still work to be done. Always, there is work to be done.

There are mouths to feed. Baby animals to be birthed. Putrid refuse to be jettisoned overboard. Rancid, reeking, sloppy-floored stalls to be cleaned. Life-sustaining vats of gruel to be prepared. Relentless leaks to be plugged. Regurgitation, from both humans and beasts, to be scrubbed and mopped from the decks. And, occasionally, at the end of the day, they are rewarded with the sweet release of a few moments of sleep.

Then it all starts over. Get up, get a little something to eat, then begin the necessary monotony once more. And again…and yet again…*and still again.*

For the most part, time is now irrelevant. For the longest, there is no sun or moon by which the ark dwellers can measure their lives. There are no stars by which they can navigate. And besides, to where would they "navigate?" There's no land to mark as their ultimate destination…at least not yet. That detail is left solely in the hands of God, as it has been so much of their lives.

For now, there is just *the work.* And a few precious moments of blissful slumber. Then more work. More pounding rain. More rocking back and forth. More irritated protestations from the animal passengers. More wretched seasickness. More filth to clean up. More holes and cracks to fill. And *more work*…today, tomorrow, and the many seemingly unending days after tomorrow.

In the midst of all that, each and every day, for forty days and forty nights, the heavens and the earth continue to cascade out their pent-up oceans of water. For 150 days, the swirling waters pound over the earth. In the last of those days, as far as the eye can see, not even a mountaintop is visible. Everything is simply gone. Vanished beneath the global ocean.

Then…Yahweh speaks to His own creation. And it listens, as it did in the beginning.

With simply the sound of His voice, He sends a mighty rushing wind over the earth. The waters buck against the gale, but the mountain-like waves now relent and begin to recede. Yahweh speaks yet again, and the springs of the deep and the floodgates of the heavens seal shut; the rain stops falling from the sky. In a mere snap of a split moment, the wind and the waves are stilled.

The water begins its withdrawal, swallowed up by the gaping fissures in the earth's crust. At the end of the 150 days, the swirling torrents of the newly created oceans have gone down considerably. And on the seventeenth day of the seventh month, the ark comes to rest on the mountains of Ararat. The waters recede until the tenth month, and on the first day of that month, the tops of the mountains finally begin to show themselves once again.

By the first day of the first month of the next year, Noah's 601st year, the flooding waters of death have begun to shrink their depths, retreating from the surface of the earth. It is as though a gigantic drain plug has been pulled open, and the earth swallows the water back into its core, in great heaving gulps. By the twenty-seventh day of the second month, the ground is completely dry.

On this day, Noah's oldest son, Shem, approaches his father, his hair tangled and matted, his beard long and shaggy, reeking of the smell of months of nonstop human work and animal waste.

"Father," he asks, "is this really the end of everything? What's to become of us now?"

Noah looks outside the portals as the clouds are parting and the first rays of sun the family has seen in months are streaming through, in all their glory. Brilliant, multicolored, arched bands of shimmering light fill the crystal blue skies above; this is a phenomenon they have never before beheld.

"On the contrary, my son," Noah answers. "This is only the beginning. This is where it starts over! *Here. Now!*"

Shem relaxes in the comforting tone of his father's infectious enthusiasm. It is one of the things he adores about his dad. Ham and Japheth move closer to their brother and father. They understand.

Noah leans in toward the three men, pulling them together in a gripping bear hug like when they were still his little boys. He places his forehead gently upon the foreheads of each of his sons, one by one, cupping their faces with his hands as he shows them his affection. "Come, my sons! Help me open this door! I'm ready to put some solid ground under my feet—how about you?"

All four men beam, wide-eyed, at their wives. They will soon step upon firm soil as earth's brand-new first family. With the eight of them and Yahweh's hand of mercy, everything will begin again.

"Hurry up!" Noah shouts as he scrambles toward the door. "There's work to be done! A lot of work. We have a new world to build!"

The family bursts into joyous laughter, dancing as they pile out of the ark, leaping about as children who have just now been released upon a wondrous and pristine playground.

However…deep within the unseen realm of abominable blackness and depravity, the ancient serpent[102] is still developing his strategy to root out the *Seed* of his swelling kaleidoscope of nightmares…and utterly destroy Him.

PART SIX

Relentless Pursuit

Scriptural Backdrop:

The Seed

And I will put enmity between thee and the woman, and between **thy seed** and **her seed**; it shall bruise thy head, and thou shalt bruise his heel. (Genesis 3:15, KJV; emphasis added)

And **thy seed** shall be as the dust of the earth, and thou shalt spread abroad to the west, and to the east, and to the north, and to the south: and in thee and **in thy seed** shall all the families of the earth be blessed.[103] (Genesis 28:13–14, KJV; emphasis added)

Now to Abraham **and his seed** were the promises made. He saith not, and to seeds, as of many; but as of one, and **to thy seed, which is Christ.** (Galatians 3:16, KJV; emphasis added)

Then Pharaoh gave this order to all his people: "**Every Hebrew boy that is born you** must throw into the Nile, but let every girl live." (Exodus 1:22, KJV; emphasis added)

When Haman saw that Mordecai would not kneel down or pay him honor, he was enraged. **Yet having learned who Mordecai's people were,** he scorned the idea of killing only Mordecai. Instead **Haman looked for a way to destroy all Mordecai's people, the Jews,** throughout the whole kingdom of Xerxes. (Esther 3:5–6; emphasis added)

When Herod realized that he had been outwitted by the Magi, he was furious, and **he gave orders to kill all the boys in Bethlehem** and its vicinity who were two years old and under, in accordance with the time he had learned from the Magi. (Matthew 2:16; emphasis added)

The dragon stood in front of the woman who was about to give birth, so that **it might devour her child** the moment he was born…. Then the dragon was enraged at the woman and went off **to wage war against the rest of her offspring**—those who keep God's commands and hold fast their testimony about Jesus. (Revelation 12:4, 17; emphasis added)

20

THE DRAGON'S LAIR

After the Flood, the history of humanity marches on–for millennia,
Satan is on the prowl–in search of the Seed.

---

nly two more quick chapters, and we're back to the narrative.

First, let's quickly examine one of the main themes of the Bible—
especially as it relates to the days in which we currently live. I believe it
will help you to make much more sense of our world, and it will make the
narrative section that follows more understandable from a spiritual as well
as an interdimensional perspective.

Have you heard the maxim that the word "history" can be more accurately represented as "His Story"? There's good reason that play on words
is considered to be so true.

For thousands of years after the Great Flood, especially from the days
of the Egyptian Empire and forward, the newly formed nation of Israel
was constantly under attack by the surrounding kingdoms. On several
ominous and history-changing occasions, Israel was torn asunder and
subsequently enslaved.

Satan's continual targeting of the nation of Israel was set in motion to
accomplish one major goal: *destroy the coming Seed* and unleash his rebellious

vengeance upon the people of Yahweh, through whom that Seed had been promised to arrive. This was Satan's psychotic obsession.[104]

The ancient serpent knew that if he couldn't stop the prophecy of Genesis 3 from coming to fruition, his own kingdom dreams, in the end, would be obliterated. So he employed the human powers he had under his sway. Down through the ages, they were the ones who would do his bidding: the halls of institutionalized religious influence, entertainment and sports productions, educational organizations, and especially the thrones of great geopolitical power. It would appear that, in this matter, not much has changed through the millennia.

Game of Thrones

The major empires of world history, especially those that directly affected the Middle East, Europe, and parts of Asia and Africa, tell the larger story in regard to Israel's history as it unfolded through those nations. At the crux of that story is Satan's murderous agenda against Israel and the "Seed" that would arise from within the population of their own generations, the One who would "crush his head."

Even though the following synopsis of major world empires is admittedly an oversimplification of the complex saga of the history's overall unfolding, it is an accurate assessment of the details as they pertain to the context of our examination.

The Egyptian Empire was intermittently *friend* and *foe* to the children of Israel once they were in the Promised Land. On several occasions, ancient Egypt even conspired with other empires for the purpose of destroying God's people and their nation.

Egypt's rulers continued these kinds of conspiratorial arrangements and attacks right up to the Six Day War in 1967. However, prior to the time of the New Testament, it can be asserted that much of Egypt's animosity toward Israel was fueled by Satan's never-ending desire to find and destroy the coming Seed—the one prophesied to abolish the ancient serpent's earthly empire.

The Assyrian Empire was one of Israel's most ruthless enemies. By 722 BC, Assyria had succeeded in becoming the ancient world's newest superpower. It also conquered the Northern Kingdom of the civil war-divided Israel. As a result, ten of Israel's twelve tribes were taken into captivity by Assyria.

Assyria set out to defeat the Southern Kingdom of Judah in order to capture Jerusalem—*the ultimate prize*—along with the two remaining tribes. They were never successful, and, in time, had to turn their attention to another rising world superpower. The brutal Assyrian Empire would soon be conquered by the bloodthirsty beast that was on the rise—the Babylonian Empire.

The Babylonian Empire under King Nebuchadnezzar was, over a period of years, able to overcome the Southern Kingdom of Judah in 597 BC. In so doing, it destroyed the city of Jerusalem, as well as the Temple of Yahweh that was built by King Solomon. In addition to carting off the Temple treasures, Babylon also took the surviving Israelites into captivity. The best and brightest of them, especially the male children, were schooled in the ways of paganism and the Babylonian language and customs.[105] Thus, we learn of the exploits of Daniel, Shadrach, Meshach, and Abednego in the Old Testament.

The Persian Empire came to fruition around 560 BC. By continual encroachments upon the Babylonians, the Persians came to possess what the Babylonians and the Assyrians before them had amassed. By default, that Persian inheritance included what used to be the land of Israel and the capital city of Jerusalem.

The Jews were hated by certain factions within the Persian kingdom, including a particularly influential government official by the name of Haman. Haman plotted to have all the Jews in Persia destroyed by a decree of the emperor. Once again, Satan filled a singular man of power to carry out his plan of destroying "the Seed" and those who were carrying it. The plot almost succeeded, except for the hand of Elohim working through the Jewish queen of Persia named Hadassah—or, as she is often known by her Persian name, *Esther.*

It was under the Persian Empire that, eventually, the Jews were allowed to return to Jerusalem to rebuild the city walls and the Temple. Even then, the satanically inspired enemies of God's people plotted, without ceasing, the ruin of the Jews and their plans to revive their Temple-centered worship of Yahweh.

The Greek Empire, by 449 BC, after a series of long and brutal wars with the Persian kingdom, prevailed, and a treaty was signed with Persia. Within one hundred years of that date, the Persian Empire ceased to exist altogether. The Greeks were then entrenched as the world's new superpower and would go on to conquer the "known world" under Alexander the Great.

After Alexander's death in 323 BC, the land of Judea, including Jerusalem, fell under the power of the resulting Greek Seleucid Empire. The process of *Hellenization*—the infusion of the pervasive customs and culture of the Greeks, including their pagan religious practices—was enforced upon the Jews without an ounce of mercy.

Consequently, by 167 BC, Jewish religious sacrifices were forbidden, among numerous other distinctly Jewish religious and cultural practices. Altars to Greek gods were set up, and animals considered "unclean" by the Jews were sacrificed upon those altars. The Olympian Zeus was placed on the altar of the Temple of the Lord in Jerusalem. Possession of Jewish sacred texts was outlawed; the law was enforced by threat of a sentence of death.

By 166 BC, the Jews revolted against the heavy hand of their Greek overlords. The ensuing war became known as the Maccabean Revolt, and it eventually resulted in the liberation of Jerusalem and the surrounding area. That Jewish emancipation lasted for about one hundred years.

However, this "freedom"—politically speaking—was due in large part to an ill-fated alliance that the Jewish leaders had struck with a fledgling empire that was gaining prominence with alarming speed...*and overwhelmingly massive power.*

The ancient people of God were getting ready to dance with the devil. But they had no idea what that deal would cost them…until it was far too late.

Yet, as evil as the next empire would prove to be, Yahweh would use it to His own glory. This is the empire that would, without any idea that it was doing so, give birth to the Savior of all humanity.

21

THE DRAGON'S BREATH

His ages-long quest now focused upon one individual in particular—a baby boy.

The Roman Empire was on the rise. Its ascent was ferocious and merciless. Rome's final grip upon the throat of the collapsing Greek supremacy closed tighter. By 63 BC, the Roman general Pompey sailed across the Mediterranean with his vast fleet of battle-hardened ships, unleashing his devastating naval supremacy on the floundering remains of the Greek Empire's reaches.

It was into this new and history-altering world that God implanted the beginnings of His strategy to deconstruct Satan's empire—one that was operated from an ever-entangling web being spun in the unseen realms of demonic darkness.

During that period of human history, Satan thought he might have come upon a bit of good fortune by cornering his coming mortal enemy— the divine messenger of his demise—*the Seed* that would come from the womb of a woman…and who would, one day in the future, crush his head. He was frantic to uncover the truth of the matter.

He, of course, would fail in his plan to destroy the child, or the man that grew from that Heaven-sent child. But, after Satan increasingly realized that he had been duped by Heaven's throne, he turned the might of the Roman Empire—mere puppets of his own dark kingdom—against the Church.

In the midst of those days, the symbol of the dragon had become an official emblem of the Roman cavalry. The armies of Rome would emblazon their soldier's breastplates and battle flags with an image of a dragon, or as they called it in Latin, the *draco*.[106]

In addition to the banners and breastplates, a draco battle standard was also created by shaping metal to form a hollow head that resembled a ferocious, sharp-toothed dragon. A cloth, tube-like tail was then attached to the neck of the head, so that it would expand when the wind passed through it as the standard was being carried high in the air at great horseback speeds. When the draco standard was displayed in this manner, as the cavalry's units raced towards their enemy targets, a hissing noise would issue forth that was caused by the airstream passing through the dragon's mouth.[107]

Satan wanted his fury and authority on vivid display at all times. This was his greatest empire to date. And, just like the serpent's veil of hypocrisy, Rome advertised its empire as one of great peace and justice. In reality, the exact opposite was true.

Rome's "peace" was accomplished only in obliterating its enemies with its incomparable and unimaginable power. It's truest "justice" was reserved exclusively for certain elites of Roman society and citizenship—those who were abjectly loyal to the throne and all of its cruelest eccentricities. The empire had taken on the characteristics of its dark and unseen overlord, the one who was truly pulling the strings on his human puppets from deep within another realm: the ancient dragon.[108]

But it was in the early days of that draconian empire that Satan began to narrow his search. His ages-long quest now honed in upon one individual in particular—a baby boy. A child born in Bethlehem, during the time of Caesar Augustus…and Herod the Great.

Following is how the saga unfolded.

PART SEVEN

The Journey

Scriptural Backdrop:

The Conception:

This is how the birth of Jesus the Messiah came about: His mother Mary was pledged to be married to Joseph, but before they came together, she was found to be pregnant through the Holy Spirit. Because Joseph her husband was faithful to the law, and yet did not want to expose her to public disgrace, he had in mind to divorce her quietly. But after he had considered this, an angel of the Lord appeared to him in a dream and said, "Joseph son of David, do not be afraid to take Mary home as your wife, because what is conceived in her is from the Holy Spirit. She will give birth to a son, and you are to give him the name Jesus, because he will save his people from their sins." All this took place to fulfill what the Lord had said through the prophet: "The virgin will conceive and give birth to a son, and they will call him Immanuel" (which means "God with us"). (Matthew 1:18–25)

The Census

In those days Caesar Augustus issued a decree that a census should be taken of the entire Roman world. (This was the first census that took place while Quirinius was governor of Syria.) And everyone went to their own town to register. So Joseph also went up from the town of Nazareth in Galilee to Judea, to Bethlehem the town of David, because he belonged to the house and line of David. He went there to register with Mary, who was pledged to be married to him and was expecting a child. (Luke 2:1–5)

22

THE DECREE

The tiny village of Nazareth, Roman district of Galilee, circa 3 BC

Nine months from now, a convergence of seemingly unrelated events will occur. The collision of those events will shake the world to the depths of its foundations—literally, and forever. From that point forward, nothing will ever be the same.

Caesar Augustus—the "heathen Roman Emperor," as the Jews call him—issued an executive fiat only a few weeks ago. The order demands that a census be taken of the entire Roman world. The decree impacts all of the lands within the empire's domain. And that domain is immense.[109]

But the truest reason for counting the empire's population is to assure that the proper amount of tax revenue flows into Rome's insatiable government treasury. The people are well aware of what this census is about, and they hate Caesar for it. But they have no choice. They have to comply.

In the Roman province of Judea—the most prominent populace being Jewish—the details of the Roman order are carried out at the bidding of

Herod Agrippa, also known as the "King of the Jews," the official title he has held since 40 BC. In reality, Herod is a mere governmental appointee, and because of this, he is fiercely loyal to Rome. He is also considered by many of his subjects to be a Jewish/Arab half-breed.[110] Therefore, the cruel and often maniacal Herod is loathed by practically the entire population of those over whom he rules.

In submission to Caesar's decree, Herod has directed that the Roman registration order will be carried out in line with the ancient Jewish custom of "enrollments." He has instructed his subjects to be registered according to families and, specifically, to be registered in the towns of their birth, according to the lineages of their fathers.[111]

In the case of Joseph, whose ancestry emanates from the line of King David and because he is originally from Bethlehem, it is natural that, in accordance with Jewish law, he will travel to Bethlehem for the registration.[112]

Because of the "mysterious" circumstances surrounding Mary's seemingly ill-timed pregnancy and the resulting veiled innuendos that have pummeled the young couple, they have grown increasingly content about finally leaving Nazareth behind them and beginning their journey to Bethlehem. The trip will not be without difficulties, though. It will be a lengthy one, and they will carry everything they need on their backs, and strapped to their donkey.

Much of the trip will be through sometimes brutal terrain. Many thousands of other travelers will also be on the move, headed to their respective places of registration. A number of truly good people will help one another along the way, but ruffians will also be scattered among the same crowds. They'll be looking for opportunities to pounce upon easy prey…like Serengeti lions stalking the unsuspecting herds of migrating wildebeests. As he plans the journey, Joseph has to take all of these factors into account.

The Jews of the district of Galilee—where Nazareth is located—are principally a rural people. Few young couples living in the area venture very far from their little villages within the course of their entire lifetimes.

The majority of Galilee's people work the land, tend their flocks, and ply their trades, seldom traveling more than a single day's journey from home. Some, however, do occasionally make the trek to Jerusalem to celebrate the Passover. And even that is no small excursion from Nazareth. It is a several-day journey, on foot, each way.[113]

Almost three hundred villages are scattered throughout the district of Galilee. Nazareth is just one of those insignificant hamlets. The average settlement is no more than a handful of acres, with a population of only a few hundred in each location. The larger villages, called towns, might cover ten acres or more and are often walled in. The tiny world of Joseph and Mary is pretty much limited to their mountainside village and the fields around it.[114]

Mary is now in the very last days of her "suspicious" pregnancy. Because of the atmosphere in the village surrounding the ordeal, Mary has insisted that she will go with Joseph to Bethlehem. She doesn't want to leave the protective care of her new husband. He agrees. So the matter is settled.[115]

But there is another important matter of consideration. The truth of it is too surreal to utter among the general populace of the village, but one that she and Joseph have pondered with each other on several occasions. They are both intimately familiar with the commonly accepted biblical teaching among most of the rabbis of their day that the Messiah of Israel is to be announced in—of all places—*Bethlehem*! And they both know she is carrying this very child. This is a detail they have been forced to keep relatively private as long as possible, lest they be held in contempt of a perceived and unforgiveable sacrilege. The circumstance that demands that they head to Bethlehem—the emperor's decree, coupled with Herod's directives—is far too incredible to be considered mere coincidence.

So, they concur: Mary *has* to accompany Joseph to Bethlehem.[116] It seems the angel's divine announcement, given almost nine months earlier, is coming to fruition. This holy child will be named Yeshua. And, He will indeed be born in Bethlehem—or at least somewhere on the way there...

~~

The young couple has gathered their families together and finalized their plans. They have spoken their goodbyes in the midst of a prevailing sadness. In that same vein, they have clasped hands and prayed together, then put the finishing touches on their preparations and loaded the donkey with their meager supplies.

As they leave Nazareth, the arid breezes lightly brushing their faces, they have an unexplainable sense of adventure in their hearts. Many among their family and friends think them to be reckless regarding Mary's attempt to make such an arduous journey. But there simply is no stopping the couple. It is as if they are on some sort of "divine mission." *Silly young people. Now…all we can do is pray, and trust them into the care of Yahweh.*

So it is that, under these particular circumstances, Mary, now the wife of Joseph—though only in the actual relationship of being engaged—will accompany her husband to *Bethlehem*…the town that bears the name that is the Hebrew word for "House of Bread."

The journey they are beginning will ultimately impact the entire planet and violently alter the course of human history. This is a fact they can't even begin to fathom at this point in the context of their otherwise "inconsequential" lives—insignificant as far as the world is concerned, anyway.

But Heaven knows something different….

Yahweh has always enjoyed confounding the wisdom of the wise by choosing to work His glory through the things that the world considers *small.*

Now, He is getting ready to do it again.

23

DREAMS

Before he can finish the sentence, Mary interrupts with
a huge smile, betraying her excited anticipation.

As they set out from Nazareth, the young mother-to-be is situated on the back of their donkey. Joseph directs the beast by the reins, leading the way on foot. Mary glances back over her shoulder toward the little village...the serene place where she has lived her entire childhood. All of it is now fading into her past. The growing droplets of moisture in her eyes escape and dribble down her cheeks, regardless of her failed efforts to fight them back. After a while, the people of her hometown began to look like nothing more than living dots, their movements only discernable because of the contrasting backdrop of the mountainous horizon.

Like a fading dream, her past is slipping behind her, but her future is still just up the road. *What a notion!* It is in that moment that her mind bursts with an exciting revelation.

Over the next several days, she discusses the concept with Joseph. "*Perhaps,*" she entreats, "if it is possible, we can make our permanent home in Bethlehem? We could start again with our lives—from there! Just the three of us. In Bethlehem!"[117]

At her first mention of the idea, Joseph pauses the journey, pulling on the reins. He turns to Mary, patting the donkey's head as he speaks. "You know. *That's really not a bad idea.* Though it could be a struggle, financially…

"But," he pulls at his beard in further thought, "if it is the Lord's will, this *could* work!" He shoots a tender look at her again, and her heart melts. She truly *loves* this man!

Mary continues her considerations: "I've grown so weary of the gossip back in Nazareth, Joseph. And the out-and-out slander that accompanies it! You're a *good* man. You've risked your life for me, and you've done so on more than one occasion.

"And," she urges, "think of our son! Think of the names they'll call him. I don't believe my heart will be able to bear it, Joseph. We will know the truth, but we'll never be able to explain it to anyone else—"

"Mary," Joseph breaks in, "I've received my word from God as well, delivered by an angel, in a dream—a dream so real it might as well have been lived in my own flesh! If it wasn't for that…well, you know the struggles I had! And, yes. I also believe it would be easier on our son, and all of us, to start life over somewhere else. Bethlehem is as good a place as any. I've got relatives and other connections there—"

"—well then," Mary interrupts, "I'm glad that's settled and you agree with me." She winks at him.

With a more serious look on her face, she persists. "But, Joseph, regardless of your humility in the matter, *my words are true!* You don't deserve what those people back there are saying. You are the Lord's servant as well, my love. It's just not fair. They don't know what they're talking about! They haven't the slightest idea."

She pouts with faintly pooched lips as she speaks, coupled with a slight girlish grin. It is a look Joseph has never been able to resist. And she knows it. *And he knows that she knows it.*

Throwing his head back as he chuckles aloud, he collects his thoughts and tugs at the reins. The donkey jolts into action. "You also are the Lord's servant, Mary," Joseph responds as they walk.

"In fact, you are much *more* the 'servant' than I am! I'm not the one carrying the child. Nor am I the one who will birth the child, Mary. *You* will! *Thanks be unto the Lord for that!*"

He laughs aloud at the delivery of his own joke. "Yes, Joseph! *Thanks be unto God!*"

The two of them appear as if they are a couple of playful children, rather than the average variety of more somber married couples who are on a burdensome journey, one that Rome means only for the purpose of registering them for a taxation census.

"And," Joseph goes on, "I'll not be His *mother*, either. It's *you*, Mary. *You*. You are God's chosen one. I'll be faithful to my anointed part in all of this, gladly. It's truly an unspeakable honor. But, never forget: *I love you Mary*. I have loved you for a very long time—"

Before he can finish the sentence, Mary interrupts again. "No one will have to know the unbelievable circumstances of our ordeal if we stay and live in Bethlehem! Think of it, Joseph! We can just live as a normal family, *on our own*, in a new community. We can make new friends. No gossip, no mockery, no disbelief, and no constant explaining. Oh, if only it could be so!"

And so it is that their mutual longing to begin a new life together in Bethlehem comes to be.

But right now, the donkey has just misstepped yet again.

Mary jolts to the side, afraid she'll fall off *this* time. She squeals as the animal stumbles, and then she bursts into a childlike hilarity, embarrassed by her own startled shriek.

This isn't the first close call she has endured with this not-so-surefooted beast. And it probably won't be the last. But, as usual, Joseph is right there, cradling her to prevent a fall, and calming the donkey at the same time.

Within moments, they're on their way again.

They still have many more grueling miles to traverse.

24

THE APPROACH

Behind them lay the valleys and hills that separate Bethlehem from Jerusalem.

The trip has, thus far, been bone wearying. The days seem much slower in their passing than they should. Frequent pauses are required. A sometimes ornery donkey has to be placated. Sore feet need to be rubbed, and rested. And a very pregnant mom requires a multitude of stops for a few moments of non-bouncing rest. But such is the drudgery, and danger, of extended first-century foot travel.

This is not a trip one would normally "enjoy" in the first place…much less under the circumstances in which they are now making it. The entire journey from Nazareth to Bethlehem will encompass the better part of a week, one way. Sometimes it can take longer, depending upon weather and other unforeseen circumstances. The food and water they carry will need to be rationed until they can replenish their meager supplies along the way. Of course, they are also concerned about a baby arriving somewhere en route…a situation they have prayed will not happen. And these factors don't even take into account the bandits, con artists, and other dangers they might encounter.

As an extra precaution, they take the most commonly considered "safe" route to Bethlehem. It isn't the shortest path; however, it is the course that will avoid the dreaded region of Samaria and its often unfriendly inhabitants who live directly to the south of Nazareth. There has been bad blood between the Jews and Samaritans for hundreds of years.[118]

So it is that the course they are now on will carry them along the eastern banks of the Jordan River, after first passing through many of the *wadis* of the rugged wilderness between Nazareth and the Jordan roadway. First-century travelers in that area are intimately familiar with the popular routes of the wadis, those deep ravines and valleys between the high hills that, during the rainy season, flood with rushing torrents of dangerous waters. But now, in this season, the wadis serve as reliable traveling passes and shortcuts.

Onward they traipse. They have several more days just to make it to the Jordan River Road. From there, the journey will become a little easier. But that targeted thoroughfare is still a long way off. So they plod along… two more days.

On the morning of the third day, they leave the wadis and are at the northernmost point of the Jordan Valley road intersection. And on that day…it rains. Constant, cold drops turn the narrow paths ahead of them into a sloppy, dangerous thoroughfare, a phenomenon that is relatively common within this area of the country. By midmorning, the rain has stopped, but the trip has been made more difficult because of it. So, they slog on.

After yet another day's journey along the southward traveling road, they eventually arrive at the well-known convergence on the banks of the Jordan River, just east and a little to the south of the ancient city of Jericho. They are now just north of the Dead Sea. Here, at the Jordan crossing, the water is shallow enough to wade on foot or on the back of a donkey. For ages, these fords have been a major junction for the passing of the vast populations that traverse this part of the province.

The baby boy Mary cradles within her womb will one day stand very close to the spot through which they are currently wading through knee-deep waters. In this area is where Jesus will be baptized by John, his cousin who will come to be known as John the Baptist. That ancient ritual, thirty years in the future, will thus begin His earthly crusade to reclaim the Paradise that was lost in the primordial Eden disaster. This is just one small piece of the puzzle that will define the coming years, a piece they still don't comprehend.

At this crossing, Joseph and Mary are in one of the warmest parts of the region. However, the fact that they are traveling in the cooler season of the year will soon become more apparent as they come nearer to Bethlehem. But several more days of travel are still ahead.

25

THE HEIGHTS

They shiver as they look in its direction.

They have arrived on the far eastern side of Bethlehem, the city still miles away. They are stopping more often now to accommodate Mary's growing fatigue. They trudge their way up the steeply inclining roadway before them. From the crest of that mountain range, they will start their final descent into the city.

As they reach the heights of Bethlehem, the most conspicuous scene within their direct line of sight, just south, is the great castle that the unpopular King Herod had built. The ornate edifice is actually miles away, but its image is unmistakable...dominating the landscape as far as the eye can see, just as Herod intended.

Roman Judea's most despised king had constructed the palace and its surrounding support city on the backs of slaves, as well as the most skilled craftsmen that his vast wealth could purchase. Embarrassing to the common people of the area, Herod named the blood-bought city castle after himself...*Herodium*. Mary and Joseph had heard the stories about the pretentious monstrosity since they were children, but now they are actually looking at it for their very first time.

Regardless of how it came to be, Herodium is indeed an imposingly magnificent palace. Resting atop the highest hill in the region some 2,500 feet in altitude, just southeast of Bethlehem; the fortress city is menacingly formidable—almost a royal city unto itself. The palace and its gardens contain all the trappings of the luxurious niceties that Herod's opulent lifestyle demands.

But such is Herod's arrogance. And he has proven many times over that he will destroy, or even murder, anyone who comes close to stepping in the way of his jealously guarded power and lavish wealth. So, while the mountaintop fortress is truly beautiful to behold, few who see it doubt the terrible price at which it was constructed. At the moment, they have no idea that, not long from now, Herod will turn his wrath towards them— and especially their newborn child.

With a sense of relief, the traveling couple turns and heads down the mountain slopes toward their ultimate destination. In the distance, east of Herodium, through the various visual breaks in the surrounding hills, the glimmer of the diamond-like sheen of the Dead Sea comes into view.

The watery vista they behold—the "Sea of Judgment," as some still call it—brings to their minds the divine verdict that had rained down upon the Dead Sea valley and its vast, more than two hundred square miles of metro area called Sodom and Gomorrah, housing millions of residents and dating all the way back to the days of Abraham.[119] The five-city area that made up the district is obliterated now, buried thousands of years ago under fiery judgment from the heavens.[120]

To the north, as they continue their descent, stretch the valleys and hills that separate Bethlehem from Jerusalem. They are the same ones that, at this moment, conceal the Holy City from their view. But they know Jerusalem is there, just out of sight, as well as the Temple of God, teeming with its priests—not to mention the potentially brutal Roman troops, hordes and hordes of them.

They also know something of what Jerusalem meant regarding the holy mission they've now embarked on. They've been there before, on feast days. And they will go there again, to present their newborn baby boy to the priests at the Temple.

They shiver as they turn to look back in its direction.

Zion...*Jerusalem*...the city of King David.

The thought of everything that now seems, in this surreal moment, to be so quickly converging upon their formerly simple lives, leaves them speechless. *Who are they, that God might somehow use them in His eternal plans?*

26

JEHOSHAPHAT'S VALLEY

By the time Jehoshaphat and his army enter the valley prepared
for a mighty war, the enemy has already self-destructed.

A sense of serenity floods over the couple when they have, at last, set foot
in the magnificent valley below.

They are now entering the sumptuous plains that encircle the ancient
city of Bethlehem. As they traverse through the basin, they pass lovely, terraced vineyards and gardens that just recently have lost their earlier beauty.
Their luster will surely burst back to life just a few months from now, as
spring begins to announce itself to what used to be known as the land
of Israel—an ancient nation now swallowed up by the mighty Roman
Empire.

The immense vale resembles a gigantic amphitheater. The back and
sides of it sweep up to the twin summits stretching out to seemingly
embrace Bethlehem on both sides.

They are now in the fall of the year, quickly approaching winter,
when, in Bethlehem, the temperatures sometimes reach into the sixties,
but the nights can plunge by more than twenty degrees. This cycle will
go on all winter long, and then the hot, arid days of Israel's spring and

summer will surge forth again. For now, it is already much cooler here than in the earlier part of their journey, back along the crowded paths of the Jordan Valley.

The thick green and winter-silver foliage of the groves of olive trees scattered throughout the valley is the prominent feature of the terrain's plant life. Those colors mingle with the pale pink of the multitudinous almond trees, which will be the first to bloom throughout Israel. They will burst into their glorious blooms in early February, just a few months from now, turning the valley into a veritable wonderland.

The lovely plains upon which the couple gaze comprise the famous swath of land that stretches from west to east between Jerusalem and the Dead Sea and beyond Bethlehem and south to Hebron. They know the story of its supernatural history. The riveting account was in their synagogue scrolls of the Tanakh;[121] they learned of it from their rabbis during their younger years.

The seemingly innocent beauty and peacefulness of the place brings to memory Boaz, Jesse, and David—the shepherd boy who would one day rise to become the most beloved king of Israel.

This greatly celebrated king was Joseph's forefather! That fact is why Mary and Joseph are here now. And it has been accomplished by a decree issued by a Roman Emperor with no earthly idea how his greed has played right into the hands of God's throne. The young couple look at each other in disbelief over what their eyes are taking in; Mary has wet cheeks and a knot in her throat. They are almost there...

The sprawling vista had been named the "Valley of Blessing" by Jehoshaphat, the ancient king of Judah. The valley encompasses the main road from Hebron to Jerusalem, passing directly through Bethlehem. Jehoshaphat named this place after God had given him victory over Moab and Ammon, as recounted in the Hebrew scroll of the Chronicles. The Moabites and Ammonites had planned for the battle to bring total destruction to God's people. But Heaven had other plans. God answered Jehoshaphat's prayer by stirring up the enemy to turn upon themselves and then kill each other in a fierce and confusing battle. By the time

Jehoshaphat and his army entered the valley prepared for war, the enemy had already self-destructed, with only a tiny remnant escaping into the surrounding hills.

The Israeli king's army spent the next three full days collecting the valuables of their enemies, including gold, silver, and precious jewels. From this great victory and the bounty it represented, the valley received its glorious name. The young traveling couple will soon play their part in bringing the true blessing of the world to fruition—from the little city called the "House of Bread" situated in the midst of the Valley of Blessing.[122]

And here they stand, in this very valley. Once again they see an ancient biblical site from a viewpoint they could have never before imagined, having spent most of their lives in the far-north village of Nazareth.

As they make their approach to Bethlehem, overwhelmed by the emotion of the day's journey, they find an agreeable spot and make their camp for the night. Sometime tomorrow they will enter the city. There, they will register for the census and look for a place where their baby can be born—a clean place, a respectable place. Maybe they can even look for a house within a couple of days after the birth—a house where they can start their lives over, live their shared dream, and make a real home.

At least…that's what they think will happen. But, seldom do life's plans follow every desired path of the human heart. In the years to come, they will learn this lesson many times over.

Mary will certainly understand the deepest truth of that lesson; she will one day agonizingly position herself below a Roman cross, in Jerusalem, just six miles from Bethlehem, and once again gaze into the eyes of her son as she chokes on her own overwhelming grief. That day will crush her heart beyond description. On that day, she will limply stand there, barely enduring the unspeakable pain—alone, without her beloved Joseph, who will have already left her in death.

However, there are many other things that have to happen first…

…such as birthing a baby—and *soon*.

PART EIGHT

The Coming One

Scriptural Backdrop:

The Mystery

Concerning this salvation, the prophets, who spoke of the grace that was to come to you, searched intently and with the greatest care, trying to find out the time and circumstances to which the Spirit of Christ in them was pointing when he predicted the sufferings of the Messiah and the glories that would follow. It was revealed to them that they were not serving themselves but you, when they spoke of the things that have now been told you by those who have preached the gospel to you by the Holy Spirit sent from heaven. Even angels long to look into these things. (1 Peter 1:10–12)

The Place

While they were there, the time came for the baby to be born, and she gave birth to her firstborn, a son. She wrapped him in cloths and placed him in a manger, because there was no guest room available for them. (Luke 2:6–7)

The Time

But when the time had fully come, God sent His Son, born of a woman, born under the law, to redeem those under the law, that we might receive our adoption as sons. (Galatians 4:4)

27

O LITTLE TOWN OF BETHLEHEM

These are no ordinary shepherds.

The relatively short day closes in upon them as the two lowly travelers from Nazareth come to their journey's end. Now, they stand within the borders of Bethlehem. There is nothing about the couple that anyone notices as "different," so they blend in with all the other "commoners" who have come for the same reason—to register for Caesar's reprehensible tax census.

They are indescribably sore, famished, and bone tired. Peeling, blistered, bleeding feet and raw, aching backs and bruised posteriors accompany them. Over the last week, they have traveled a little over a hundred miles. It was a grueling trip, especially with a very expectant traveler as the centerpiece of daily concern. But, for the present, there is the pressing necessity of finding shelter and, before long, a proper birthing place.

The little town of Bethlehem is already teeming with those who have come from the outlying districts in order to catalog their attendance for the registration. Every house is fully occupied, guest rooms rented out—some to overflowing, because of the sheer influx of people pouring into the area. Caesar's decree had created a financial windfall for the town.

By the time they arrive, it is already growing late in the day. To their dismay, they find the city's small inn is already "filled" as well—or at least that's what the innkeeper claims. He tells them this bad news while gazing at Mary's extremely rounded belly, ripe with child. And that's not to mention the fact that she is beginning to grimace in the midst of the early onset of birth pains. Few innkeepers would want that extra burden. Neither would they welcome the accompanying noise, mess, and responsibility. Plus, there would be complaints from the other residents. To further complicate the matter, there is the Jewish *law of separation* regarding women in the throes of childbirth.[123] This is a disaster waiting to happen, as far as the innkeeper is concerned; he will have no part of it. It's not that there are no more rooms…it's simply that there are no more rooms for *her.*

So, trying to manage his business in a decent and lawful manner, appealing even to the most Orthodox of his renters, he asserts to Joseph that there are "no more rooms available." The proprietor's solution is straightforward, and unmovably final: He tells Joseph that he "wants to help," but he is overwhelmed by the almost-full house he already has.

Joseph begins to panic as once again he finds himself standing outside in the midst of the bustle of Bethlehem's busy streets, which are laden with even more newcomers. *What are they to do?*

Mary grimaces again, her discomfort growing increasingly obvious. It is then that her water breaks. The time for the child's arrival is getting closer. Silently, in the confines of his hastily mumbled prayers, Joseph seeks wisdom from Heaven. *Is this insufferable insensitivity from an innkeeper really to be Heaven's final word? Is she to give birth to Heaven's divine child in the middle of the street?*

It is in that very moment of his heart-wrenching appeal to Heaven that the idea comes to him.

When they had first entered the town, they passed through the shepherd's fields at the northernmost part of the city less than a mile back. That road, had they turned and traveled in the opposite direction as they were entering Bethlehem, would have led them straight into Jerusalem and up to the Temple Mount. In these renowned and specially selected fields along the road, the Temple-ordained shepherds performed a very important priestly function. These were no ordinary shepherds who worked these fields and these sheep. They were the ones expressly selected and trained by the priestly order that served in Jerusalem, at the Temple.[124]

These shepherds, above all others in Israel, had been designated for the important duty of raising and caring for the sheep that were to be used in the daily sacrifices—the *Tamid sacrifice*—in Jerusalem's Temple. Twice every day, in rotating units, they would make the six-mile one-way journey to Jerusalem, carrying their holy cargo of "perfect male lambs" up to the Temple to fulfill the sacred rituals of the sin offerings.

The shepherds of Bethlehem's fields were also responsible for the tender care of the sacrificial lambs. Everything about the birthing, swaddling, handling, and daily attention given to those little lambs had been prescribed by the priests and was carried out with precision by the special caretakers.

As it happened, just outside the hub of Bethlehem's activity, but still considered a part of the city itself, was a "birthing room" for the lambs destined for the Temple sacrifices. That place was called the "Tower of the Flock,"[125] and it was the birthing room nearest to Bethlehem.

The shepherd's tower was an ancient landmark to the inhabitants of Bethlehem. Everyone knew its location and its purpose. It was here, as recorded in Genesis, where Jacob had fed his sheep.[126] But to the common village resident in this day and time, the tower went largely unnoticed. It was simply a necessary "tool" in the daily life of Bethlehem's current Temple shepherds.

The Tower of the Flock was used for the newest lambs among the huge flocks that grazed upon Bethlehem's hills. Even though this specific landmark was somewhat special—being so near to the actual city of Bethlehem and with such a rich biblical history behind it—many similar structures were scattered throughout the vast fields.

Those watchtowers that dot the fields and hillsides possessed a dual purpose. They were built as lookout towers, so that the shepherd priests could more easily spot the sheep-snatchers…and the even more plentiful wolves. But, in the bottom section of the towers were special "mangers"— enclosed *birthing rooms*.[127]

Here, in these birthing rooms, the baby lambs were prepared for the Temple sacrifices from the moment of birth, when they were first swaddled. This special wrapping process was accomplished with the use of priestly sanctified cloths, stripped and fashioned into "bands." These bands were used so that the little lambs might not break their legs or otherwise injure themselves before the shepherds could deliver them to the Temple. The lambs had to be "perfect" upon delivery, or they couldn't be used as the *sin sacrifice* for the people.[128]

The manger birthing area was therefore kept very clean—as clean as a first-century place such as this could be made. No other animals were allowed in the birthing rooms, only the lambs.

However, tonight, with God's hand of blessing, there might also be a baby boy in one of these mangers. More than likely, this will be the first human birth to occur in such a place. But, it will happen tonight only if Yahweh wills it—and, if the shepherds allow it. And, if they can get to one of these birthing rooms in time—before the child arrives on his own. The prospect of actually arriving prior to that time is looking pretty grim to Joseph at the moment.

Mary is breathing hard now, holding her belly in noticeable distress. She grimaces—then screams out before she can even consider holding it back.

The time is growing closer.

28

THE PRECISE PLACE

His first angelic cry pierces the stillness of the star-splashed Bethlehem night.

J oseph had noted, as they entered the city about an hour ago, that one such tower and birthing room had been unoccupied. Perhaps…if they hurry to the nearby outskirts, maybe they can secure this one—just for the night, or maybe for only a day or two at the most. He gathers up their belongings and rushes Mary towards the tower. Every few minutes, he calls out for Yahweh's help as he scurries along the path with the donkey, Mary, and the soon-to-be-born child.

It is right in the middle of this horribly inconvenient time that their donkey decides it has endured enough. The distraught beast defiantly shoves his front hooves into the dirt, both at the same time, comes to a grinding halt, and bellows out a shrill protest as if it's insisting, "I'm not going any farther! This is my last step!"

Joseph approaches the animal, soothing it with encouraging words. In a matter of seconds, it relaxes and complies with his master's reassuring manner. He pulls on the reins. The donkey finally follows, having no idea of the precious cargo it carries.

He continues to pray aloud as he hastens toward the shepherd's tower. *Please, don't let this ornery donkey stumble again! Make its paths straight! And Lord, please arrange for this baby boy to hold off just a little bit longer!*

Joseph had hoped to be able to employ the services of a seasoned midwife upon their arrival in Bethlehem. He was certain they would need some help, especially after such a grueling journey. But there's no time for that luxury now. Since the pains have already started, they now keep coming with increasing frequency and ferocity.

The tower is now before them. They have arrived just in time. The pains are getting closer, much closer. It won't be long. It will be just the two of them, no assistance, no attendants—just them, but soon to be *three.*

Joseph bounds to the door and snatches it open, glancing from one end of its chamber to the other, checking its general cleanliness. This will have to do. *Thanks be unto the Lord…the manger is empty!*

There aren't any shepherds in sight who might disagree with what we're about to do! Better to beg forgiveness later than to have to beg for permission now!

He helps Mary down from the ornery beast that has vastly improved its attitude from the previous moment of panic, leads her through the opened door, and maneuvers her inside.

"We're almost there," he sighs.

"*You* are almost there!" Mary ekes out a slight tease, though with her voice steadied against the pain. "*I* am not anywhere near *your* imaginary 'almost there'."

"Well," Joseph rejoins, "at least you have your sense of humor. That'll come in handy in a few moments from now…I'm certain of it!"

Mary faintly smiles, but says nothing. She rubs her belly, purses her lips, and quickly blows out a stream of labored breath, grimacing as if her stomach contains a pot of boiling water.

The night air is growing chillier by the moment. Soon it will be downright frigid. Joseph hastily throws together a soft bed of straw, also using the meager supply of blankets they brought with them as extra padding and warmth. This will have to do, considering the frantic nature of the circumstances before them.

Mary grabs her abdomen again and cries out a pitiful wail, announcing her swelling labor pains. There will still be more of this to come, and it will come much more often. She is in full labor now.

Joseph coaxes a blaze of warmth from the manger's little fireplace. The birthing room has been well stocked with fresh firewood and kindling. During certain times of the year, the quarters need to be warmed, not only for the little lambs born here, but also for their miserably pregnant mothers. *Perfect!* Everything has been provided. It is as if God knew exactly what He was doing. Joseph bathes in the wonderment of it all as the fire begins to crackle.

He glances around their tight quarters. *So, this is where our holy child is to be born?* he wonders to himself. *But, why here?* He eases over to Mary and strokes her hair, attempting to bring her a few moments of comfort before the child begins to show himself. As she lay in her makeshift bed, he lifts a small cup of water to her lips, a little something to hold back her currently parched condition. She gulps down its meager contents.

Then she moans again, breathing in short, labored gasps. In that moment it hits him.

⁓

Wait a minute! What's happening here? Can this really be true?

Has not this very location in which they are currently concealed been directed by Yahweh Himself? Of course it has! How can it not have been? If God is in control of all of their circumstances, if this is truly the Messiah they are carrying, then this place is no accidental birthing room! The Scriptures come flooding back to Joseph from his boyhood memories of synagogue teachings.

The Messiah that the Jewish people yearn for was long-ago prophesied through the words of the prophet Micah to come from Bethlehem. *Everyone knows that.*

Not only that, but Messiah was also foretold to be initially "revealed" from a very specific place in Bethlehem. Even the shepherds know this! A great number of the rabbis speak of it as well. Why has this not been obvious to him all along?

Yes! Yes! This all makes sense now!

Joseph begins repeating the two passages—rapid-fire—both given from the very same prophet, only verses apart. He repeats them over and over. Mary listens, with startled eyes, wide open with wonder, while the child rumbles around in her womb—longing to come out. She, too, remembers the promises spoken by the prophet Micah.

> But you, Bethlehem Ephrathah, though you are small among the clans of Judah, out of you will come for me one who will be ruler over Israel, whose origins are from of old, from ancient times.[129]

After several times through, Joseph pauses. With incredulity dripping from his quivering voice, he recites another verse. This is the one that flooded his memory just moments ago. It is found in the scroll of Micah as well, not many verses before the one he just spoke aloud. He emphasizes certain unbelievable words as he delivers it from memory, looking into Mary's eyes as he speaks:

> And you, *O Tower of the Flock*, the stronghold of the daughter of Zion, *to you shall it come*, Even the former *dominion shall come*, the *kingdom* of the daughter of Jerusalem.

And here they are…in Bethlehem! And now, at this very moment, they are inside the *Tower of the Flock*, a place known by everyone in Bethlehem—and foreseen by the prophet! Now…it is happening. *To them.*[130]

Does this mean—? Yes! *It does!* That ancient prophecy is about *them*, a lowly and apparently preordained couple from Nazareth! This is too much to take in. Joseph chokes on the lump in his throat, sipping a little water to compose himself. Mary weeps as they embrace each other in holy awe of what God is doing through their humble lives and their simple obedience.

The young woman yelps again…and then *again and again*. Her labored breathing and sounds of guttural groaning become almost inhuman in their resonance. This latest pain is far more agonizing than anything before it. There's no doubt now. Soon, there will be a baby boy in the Tower of the Flock!

Mary pushes and pants—soaked in perspiration. She heaves deep, raspy breaths *in and out…in and out.* Joseph consoles and encourages, keeping her forehead damp with a rag and her parched lips soaked with cool water. Mary screams out again as tears pour down her face…but she is resolute. Mercifully, there finally come a few welcome moments of relief.

But those merciful minutes slip by ever so quickly. Then the pains return. More yelps…panting, consoling, sweating, pushing, and crying. In the next moment, the baby's head crowns. And then, the child comes forth—at just the right time, according to Scripture, and at just the right place.

He is here. In Bethlehem! In this preordained spot! Arranged by a Roman decree, without the author of that decree having any inkling of what the stroke of his pen had just assisted. However, a *heavenly decree* has indeed come to fruition. In this very place. In this very moment, and in this very town. Soon, the Temple shepherds will know about His arrival as well.

But not yet.

⁓

His first angelic cry pierces the stillness of the star-splashed Bethlehem night. The newborn yaps of this precious little one fold in with the common night sounds of the city that surrounds them. Dogs bark in the nearby fields and byways. The last far-off sounds of the city's residents making their final preparations for the night punctuate the moment. A distant bleat of lambs in the pastures fill in the refrains of the evening's noise.

The producers of each of those sounds are oblivious to what has just happened at the Tower of the Flock. Yahweh's divine plan is unfolding all around them, yet the entire event is still a mystery to the town's inhabitants, and to the *world*—and, most importantly, to Satan's dark domain. The "seed of the womb of a woman" that he has been frantically searching out down through the ages has just arrived.

Moments later, Mary cradles the "Lamb slain before the foundation of the world" to her breast.[131] Joseph cuddles both of them in a tight embrace. For the time being, they are a family. They are the *chosen ones*... ordained by the Creator of the universe Himself. They have been "raised up" for this very moment, and to be coworkers in the accomplishment of this prophetic and divine task. Together they weep. And wonder. And worship.

It...has happened. Immanuel has arrived.

And now, they are holding Him in their arms.

29

MOTHER AND CHILD

In a secluded instant, secreted away at a manger, everything has changed.

On this night, in the Tower of the Flock birthing room—in the City of David—Mary has brought forth her firstborn son, just as the Scriptures long ago predicted.

She has wrapped Him in swaddling bands—strips of cloth that have been prepared by the shepherd priests—just like the perfect Lamb that He is. Those priestly anointed bands were fashioned for little mewing lambs, the ones meant for the daily sacrifices. But Joseph has collected the strips into a bundle and brought them to Mary, now to be used to gently safeguard their brand-new baby boy.[132]

Surely the shepherds won't mind—not when they see this!

After securing her son, Mary enfolds Him further in warm blankets and lays Him in the feeding trough built into the side of the wall in the manger. She whispers His name in His little ears as she bends over and lowers her face towards His.

"Yeshua?" she coos as she seeks His attention.

He opens His eyes, and they meet hers—a moment of holy connection: mother and child. Of course, He can't smile back yet. But His eyes say it all. Mary melts into them, and weeps.

137

"Yeshua" is indeed Heaven's name for Him, just as Heaven's angelic messenger had instructed her nine months earlier. The angel had introduced himself as Gabriel. He had said he was the one chosen by God to deliver the message of the divine task—and the challenge of it—to Mary. He had seemed just as honored to be a part of the mission as Mary was.

Eight days from now, she will declare *Yeshua* as His given name. She will announce this fact before the priests in Jerusalem as her newborn boy is being dedicated at the Temple.

But in this moment, once mother and child are safe, Joseph eases the door open and looks outside. The sky is blanketed by uncountable pinpoints of glimmering lights. The temperature has already fallen significantly. Joseph pulls his collars up around his neck, closes the door behind him to keep the heat in, and shudders in the chill of the night air as he stands there, still immersed in the wonderment of this journey…this night…this child. Mary is napping, utterly exhausted.

After ten minutes or so, Joseph steps back inside the manger. He lights the lantern and hangs it just inside the door. The windows glow orange, brighter even than the light that has been produced only from the tiny warming fire.

❧

The shepherds are in the distance, keeping careful watch over their flocks during the night hours, the time when the little lambs are the most vulnerable. A number of shepherds are still sitting around the campfires, waiting for their shifts among the sheep and their turns in the surrounding guard towers. Joseph can see the fires dotting the countryside, like candle lights casting their dancing images in a huge banquet hall. This is the little town's legacy. The sacred mission of the shepherds had been going on since the days of the First Temple's construction and had resumed again with the rebuilding of the Temple during Israel's Persian captivity.

Tomorrow will be yet another long and routine day for the rotating shift of shepherds that will deliver more male lambs to the Temple. The parade of shepherds and sheep will once again begin plodding down the Bethlehem-to-Jerusalem roadway, just as it did yesterday, and the day before that, and for ages past. So, for the shepherds, this is a night just like all others before it and all the others that will come after it. It is all merely a part of the expected stuff of life in the first-century Roman Empire, in the province of Judea.

Birthing sheep and paying taxes.

At least, that's what they think.

But they are mistaken. This night is different, beyond anyone's wildest imaginations.

In a secluded instant, secreted away at a manger, everything has changed.

As will their very lives…in just a few more moments.

30

OF SHEPHERDS AND ANGELS

A burst of light renders the shepherds temporarily sightless.

The shepherds who are still out in the fields, and even those relaxing around their campfires, jerk their faces toward the heavens as every one of them hears a distinct popping sound in the skies directly above.

In a prismatic flash, heaven and earth appear to mingle as the two dimensions fold together as one. It is as though a thick veil separating two distinctly different realms of physical reality have been pulled back. Now, the human realm will get a unique glimpse of the indescribable glory just behind the cosmic curtain—the dividing drape that has always been there, unseen, but that has now opened up before them.

With a pulsating blaze of multi-colored light, a mighty angel of the Lord appears to them, in their realm, and positions himself before their astonished eyes! At the crack of the air, he simply is *there*, seemingly out of nowhere. He is now peering down at them.[133]

The gigantic, humanlike figure stands just above them—on nothing—in all of his shimmering aqua-golden brilliance. The *Shekinah* glory of *Yahweh Elohim* fills the sky around this mighty one of the hosts of Heaven. The shepherds' legs fail them and buckle, almost in unison, as they fall to their faces upon the ground.

141

The enormous being of glimmering light speaks, his voice sounding like deep, resonant thunder:

Do not be afraid! I am a fellow servant, and a messenger of the Most High. On this night, I bring you good news of exceeding joy, and it will be glorious news for all who have longed for its proclamation. It is God's promise of redemption for all who will believe! The announcement for which even your forefathers had waited![134]

The shepherds are still paralyzed by his presence. The angel continues to bellow out his heavenly decree:

Today in the town of David the Savior has been born to you; He is the Messiah, the Lord. This is how you will know where to find Him: You will find the child wrapped in swaddling bands, and He is lying *in the manger*—the very one of which the prophet spoke. Go…see where the child lays. *You know the way!* You know the place! Messiah will now be presented to you, exactly as it was written! You will see Him with your own eyes![135]

Then there is another blinding burst of light that washes over the shepherds, who are still paralyzed in wonder, followed by another fold in the atmosphere…another loud popping sound. Now the heavenly host, ten thousand times ten thousand of them—the entire army of Heaven—accompanies the mighty angel of God on both sides and behind him. As far as the human eye can see, their presence fills the skies, their true numbers disappearing into the distance.[136] They shout their celebratory praises to the throne of God, and then they sing with melodious voices a tune no mere mortal has ever heard before:[137]

Glory to God in the highest, and on earth peace among those with whom he is pleased![138]

Over and over they sing. Each time they repeat the refrain, the message becomes more joyous, more powerful. They are teaching the song to the shepherds! They are actually coaxing the Temple servants to join with them in the song! The shepherds slowly begin to stand and join their voices with the heavenly host.

"Glory to God in the Highest!" Men and angels…singing together, declaring the praises of Heaven. Just like it had been in ages past, in the very beginning…in the Garden, around the throne of Yahweh.

Suddenly…the magnificent being raises his hands toward the heavens, and the air sizzles again, as though it might burst into flame. Then, an instantaneous eruption of blinding light renders the shepherds temporarily sightless. Suddenly, the hymn has ceased. The night air is ominously still…silence engulfs their presence. It is as though the host of Heaven has never been there at all.

Not even a sheep bleats. A holy hush falls over the entire area. The remnants of the light fade from the sky. A glittering substance rains down upon the earth and dissipates as it touches the soil, like winter's first snow falling in the starlight. The shepherds are alone again. But they are changed. Gloriously changed. One thing is certain—they will never forget this night, nor will they ever again be the same!

When the angels leave them, and they have composed themselves enough to speak, the shepherds say to one another, "Let's hurry, and see this thing that the Lord has told us about." [139]

So they rush off toward Bethlehem. They know exactly where to find Heaven's child. There will be no need to search the town from top to bottom, no need to ask directions. These are, after all, the shepherd priests. They *know*… [140]

There is only one place where they will find a birthing room, complete with swaddling bands, that is located at Bethlehem itself—the place *has* to be the *Tower of the Flock*! Hadn't the prophet Micah left them the instructions through a pronouncement they all know so well—a message proclaiming that their Messiah will one day be presented to them at the

Tower of the Flock? Certainly Micah had prophesied this place! The rabbis and priests have often spoken of it.

Today is the day! Oh, what a glorious night! The shepherd throng streams from every corner of the fields. As one huge group, they race up the terraced heights to where—at the entrance to the town of Bethlehem—stands the Tower of the Flock, its lamps lit, and one swinging over the doorway just inside, its windows glowing a chocolatey orange.

As they draw closer, they see him. There is a very nervous man who stands in the doorway. And, in the next moment…they hear a baby crying! There's no way to miss it! This is the place! With an air of reverence about them, the shepherds ease toward the manger birthing room.

Joseph turns to Mary with eyes widened like a three-year-old having seen a particularly majestic site for the very first time. Mary is still lying upon her bed of blankets and hay, and, after a brief nap, is holding her son again. She sees Joseph's face, and wonders…

"They're here!" Joseph whispers to her in tender, hushed tones. "The shepherds of God's Temple have come to inspect the little Lamb of Yahweh! *Your Lamb.*"

Mary's eyes dampen. She can't believe the dream she is living. Except, this isn't a dream at all. It's actually *happening*, in real time. Right here. Right now.

As Joseph greets the men, they relate to him the description of the heavenly host's visit. They can barely contain themselves as they recount all that has just happened. Joseph, who had been the recipient of an angelic visit himself, doesn't doubt their saga. He quickly relates his own angelic encounter and welcomes them inside.

Small groups wait their turn outside until they can enter the cramped birthing room. Without prompting, each one who approaches the manger falls to his knees in worship. Many pray aloud. Some weep openly, shamelessly. They are overwhelmed in the presence of this little one. The Lamb of God has come…and He has come *to them!* And they are now looking at Him, with their very own eyes!

They're flabbergasted that they have been tapped by Heaven's angelic host to be the first witnesses to Micah's four-hundred-year-old vision. The prophecy had been *for them*! And *about* them! Even those who have come into the child's presence to worship can't stop weeping as they go outside to rejoin the others. It is a holy night, a silent night, a heavenly night... in Bethlehem.

After a while, the shepherds dismiss themselves and allow the young family the privacy they so desperately need. In leaving, they pledge to watch over the premises as long as the three of them are living there. As the massive wad of shepherds make their way back to the fields, Mary and Joseph hear them singing, praising, and weeping for many more minutes, until their sounds fade into the night air.

When even their visages have melted into the darkness, Joseph steps back inside and closes the door behind him.

But the prophetic event isn't over yet—far from it.

Because now, Heaven's plan is fully underway.

There's no turning back.

31

THE HUSH OF WONDER

This is the eternal question of two thousand years of humanity's travail.

In the collection of the moments making up this tiny little dot along the timeline of civilization's storied history, only two people on the planet truly understand—at the very depths of its meaning—why this specific child is so ineffably different from all the others before Him *and after*. As they gaze into His searching little eyes, they are overwhelmed by what they are privy to, and by what this moment really means.

Mary will ponder this night in her heart for the rest of her life. The simple, unbelievable truth of the matter is that none of this has taken place within a famous rabbi's family, as so many of the rabbinical class predicted. Neither has it come to pass through the household of a renowned Temple priest, as many from that class of people anticipated.[141] Mary is only a farmer's daughter from a tiny village, and her husband...a simple carpenter in that same unimportant Galilean community, a speck on the map that is more than a hundred miles and a week's journey from here. And *they* are the ones Yahweh chose to use for His plan of redemption! Who are they that all this should happen to them?

Everything happening now will certainly begin to make much more sense on that dreary late afternoon, still thirty-three years into her future. She will helplessly stand on Golgotha's hill and watch her son die, spiked to a Roman cross like an animal, beaten beyond human recognition.[142] But, of course, mercifully, she knows nothing of any of that...yet.

Within several weeks of Yeshua's birth, after Mary and Joseph have quietly faded into Bethlehem's daily life and the census crowds have departed the village, the young family is able to find a small house to accommodate the beginning of their dreams of staying in Bethlehem.[143] They are ready to settle in and start life afresh, just as they discussed on their long journey from Nazareth.

But not long after their new life in Bethlehem has begun to take hold, they are once again visited with a parade of excitement. Another group has arrived in the small town for the purpose of honoring and celebrating the arrival of this new child. Yeshua isn't visited by shepherds this time, but by magi—wise and highly learned men—from the East. Like the shepherds, these newest and distinguished visitors have also been guided to the divine child by the supernatural direction of Yahweh Himself.[144]

The initial arrival of the magi in the greater area of Judea—back in Jerusalem—had caused a huge stir among the people, especially among the Jewish Orthodox elite.[145] The visitors had brought with them the claimed knowledge that the king of the Jews was born, not too long ago, somewhere in the general vicinity. They told King Herod that they had been watching His "star"—a specific and exceedingly rare alignment of "wandering stars"[146] that had been growing in splendor over the last two years.[147] They explained that they had been observing the phenomenon from the vantage point of their headquarters back in the East and had traveled for months to make their way to Jerusalem to seek further guidance—namely, the exact location of where the Jewish Messiah was prophesied to appear. They needed this information so that they might align themselves and their exact direction of travel with the star's orientation in the night sky.

When asked the question from Herod and his entourage, the Jewish scholars in Jerusalem collectively appealed to Micah 5 and announced, "The Messiah is to come from Bethlehem." Once the reason for the visit from the magi was known and the particular details of Messiah's place of arrival was revealed, it would eventually send the maniacal, paranoid Herod into a murderous panic. This condition defined the well-known character of the man, a demonic trait that had arisen on several other occasions during his tyrannical reign of terror.[148]

From this point on, the lives of the new family will be in the gravest of danger. And, of course, they still have not endured the coming wrath of King Herod that is just around the corner. That psychopath lives and rules less than ten miles down the road from where they now make their home. It won't be long, and they will once again need to pack up and get on the move. They will have to escape into obscurity until their child is safe.

They have no idea that their Heaven-sent child will so immediately cause such an outrage among the powers of the earth. When the magi do not return to Jerusalem with a report of this new "king's" whereabouts, Herod gives orders for his soldiers to make haste to Bethlehem and, without prejudice, slaughter all the male children under two years of age...just to be certain he kills the "right" one.

Joseph has been warned by an angel, in yet another Heaven-sent dream, that danger is bearing down on them. So, they flee into the night. As they make their harried escape, they hear the screams of horror spilling through the streets behind them—mothers crying out for the lives of their toddlers, their children murdered in a blinding rage as they are forced to witness the butchery.

During the earliest days of their new-parent bliss, they had never dreamed that they would soon be living in the distant Roman province of Egypt. Thankfully, they now possess the incredible wealth with which to accomplish this next phase of their remarkable journey. It had been laid right at their feet by the magi: great armfuls of gold, along with large containers of the insanely valuable commodities of frankincense and myrrh.[149]

The family will abide in Egypt for several more years, only to eventually return to Nazareth after the death of Herod the Great.[150] And so it is that, from the little village of Nazareth, they will commence, yet again, in the location of their humble beginnings as a couple—but this time with a four-year-old boy in tow.[151]

For now, in the ensuing days and months after Yeshua's arrival, the hush of intimate wonder falls upon all who hear the account. It is a message that is being shouted about through the witness of the Temple shepherds—a missive that quickly travels from Bethlehem to Jerusalem, and even from the Temple area itself, eventually spoken from the mouths of prophets.[152]

The child and His new family will eventually come back to Galilee and settle into an obscure and protective silence. He will grow up, during the majority of His life, in the village of Nazareth, the original starting point for His mother and father. He will be known in the village as *Yeshua ben Joseph*—"Jesus the son of Joseph"—or simply as "the carpenter's son." After His father's death, He will most commonly be known as "Jesus of Nazareth."

But, several decades after returning to Nazareth, at just the right time, He will reappear to the full view of the people—in a very public way.

The advent of His regional ministry—His baptism at the Jordan River—will mark the day upon which His name, from that day forward, will be forever spoken from the lips of humanity. The daring proclamation that Jesus is indeed the true Lamb of God will first issue forth from the fervent declarations of a rugged and controversial character, one who was prophesied more than seven hundred years earlier...*a voice crying in the wilderness.* The world will know him as "John the Baptizer."

Jesus will call him "Elijah."[153]

And on that day at the River Jordan, in the presence of that rugged prophetic *voice* and a huge crowd of witnesses...the One whom they have been yearning to behold will be standing right before them. In the flesh.

The Messiah is here.

But only for those who have eyes to see...or ears to hear.

This man, Jesus of Nazareth, now has Satan's fullest attention.

PART NINE

The Hunter

Scriptural Backdrop:

About Four Years of Age[154]

After Herod died, an angel of the Lord appeared in a dream to Joseph in Egypt and said, "Get up, take the child and his mother and go to the land of Israel, for those who were trying to take the child's life are dead."

So he got up, took the child and his mother and went to the land of Israel. But when he heard that Archelaus was reigning in Judea in place of his father Herod, he was afraid to go there. Having been warned in a dream, he withdrew to the district of Galilee, and he went and lived in a town called Nazareth. So was fulfilled what was said through the prophets, that he would be called a Nazarene. (Matthew 2:19–23)

Twelve Years Old

Every year Jesus' parents went to Jerusalem for the Festival of the Passover. When he was twelve years old, they went up to the festival, according to the custom. After the festival was over, while his parents were returning home, the boy Jesus stayed behind in Jerusalem, but they were unaware of it. Thinking he was in their company, they traveled on for a day. Then they began looking for him among their relatives and friends.

When they did not find him, they went back to Jerusalem to look for him. After three days they found him in the temple courts, sitting among the teachers, listening to them and asking them questions. Everyone who heard him was amazed at his understanding and his answers…. Then he went down to Nazareth with them and was obedient to them. But his mother treasured all these things in her heart. Jesus grew in wisdom and stature, and in favor with God and man. (Luke 2:41–47, 51–52)

John the Baptist: At the Jordan River Fords

In the fifteenth year of the reign of Tiberius Caesar—when Pontius Pilate was governor of Judea…the word of God came to John son of Zechariah in the wilderness. He went into all the country around the Jordan, preaching a baptism of repentance for the forgiveness of sins. (Luke 3:1–6)

About Thirty Years Old

When all the people were being baptized, Jesus was baptized too. And as he was praying, heaven was opened and the Holy Spirit descended on him in bodily form like a dove. And a voice came from heaven: "You are my Son, whom I love; with you I am well pleased." Now Jesus himself was about thirty years old when he began his ministry. (Luke 3:21–23)

32

THE IMPORTANT ONES

John the Baptist, at the Jordan River approximately thirty years after Jesus' birth, in AD 27, during the reign of Tiberius Caesar Augustus (known as the Divine Son of God)[155]

Three decades after the secret birth of Heaven's Son, Satan is the one being hunted. He just doesn't know it yet.

When it dawns on him that the divine safari—emanating from the throne of Elohim—is aimed squarely at the demise of his fraudulent kingdom, it will infuriate him. His suffocating conceit will not abide such a scheme. So, he'll unleash his counterattack.

Satan has ruled as prince of the earthly dimension for thousands of years. He believes it is his rightful domain. In his perverted arrogance, he is certain that he has come about ownership in a "legal" sense.[156]

The vast majority of the Roman Empire's government officials—including the emperor himself—have unwittingly operated within Satan's firm clutches, serving him as human foot soldiers and pawns. And, it has been the same with most of those among the ranks of the Jewish religious elite.

In his perpetual state of dark delusion, Satan has presumed this is *his* exclusive principality, and nobody in Heaven or on earth will take it

from him. Thus, he will soon launch every power available to him in an
attempt to thwart Heaven's strategy to wrest that kingdom from his grip.
And that assault will be saturated in ravenous fury.

The saga unveils in the Judean countryside, at the Jordan River. This
is where the prince of darkness first begins to sense that a grand scheme is
taking form, as he observes the gathering array of humanity. The people
are daily flowing to the river's edge to listen to a bellowing preacher proclaiming that God's Kingdom is on its way. He is assuring the people that
the Messiah will soon appear. This is good news to the dark prince. Perhaps his nemesis *Seed,* the one for whom he has been searching for ages, is
drawing closer to revealing Himself?

It is at this time that Satan snatches at the strings of his earthly puppets, summoning the power of the thrones that he and his demonic hordes
manipulate so deftly. As a result, his mortal marionettes are all too eager to
play their parts to do his bidding.

⁓

"The Baptizer" has just lifted another convert out of the cool Jordan
waters. Dozens stand in single file in the waist-deep waters of the river's edge waiting their turns with anticipation. Thousands more line the
shores. John shields his eyes from the blazing Judean sun as he focuses
upon the advancing confederation of gloomy-looking religious authorities and the cloud of dust that trails their heavy footsteps.

He knows these approaching black-robed men are powerful emissaries. They have been directed here by the prestigious Sanhedrin Council,
headquartered in Jerusalem. They consider themselves *the essential ones,*
in the Sanhedrin's ever-present efforts to keep "rabbinic order" among the
Jewish faithful. John has already been warned of their imminent arrival.
The word of his recent ministry endeavor has apparently spread faster
than he imagined it would.

John chuckles to himself. There is certainly no mistaking this envoy or
the nature of their mission. Adorned in their flowing Orthodox garb and
long phylacteries, their exalted station in society is unmistakable. John

wonders if they even have a clue as to who their master truly is—the vile prince of this world, the cosmic enemy of Yahweh.

In truth, John thinks, *they are a ridiculous-looking, swaggering gaggle of self-important men.* They pick, demand, and push their way through the conflux with their usual air of entitlement and pomposity. If the scene wasn't veiled in so much evil, it would be downright comical.

However, most of the people fear them. Knowing this, the approaching *important ones* bask in the crowd's obvious awe, immersed in the pageantry of their own grand entrance. Not only do these men hold places of prominence in presiding over the religious and social life of the Jews, but they also hold weighty connections to the local Roman governing authorities. Within the confines of proper procedure, the Sanhedrin—made up of seventy elite Pharisees and Sadducees—can even arrange for a fellow Jew to be crucified.

Seen from above, this line of men—dressed all in black, circumnavigating through the crowd—take the form of a viper. They appear to be slipping and winding their way toward their intended prey. The uneasy crowd defers to them, almost genuflecting as the powerful men slither through their midst. Soon, the bearded brood stands on the sandy shore of the Jordan, looking like a flock of vultures roosting in the sun-bleached branches of a rotting treetop.

～

The Baptizer, resembling a rugged prophetic figure right out of ancient times, has been in the area of the Jordon River for several days. He will remain here for months. Every day, thousands are flowing out of the surrounding countryside to take part in the messianic fervor that has recently saturated the land. They so desperately wish to be free of their Roman bondage and the suffocating circumstances of their ever-disappearing liberties. They *need* their Messiah, their deliverer. And they need Him soon! The crowds continue to move into the waters of baptism. This is why they have come, to prepare themselves for Messiah's appearance.

Some in the crowd ask, "What should we do then? Since we are here to repent, where should we begin?"[157]

John answers, "Anyone who has two shirts should share with the one who has none, and anyone who has food should do the same. Love each other. Care for each other's needs."

The masses are surprised when even a number of tax collectors come to be baptized by John. "Teacher," they ask, "what should *we* do?"

"Don't collect any more than you are required," John replies. "Treat the people fairly—as you would want your own family to be treated."

And to the utter shock of many, even a few Roman soldiers also step forward for baptism. "And what should *we* do?" they ask John.

"Quit extorting money from the people," he answers. "You know in your hearts this practice is evil. And don't level false accusations against the people—be content with your pay. Serve your masters with dignity and honor. These are the things that bring honor to the Lord and to the glory of His coming kingdom."

The crowds agree. Never have they heard a preacher speak such bold words—proclamations spoken to not only the common people, but also to some of the most powerful people in the empire. But it is for this very reason that the religious authorities and their governmental counterparts are here: The huge collection of those at the Jordan are actually listening to this man.

The Sanhedrin emissaries desperately need legal ammunition against this dangerous wilderness preacher. His zealous movement has the potential of going terribly wrong, and soon.

What they actually need is evidence of sedition. They will shortly get the proof they want. John will willingly serve it up to them on a silver platter.

33

THE VIPER'S PIT

After the initial collective gasp of the crowd, the silence that follows is stifling.

atan's befuddled ambassadors—that federation of Sanhedrin moles—grow increasingly incensed as John preaches what they consider to be unqualified heresy. They are certain the Jerusalem overlords will agree with their assessment once the report has been delivered. *This man must be brought to account.*

Looking directly at the black-robed infiltrators, the Baptizer's booming voice splits the air again, this time with a particularly penetrating invective: *"You brood of vipers!"*

John's brow wrinkles in righteous anger as he speaks. He knows that by identifying these men as children of Satan,[158] he will be stirring an already bubbling, vitriolic stew.

But one of the goals of John's mission is to "flush out" the great hunter of men's souls. Satan is the prime cosmic target of this operation, and John has just fired the first shot into the demonic jungle—straight into the unseen realm of Satan's lair.

But the other objective of John's mission—by far the most important one—is to introduce *the One* for whom the people have been waiting...

the long-expected Messiah. For now, however, that indulgence will have to be set aside. There is a little matter of business that needs John's attention.

He singles out the approaching rulers of the Jews by punctuating the air with the stabbing point of his index finger. At the delivery of his caustic accusation, the men stop dead in their tracks.

John continues his tirade as he levels his arm in their direction. "*You! You hypocritical offspring of everything that is evil! Who warned you* to flee from the coming wrath?"

They are appalled. *Who is this loathsome beast, this lowly and disgusting preacher, to point us out with his bony finger and to bellow at us with such blasphemous indignity? Does he not understand who we are? Does he not know who it is we represent? Is he really that ignorant of our far-reaching and fearsome power?*

As if its presence has been orchestrated for this very moment, a circling hawk screeches overhead. Several in the crowd look up at it, startled by its piercing outburst.

"You must produce fruit in keeping with repentance!" John shouts at them again. "And do not even *begin* to say to yourselves, 'We have Abraham as our father.' For I tell you that out of these stones God can raise up as many children for Abraham as He pleases! Take heed! The ax is already at the root of the trees, and every tree that does not produce good fruit will be cut down and thrown into the fire."

He stops for a moment, taking a much-needed breath. He wipes the sweat from his brow. Straggling dogs that had followed the crowd, scrounging whatever morsels they could find along the way, are barking at the sharp report of John's commanding voice. The air hangs heavy with words that, once released, have almost cracked open the atmosphere of the surrounding countryside.

The slight shivering of his body betrays his raw, spiritual emotions. It is as though the prophet can see something the crowd cannot. It is as if he is peering into another realm. Just then, a murmured curiosity ripples through the crowd. *Why has John so pointedly connected these religious leaders with the Garden of Eden?*[159]

What does the Baptizer see in those approaching men? His accusations are that they are somehow directly associated with the Garden serpent. John has further identified these men as "bad trees" producing "bad fruit." With that comparison, the Eden imagery quickly becomes embarrassingly obvious, and perhaps even hazardous for John to announce with such bold assurance. These are, after all, the religious elite. Many of the people still revere them. How can this desert preacher dare to address them in this manner?

But there it is for all to hear. After the initial stunned gasps of the crowd, and in the resulting hush of the moment, the only thing that is heard by the human ear is that same screeching hawk and a few muffled murmurs among the gathering. As the throng stands there looking at John—most of them shading the sun from their eyes—the breeze slightly moans across their eardrums, and the flow of the Jordan River endlessly trickles. What will the prophet say next?

Now the consortium of important men draws even closer to the water's edge, seething with indignation as they come: *This popular preacher is clearly out of control. His crowds are enormous. His words are caustic—and look! See how the people love him! This man has to be stopped! He has to be silenced…now!*

One of the Levites in the group asks the next question. "So, you are claiming to be *Messiah*, then?"

In reality, the query is one of accusation. Just one slip in John's next words might give them what they need to bring charges against him. They hold their breath and wait for his reply.

John answers—his face emotionless, his penetrating gaze never wavering. "I am *not* the Messiah," he replies with an icy-cold resonance. Their countenances darken with disappointment.

"What then? *Who* are you? Are you claiming to be the prophet Elijah, perhaps?" one of them goads the desert preacher.

Anything, just one careless word, is all it will take. If John will just give them *something*, then they can begin the process of filing the charges of blasphemy.

But John isn't playing their game. "Nope," he says. He picks up a stone and skips it across the river's surface as he replies. "That is not a title that I use for myself."

If they had not broken the following silence that still hung heavy in the air after the last word had fallen from his lips, it appears doubtful that John would have uttered another word to them.

In growing exasperation, they ply forward, "*What then?* Do you claim to be a prophet—*any prophet?*"

"No. I don't make that claim, either."

The circling hawk, riding the afternoon updraft, continues his relentless shrieks—almost annoyingly so. It is as though that lofty bird has purposely joined its voice in the harassment process.

"Well, then! *Who are you?* Give us an answer to take back to those who sent us! What do you say about yourself? In the name and authority of the venerable Sanhedrin Court, *we demand an answer!* Surely you have a title? Surely you have a mission?"

John responds by using the words of the prophet Isaiah: "I am the voice of one calling in the wilderness, 'Make straight the way for the Lord'."[160]

The snooping religious ones are thinking only of John's person, and of his present work. He thinks of neither. His eye is fixed on the Coming One…the Lamb of God who takes away the sin of the world. In Yeshua's presence, his own personality will have no existence whatsoever. John must become less, as He grows greater. John is only serving as the voice of a loyal ambassador—not to be inquired about personally, only heard. But *they* are acting as men who ask questions about the messenger of a great King who might be, one day, coming to them…instead of hastening with every effort to make ready for Him.

They are blinded by their own imaginary importance, John thinks to himself. *Boy, are they getting ready to be shocked!*[161] The Baptizer grins as he looks at his interrogators. They see it. They do not appreciate, at all, John's smirking countenance. Their rage grows stronger.

The spokesperson of the group speaks up again, "Why then do you baptize if you are not the Messiah?" His newest inquiry now possesses a syrupy intonation of condescension.

"I baptize with water," John responds, "but among you, this very moment, stands one you do not know. He is the one who comes after me, the straps of whose sandals I am not worthy to untie."

Several among the elite snap their heads around, apparently expecting to immediately gaze upon this "one among them" to whom John has just referred. Instead, they only see a crowd of thousands of faceless, nameless people—as far as the eye can see.

Yet, standing only a few feet away, unbeknownst to them, is the *one*. He had, just an hour ago, arrived from Galilee and now lingers at the water's edge. He gazes into their faces—even into their souls. They have no idea. They may have seen Him as simply one among thousands, but this Yeshua, from Nazareth, does not stand out in the crowd. He has no features that draw them to believe that He is the portentous one of whom John has spoken.[162] A faint expression of satisfaction forms at the corners of the Galilean's mouth as He looks John's way and knowingly nods at him. The divine plan continues to come together.

John slightly returns the greeting, with only a subtle movement of his head, and then resumes baptizing the people. He never again looks back at the Sanhedrin's entourage of spies. To him, they no longer exist. They are now irrelevant in his world. The gathering of folks follows John's lead, pushing closer to the river's edge and ignoring the pack of black robes.

The enraged essential *ones* spin on their heels, picking their way back through the crowd. Every step they take oozes with their outrage. They head back to Jerusalem to report what they have seen and heard.

John looks at the growing masses that patiently stand there, awaiting their turn in the water. This is going to be a long day.

But the coming days will grow even longer…*much longer*.

34

THE ORDINARY ONE

This man standing in their midst simply does not look
like their notion of the true Messiah.

Early the next morning, John returns to the Jordan Valley.

The multitudes have returned as well. Many of them have spent
the night along the river's shore. Additional caravans have also arrived, a
number of them from far-off communities with weeks of travel behind
them. Yeshua is there as well, moving quietly among the people again, still
unnoticed as anyone special.

When John enters the waters, the crowds begin to form a line, eager
to partake of this growing national movement of repentance. It has been
the historical teaching of the rabbis that the Jewish people, *en masse*, have
to repent and express a collective desire for their long-awaited Messiah to
appear; only then will He make His presence known among them. They
are hoping that John's powerful urging of God's people to come to these
waters and participate in the nationalistic fervor will affect that goal.[163]

But it is today, along these shores, where a great cosmic irony will soon
take place. Messiah *will* truly appear to them, right before their eyes. John
will even single Him out with an unmistakable pronouncement. While

some will be excited by the potentiality of the moment, most won't even come close to receiving John's shocking disclosure in its fullest sense.

This man, standing in their midst, simply doesn't look like their notion of the true Messiah. What they most desperately want is their immediate deliverance from Rome's suffocating and brutal grip upon their meager lives. They long for the nation of Israel to burst back into life—to its former Davidic glory—and they ache for it to happen *now*. It is absolutely necessary, so they think, for this miracle to come about by being wrapped in the visage of a militaristic and authoritative personality—one that the Romans would fear when their Jewish Messiah commands His revolutionary troops against the empire.

Yeshua holds out His hand and motions to the Baptizer, indicating that He will now be joining John in the baptismal waters. When He has drawn near, John leans into His ear. "What are you doing?" he says quietly. "I need to be baptized by *you*! The people must understand that *you* are the one—not me! You have no need to repent!"

"John. I *must* do this," Yeshua says. "This act will fulfill all righteousness. From this moment forward, those who follow me must become one with me, as I am one with my Father. They must identify with me in this holy ritual of commitment. Today, I will lead the way, like a bride and groom exchanging vows at the altar of marriage. In doing this today, I will declare my vows first. This must be done, John. Let it be so…*now*."

With an expression of anticipation, Jesus juts His chin toward two young men standing close to the shore. "A couple of my true disciples are already here," He says. "They just don't know it yet…but they will follow me *to the end*. What we will do today is for them as well."

The two men that Jesus references are Andrew and John.[164] John will go down in history as "the disciple whom Jesus loved." He will later give the world five New Testament books, including the Gospel of John and the book of Revelation. Andrew is Peter's brother. Soon, Andrew will convince his brother to meet the Messiah for himself. Peter will become the chief pastor of the world's first Christian church, born in downtown Jerusalem at the Feast of Pentecost. All these things are still years into the future. What happens next, however, will be the seed of them all, and so much more.

With the Baptizer's gentle guidance, Yeshua goes under the water. Jordan's cold waters ripple around His submerged body. For John, the moment unfolds in slow motion, on a seemingly separate plane of reality.

The people assembled at the river's edge fade into a mere blur in the background. The deafening sounds of life: men, women, children, dogs, the hawk, and the water—all of it—are immediately blocked from John's ears.

35

THE PORTAL

Yeshua grins. "Now do you believe, John? Did you see it, John?"

Like the prophets of old, the Baptizer is suddenly transported to another place—yet, at the same time, he physically remains where he is.[165]

A portal to Heaven's seat has opened upon him. He is cosmically enveloped in it. John hears the voice of seven thunders pealing from Heaven's throne.

"This is my Beloved Son. With Him I am very pleased!"

John will later describe the scene:

"*I heard the voice!* It was as clear to my ears as my own. It was as real as that of any man standing beside me. The sound of it was thunderous, yet it was filled with an unearthly and indescribable love. I could not see the actual face of the one upon the throne; His countenance was bathed in an indescribable glory. It was the most luxurious *Light* I had ever beheld!

"But it was the same voice that had spoken to me months ago, telling me that this day would soon arrive. He had assured me that I would see and hear His very own confirmation upon the Messiah, the one that He Himself would bring to me—at the Jordan.

"It was at the booming of that voice that I also saw the appearance of another bodily form. It was a holy countenance. He emanated from the throne of Yahweh and enveloped Yeshua—filling Him…covering Him.

"The whole process was as if a gentle dove had landed upon His head. The event was beyond earthly description. That's when I knew…that's how *I knew that I knew*! This was truly Him!"[166]

Just then, Yeshua comes up from the water. Suddenly, John is snapped back into the present reality. From just beneath the water's surface, Yeshua's face peers into John's—seemingly in slow motion, at first. Then, as He breaks back through the water, everything returns to normal. The regular speed of earthly life resumes. The sound of the people, the barking of their dogs. The birds. The breeze. The rippling water. It's like He never left the river's waters.

Yeshua's eyes sparkle. "*Now* do you believe, John? Did you *see* it? Did you *hear* it?"

John can barely speak. His vocal cords quiver out an answer. "I heard…I saw…and *I believe*."

"That is why I told you, John—this *had* to be done. It had to be done for *them*." He motioned with His head toward the swarm of humanity behind Him. "And, just as importantly, it had to be done for *you*—just a little glimpse of the divine splendor—for confirmation. *It had to be done, for you*. But, blessed are those who do not see, *yet still believe*."

Yeshua grasps John's shoulders and peers into his teary eyes. "You truly did hear from Yahweh!" He says. "You *were* chosen for this very moment, John. From this day forward you'll minister with an unction and courage you have never imagined you possessed. All of history will remember what you have done here this day, and they will tell of this moment and your faithfulness, forever."

John nods. Now, he understands. Immersed in a boldness he has never before felt, he cries out again. But this time, his eyes are welled with moisture….

"Behold!"

John pauses as he surveys the crowd. No one speaks as they wait for his next words.

His deep, thundering voice splits the air again. "*Behold! This* is the Lamb of God who takes away the sin of the world!" The people gasp at John's stunning declaration.

"*This* is the one of whom I spoke! This is the one you've been waiting for! This is the one whom the Father has revealed to me! I have baptized you with water. But He will baptize you henceforth with fire—and the Holy Spirit!"[167]

Yeshua never takes his eyes off of John's face while the Baptizer instructs the crowd. When John is finished, Yeshua reaches out and hugs him. He whispers in his ear, "Well done, John. *Well done!* You are a good and faithful servant."

Some in the crowd begin to complain. How can this nondescript one from Galilee be the leader to bring forth their long-awaited dreams of deliverance? He is so very ordinary! He doesn't look like a military leader! He doesn't look like a king that men will fear. Many begin to think they have come to these waters for nothing. Perhaps John really *has* lost his mind, just as many of their religious leaders have claimed.

Yeshua turns to walk out of the water. He takes a few steps, then stops and looks back at John.

"Now, everything will surge forward, John!" He says. "The enemy is at the gate, and he's there for both of us. He prowls around like a roaring lion seeking whom he may devour. *Be strong.* Be alert."

The Baptizer affirms with another slight nod of his head and a resolute sparkle in his eyes. "Now, it surges forward," he repeats.

With these last words, the *plain one* eases out of the water and once again melts into the crowd. He has somewhere else that He needs to go.

PART TEN

The Pillaging

Scriptural Backdrop:

Jesus, full of the Holy Spirit, left the Jordan and was led by the Spirit into the wilderness, where for forty days he was tempted by the devil. He ate nothing during those days, and at the end of them he was hungry. The devil said to him, "If you are the Son of God…". (Luke 4:1–3)

How can anyone enter a strong man's house and carry off his possessions unless he first ties up the strong man? Then he can plunder his house. (Matthew 12:29)

36

THE STALKING

And this is why Yeshua is here as well—watching, waiting, and calculating.

He is seated upon a ledge, a slab of flat rock jutting out of the side of the mountain face. A rough trail has led Him up to the perch, but the view of the terrain before Him is superb…the perfect place for the *Hunter* to wait upon His prey.

He surveys the gloomy Judean badlands endlessly stretched out beneath Him. Another ledge above Him forms an overhang—a roof, as it were—a shelter that will protect Him from the sweltering midday sun. This will be His base of operation for a full month…and ten days.

Yeshua remembers the look on John's face only a few days back, when He first came up out of Jordan's waters. It was a moment He will cherish to the end. That rugged man, wearing rough camel's hair clothing and bulging with a muscular frame, had displayed the innocent look of a child's wonderstruck gaze. It was as if John had peered for the very first time upon the earth below from atop a soaring mountain peak.

In reality, John had glimpsed behind the other side of the celestial veil. For just a moment, he had seen something that his mere fleshly mind never could have imagined, and that very few mere mortals had ever experienced. The curtains parted, and he had been given a glimpse of the throne of Yahweh.

Yeshua's thoughts turn more somber. *Dearest John. How I pray for you, that you will have an unwavering strength equipping you for this mission which you must now endure—for my sake.*

The terrain before Him is desolate and treacherous. It is about as isolated as one can get in this part of the country, and it is deceptive...one's imagination could run wild because of the shifting shadows, mirages, and night sounds that echo off the jagged rocks and ledges. This will be a hellish ordeal; He knows that fully well. But this is why He is in this specific place.[168]

This part of the plan *has* to be successfully completed before Yeshua can proceed with anything else. He is here to plunder Satan's house, to begin binding up the strong man.[169]

Yeshua is taking the first blow directly to Nachash, right to his front door and into his demonic lair. *A wilderness, teeming with wild animals. How fitting.*[170] Now He waits.

The vultures circle overhead, scrutinizing everything that stirs in the desert wilderness below. They float on the currents of warm air rising from the blistering-hot sand. They wait for things to die—*anything*.

There will be forty days of this dreadful battle. No food. Scant water. No human companionship. No delivery of emergency supplies. Sizzling heat by day, frigid air by night—every single day. At least 960 grueling hours are still ahead.

But this is how it has to be done. It can be accomplished no other way.

The number forty has often been used, since the primordial times, as a divine signal of judgment or testing. The enemy knows this all too well.[171]

Jesus' forty days in this barren wasteland—the dominion of the "strong man"—now send a message that cannot be missed: *"The Stronger One is here. The Seed has arrived. I am here to crush your head."*[172]

These next days will prove to be eternally significant. They will remind the ancient serpent of his profane defilement of the Garden of Eden.[173]

The *Second Adam* has arrived. Soon, He will set in motion the reclamation of the Garden—the reality of which will eventually be delivered to Heaven's throne as the grand prize in this cosmic war.[174]

Try as he might, the serpent will not be victorious in this newest, soon-coming enticement. The "tree of temptation" will have no sway over the Second Adam. This time, the "fruit" will not be eaten. The lies and false promises will not be believed. The beckoning to rule Satan's stolen kingdoms will hold no sway over the Seed.

This mission will not be defiled.[175]

Jesus is certain of it. Soon, *Nehushtan*[176]—the brazen one—will eventually show himself, in the wilderness, somewhere near to where He now positions Himself. But right now he is still out there…in the darkness… watching, waiting, and calculating.

And this is why Yeshua is here as well…watching, waiting, and calculating.

Through the human presence of the promised Divine Seed, the process of the repossession of the Garden of Eden is officially underway. And Elohim's Garden promise is now coming to pass.

Divine judgment has arrived, in the flesh.

So He sits…waiting for the enemy.

37

THE GOD OF THIS AGE

Yeshua's unabashed public appearance at the Jordan River
had been the casting of the first lure.

The passing of the forty days in this wasteland has been unspeakably miserable, and slow.

Not a morsel to eat. Precious little to drink. Blistering sun. Harsh, frigid nights. During the entire ordeal thus far, not another living soul has traversed through the immediacy of this desolate area.

Yeshua's strength long ago faded into a faint whisper. Heaven's throne has been purposely silent. This is how it has been planned from the beginning. This feat must be accomplished alone, inside the fleshly camouflage of a mortal being and wrapped in the enigma of a divine plan.

It is during the midst of this torturous ordeal that *the beasts* come. Every single night they return—the wild animals. They watch, and snarl their occasional guttural threats into the darkness. Creatures of the blackness…the forward sentinels of the evil one's imminent arrival.[177]

Each day brings a mortal battle of the mind and spirit. Jesus' body is beset with pain and almost intolerable hunger. Within the first few days, the thoughts that come to Him are in the form of the constant dripping of another voice from an unseen source—a dark, sugary sweet, and faintly vulgar voice that is yet bathed in an almost melodious intonation.

There it is again—*the voice.*

"Look how you suffer. If you had any sense at all, you'd abandon this idiotic ploy! Did Elohim truly *sssay* you were to come here, to *thisss* place? He knows you shouldn't have to do this*ss* thing…it's simply preposterous*sss!*"

The temptations ceaselessly pound His mind. But so far, the attack has only been through those deeply internal vocalizations whisking through the recesses of His subconscious. A persuasive voice, to be sure, and one that attempts to coil itself around the depths of His inner being, but nothing more. However, that particular mode of attack is about to change. The assault will soon be elevated to a much higher level; it will quickly become intimately personal.

～つ

After the fortieth day—*he comes.*[178]

Yeshua, resting upon His partly sheltered ledge, barely able to hold His own head up, first observes the slight parting in the atmosphere. The cosmic portal before Him appears as a silken curtain flapping in a gentle breeze. The spectacle first drew His attention because of a loud snapping sound. His senses hasten into a mode of high alert. He surveys His surroundings.

Is this the strong man?

Perhaps it is just a mirage? An illusion borne out of the deprivation of nourishment? No. This is no illusion. Even the circling crows have scattered at the sound, squawking out their startled protests.

There he is…

A discernable figure off in the distance is just now emerging to present itself, materializing out of the shimmering mist as though he were an *angel of light.* The *god of this age* is finally revealed.[179]

There is that eerie melodic sound again. It has accompanied his arrival, as if some unseen ensemble were subtly playing a grand-entrance theme song. Nachash merely stands there glaring at Yeshua.

A fiendish smirk forms upon his face. This is the signal; what Yeshua has come for is standing right before Him.

For the first time since Yeshua has been in His earthly form, He is looking upon the seductive visage of Satan—the cosmic father of lies and the originator of murder. The old serpent has taken the bait. So far, so good.

Yeshua's unabashed public appearance at the Jordan River had been the casting of the first lure. But His presence here, right in the center of Satan's Judean domain, is more than the ancient dragon's curiosity can resist.

Had travelers passed by at that very moment, they would have beheld only a single, isolated man seated upon an imposing rocky ledge. They would have also observed this man to be in an apparent trance—a lonely soul—seemingly lost in another world, a world unseen to the mortal onlooker's eye—yet, a very real world indeed.[180]

The *prince of the power of the air*[181] knows fully well how to traverse these interdimensional planes of reality. He has long been known to roam *to and fro* over the face of the earth, and yet also to be able to appear in the heavenly dimension as well.[182]

Nachash also understands the mystery of how to bring one dimension in touch with another, either within the confines of a person's own mind or, sometimes, by helping the thought morph itself into a literal, physical reality.[183] He is the holder of the key to such secrets as these. They are the secrets of the knowledge of good and evil. He was the tree of that knowledge, the one that held its fruit within his gnarled branches.[184] And he unfailingly uses these ill-gotten powers to his own fiendish advantage, turning them into mere playthings of bewitchment. This is how he has operated since the beginning.

Today is no exception.

38

THE SHINING ONE

---

*Yeshua still looks straight ahead, not yet making eye
contact with the liar who sits beside him.*

He approaches.

In fact, he almost floats, until he is standing just below the ledge where Yeshua sits. From there, the serpent gazes upon the fasting one, as a rattlesnake might scrutinize a field mouse it is preparing to devour. A venomous lust for increased power consumes him. *This,* he thinks, *might be the chance I have waited for!*

In a flash, the ancient serpent is seated right beside Yeshua. He is on the ledge with Him, attempting to make himself equal to—or greater than—this "Son of God."[185]

Nachash's countenance is indescribably beautiful by mere mortal standards. But Yeshua knows that even this particular presentation of himself is not the genuine thing. There is something hideous there, in his fallen condition, lurking behind the shimmering soft glow of this master of profane masquerades.[186]

The *shining one* speaks.[187] "I presume you're hungry?" Nachash mocks. "Horribly famished, I would guess? Actually—I can see it in your eyes!

Forty days? Really? For the life of me, I don't know how you pulled *that* off."

Yeshua does not reply, nor has He yet acknowledged the actual presence of Nachash. It is a move meant to unnerve the adversary. And it is working.

The serpent continues the taunt as his smirk vanishes. "Why in the world did you do this to yourself?" he says. "What can you possibly hope to accomplish by this vainglorious act of self-deprivation? All these theatrics—bringing you to an unnecessary point of utter starvation—are so unnecessary."

A twinge of exasperation defines his voice. "Surely you understand that your flesh will not tolerate this treatment much longer?"

Yeshua looks straight ahead, His eyes still fixated on the horizon before Him. Soon it will be dark.

The sarcastic one mocks again. "You know that if you don't eat something shortly…you shall die! And what a horrible shame *that* would be."

Nachash picks up a stone, leering as he holds it. He studies the suffering "wretch" before him, lifts the rock to his lips, and begins to lick it—almost in a vulgar manner—but as if he were tasting a wonderful morsel of a small loaf of bread. "*Mmm*! So tasssty! So delectable!"

Yeshua merely continues His forward gaze, not yet making eye contact with the liar that sits beside him. He closes his eyes, slightly moving His lips as He prays.

"Oh, quit being *ridiculous!*" Nachash mocks. "There's no one out here, or anywhere else, to listen to you! That ought to be apparent to you by now. Where is your help? Where is God now? Behold how even *He* has abandoned you! It's been forty days, and not one appearance from His throne. I know! I've been watching."

Turning his head from side to side seeming to scan the horizon for someone, his derision continues. "By the way, where are His holy ones? *Hmm?* It appears you may have been abandoned!"

The jabbing of the serpent is relentless. "Perhaps they've all forgotten you! How is it that you can be the Son of God, when even Heaven's throne refuses to acknowledge you? You may as well call upon *me* for your help. After all, I'm sitting right here. And *they* are nowhere to be found! Say the word, and I'll have a feast spread before you. You are now in *my* house."

Yeshua has not spoken a word to His loquacious visitor. But that circumstance will soon change.

Moving closer to Yeshua and leaning over into His ear, the serpent hisses, "How long will you cling to this*ss* outlandishly inflated confidence—this*ss* delusion that you are somehow the Son of God? Do you truly believe those preposterous*ss* claims made about you at the Jordan? Use your head for a moment!"

Yeshua closes His eyes. Satan sits up straight and carries on with his taunts. "You came here through a birthing room for sheep, for goodness' sake! No one else would have you! Oh yes! I've heard all about it by now! Yet *you* are supposed to be the Son of *God*? Really? Please explain how *that* works! Just how delusional have you become?"

The insults rage on. "And everyone knows you're nothing but the son of a poor and unsuccessful carpenter. On top of that, this same illustrious father of yours chose to raise you in a despicable little raggedy village—a nondescript, tiny dot on the map—and in *Galilee*, of all places! How do you expect anybody to take you with even a grain of seriousness? And where is your father now? He's not even in your life anymore, long ago dead! *Pffft!*"[188]

Satan is on a roll, and he believes he's beginning to make some headway. "Thirty years you spent living in that nondescript hole!" he spits out. "And...you know what everyone says—'*Has anything good ever come out of Nazareth?*'[189] Now, you want the world to believe that a 'voice from heaven,' whispered only in *your* ears and the ears of that empty-headed cousin of yours, a mere desert preacher, who claimed that *you*, of all people, are the Son of God? A little presumptuous, don't you think? How embarrassed you must be, now that all the fanfare of that day has settled?" Satan chortles aloud, slightly cocking his head to get a better look at the object of his bullying.

After a few hushed moments, Nachash speaks again, his words dripping with enlarged sarcasm. "Your days of hiding in this lonely place should end! Why linger for weeks in this desert, wandering among the wild beasts and jagged boulders? You are ignored, unattended, unpitied, and right at the point of starvation! Think of it! Is this truly an existence fitting for the supposed *Son of God*?"

Yeshua still does not respond.

But Nachash is nowhere close to giving up. "Okay then, have it your way. Obviously, you're completely deranged by now. No food. The heat. *I understand.* So, let's play your game then…shall we? *Since* you are the Christ, the Son of God—for that truly is what some are claiming about you—*well then*, surely you will have no problem—"[190]

He pauses midsentence and holds out the small, loaf-shaped rock he picked up a few moments earlier. He flips it around in his hand…taunting…thrusting it in Yeshua's direction. He licks it again, clutching it with both hands, appearing to savor its taste and aroma.

"You should have no problem turning this*ss* stone—into a loaf of bread, for example. Imagine how a gloriously sweet-smelling chunk of soft bread would ta*ssss*te right now! Hmm? Here…just *sssay* the word. *Sssay* it!" Nachash holds the stone out to Him. "Surely…you, of all people, can do thi*ss* one little thing?"

Here he is, the long-awaited object of Heaven's interdimensional safari.

Well. Look at this! Yeshua thinks to Himself. *The deer has walked up to the pile of honey-mixed grain, right under the hunter's perch, just like an overly confident beast slinking out of the woods, curious to get a whiff of this strange intruder, and not having a clue about what this moment actually means.*

This is exactly why Yeshua has come. He hasn't minded the wait. The elements, the insults, and the taunting—along with the wild animals, the cotton-mouthed thirst, even the horrible, gut-wrenching hunger—had all been worth the effort. Now, Yeshua's first words to Nachash are about to be spoken. With these words, the cosmic reclamation process is well underway.

"It is written," He begins, "'Man shall not live on bread alone, but only upon every word that comes from the mouth of Elohim'." He emphasizes the word *Elohim.*[191]

A brooding darkness falls over the serpent's brazen countenance. *That word! That name!* It had pierced his ears with a wracking pain...*Elohim!*

It was Elohim who had pronounced the prophetic primeval curse upon his head—all the way back in Eden. Can it be that this truly is the *Seed* whose mission it is to crush his head?[192]

In fact, the more Nachash studies the matter, the possibility appears to be growing right before his eyes. This is not good.

But the serpent is determined to answer Heaven's insult.

39

THE HIGH PLACE

Yeshua looks at the ancient serpent, His eyes piercing into
the soul of the creature standing before Him.

Who *is* this man?

The pitiful-looking human figure sitting upon the ledge…is this indeed the Son of God seated before him—clothed in the frailty of mere human flesh?[193]

Is this the best Elohim can throw at him? Nachash's demeanor drips with arrogance as he attempts to reassure himself: *Surely, Elohim is smarter than this. On the other hand, maybe He's not. Oh well—if He has made that mistake, then it certainly is to my fortunate advantage!*

Nachash whips his hand through the air as though he were slashing it with a knife. With that movement, he peels back yet another cosmic curtain. The atmosphere *snaps* again, like the sudden crack of a bolt of powerful static electricity.

Instantly, far below them both, a panoramic view of the Temple courtyards in downtown Jerusalem is on display. *The two of them are there.* All the sounds of everyday life echo below them as the worshipers bustle about in the matters of their daily routine, with their animals of sacrifice in tow, unaware of the interdimensional visitors in their midst.

Yeshua and Nachash clearly have not left the wilderness. Yet, they are most assuredly in Jerusalem, at the actual Temple Mount.[194] Through the command of the serpent's wizardry, Yeshua is standing on the peak of the Temple edifice. They have crossed into yet another dimensional plane. They are in two different places—at the same time.[195]

The *prince of the power of the air* has not only brought Yeshua to this place in order to tempt Him, but also to parade his own possession of this particular realm of supernatural knowledge. He wants this Suffering One to know, beyond any doubt, that he has mastered certain secrets that should not be taken for granted. He is the cosmic master thief, and he is proud of it. He drips with putrid vanity as he stands atop the Temple with Yeshua.

The adversary speaks again. "*If* you are the Son of God—that is, *sss*ince you *claim* you are the Son of God…prove yourself! Prove it to the people below. Throw yourself down from here. For it is written: 'He will command his angel*sss* concerning you, to guard you carefully; they will lift you up in their hand*sss*, so that you will not strike your foot against a stone'."[196]

"You would quote Scripture to me?" Yeshua poses the challenge in a manner that unnerves the arrogant serpent.

Nachash looks at Him, feigning innocence, and shrugs. "Well?" the taunt continues. "Will you do it? *Can* you do it? The promise is right there…it's in the Word."

Yeshua looks down at the assemblage of worshipers below. He already knows the response He will give. But He wants the serpent to squirm for just a moment more.

After another few moments, Jesus matter-of-factly replies, "The Word of Elohim also says: 'Do not put the Lord your God to a foolish test.'"

The serpent's haughtiness turns to visible exasperation. *Nothing is working on this one!*

But, Yeshua also knows that Satan has failed to quote the next, most important, verse of that particular passage:

You will tread on the lion and the cobra; you will trample the great lion and the serpent. (Psalm 91:13)

No wonder Satan conveniently omitted that particular portion. The verse perfectly describes Yeshua's current mission. Today has become a huge part of the fulfillment of the Garden prophecy: The serpent's head will be trampled upon and eventually crushed. And through that divine declaration, that great roaring lion, the devourer of humanity,[197] will ultimately be destroyed...forever.

But, not yet...there are still a few more details that need to fall into place.

Snap!

The air crackles again.

In an instant, Nachash and Yeshua are transported from the Temple at Jerusalem to what appears to be the highest imaginable mountaintop on the planet—one from which they can see all the kingdoms of the earth... at once. Only, they aren't really on this planet. No such mountain exists, at least not in the earthly realm.[198]

A thick mist envelops their ethereal perch. Smoke swirls above their heads as though the mountain has recently been on fire and is smoldering in the aftermath. Out of that mist, a panoramic, glittering display appears before their eyes. Instantly, in a flashing moment of time, representations of all the kingdoms of the world, like trophies adorning a fireplace mantle, are made visible to Yeshua.

"All this*sss* I will give to you," Nachash murmurs, "if you will only bow down and worship me. This*sss* is mine to give. Only I can deliver it to *you!*" He looks deep into Yeshua's eyes, slightly tilting his head to one side in an eerie expression of curiosity.

"It's only a little thing," the serpent tempts. "We *can* rule together! Yes—that's it! *Together!* As a matter of fact, what I am thinking is—"

"Away from me, Satan," Yeshua pointedly rebukes.

He does this right in the middle of the serpent speaking the drippy words that ooze from his deceitful mouth. Yeshua doesn't even shout the admonishment. He merely utters the command—calmly, yet firmly. His reprimand is spoken with an unearthly assurance and with a thorough absence of fear. His words and His dismissive demeanor demoralize the serpent in the face of his abject arrogance.[199]

Nachash recoils in shock. This is the first time the Suffering One has called him by that name, much less has possessed the unmitigated gall to command *him*—the prince of the earth—with such an air of authority.

Heaven's Son speaks again. "For it is written: 'Worship the Lord your God, and *serve Him only!*'" His voice booms this time…such that His words pierce the evening air, ricocheting from cliff to cliff.

"Ahhhhhhghh! Have it your way then!" A string of vile expletives flows from the serpent's blackened heart. "You have no idea what you are doing! You may, in fact, be the *Son God*…whatever *that* designation means. But…hear me in this: You will never, and I mean *never,* win this battle! This earth is mine! It is legally mine! I don't care *who* you are! And, in the end, *I will* ascend to the throne of the Most High!"[200]

Yeshua looks at Nachash, His eyes piercing into the soul of the creature standing before Him. The serpent glares back, and hisses, "Mark my word*sss.* This will not be the la*sss*t time you see me—nor will it be the la*sss*t time you hear from me. I will come back to you—over and over again I will return, in any form that I choo*sss*e…until you submit…*to my will!*"

The air sizzles—then *cracks.* The serpent is gone—for now.

An uncanny silence follows. Yeshua is back on His ledge, seated there as if He never left.

There is no doubt: He will, in fact, see Nachash again. But that old serpent still has no idea what lies in store for his kingdom. The first divine snare has been set. The serpent has unwittingly slipped his head into the noose. And he knows no more now than he did by his examination of the activities at the Jordan, just forty days back.

⟿

A lone wolf howls in the distance. Others of its kind soon join in the cacophony, instructed by an unseen conductor. The sun slips into the dust of the rugged horizon, bursting its multi-hued pallet across the earth like a painter's masterpiece.

Then, suddenly, the fiery ball drops out of sight, as if snatched from underneath by an unseen cord. The darkness seeps across the landscape, spreading itself like a thick, weighty blanket. The night creatures will soon begin their rummaging through the wilderness—bobbing and weaving eyes occasionally sparkling in the ever-brightening moonlight.

Within moments, and in an instantaneous burst of blinding light, divine messengers from Heaven's throne appear beside Yeshua. They, too, enter through a dimensional portal, one over which Satan has no authority. Those keys were denied to him long ago.

As Yeshua lies back upon the hard, stone floor of the ledge, exhausted beyond words, the holy ones attend to His physical needs of nourishment and refreshment. Tomorrow will be a day of new beginnings, and of a much longer road than the one He has just traveled.

The cosmic chess match has begun. The prize is going to be the collective soul of humanity...and ultimately, the restoration of Eden itself. But there are still three long years of grueling work to be accomplished. All of Heaven, and the generations of humanity yet unborn, are counting on Him.

He will not disappoint.

PART ELEVEN

The Incursion

Scriptural Backdrop:

Immediately after His Baptism by John

Jesus returned to Galilee in the power of the Spirit, and news about him spread through the whole countryside. (Luke 4:14–15)

Jesus Returns to Nazareth and Preaches in the Synagogue

When he came to Nazareth, where he had been brought up, he went to the synagogue on the Sabbath day, as was his custom. He stood up to read, and the scroll of the prophet Isaiah was given to him. He unrolled the scroll and found the place where it was written: "The Spirit of the Lord is upon me, because he has anointed me to bring good news to the poor. He has sent me to proclaim release to the captives and recovery of sight to the blind, to let the oppressed go free, to proclaim the year of the Lord's favor." And he rolled up the scroll, gave it back to the attendant, and sat down. The eyes of all in the synagogue were fixed on him. Then he began to say to them, "Today this scripture has been fulfilled in your hearing."

When they heard this, all in the synagogue were filled with rage. They got up, drove him out of the town, and led him to the brow of the hill on which their town was built, so that they might hurl him off the cliff. But he passed through the midst of them and went on his way. (Luke 4:16–21, 28–30)

Jesus Gives a Glimpse of Glory

This act in Cana of Galilee was the first sign Jesus gave, **the first glimpse of his glory**. And his disciples believed in him. (John 2:11, The Message; emphasis added)

Jesus Goes Down to Capernaum, Then Up to Jerusalem

After this he went down to Capernaum, he, and his mother, and his brethren, and his disciples: and they continued there not many days. And the Jews' Passover was at hand, and Jesus went up to Jerusalem.... And found in the temple those that sold oxen and sheep and doves, and the changers of money sitting: And when he had made a scourge of small cords, he drove them all out of the temple, and the sheep, and the oxen; and poured out the changers' money, and overthrew the tables. (John 2:12, KJV)

John the Baptist Imprisoned, Jesus Heads to Capernaum

Now when Jesus had heard that John was cast into prison, he departed into Galilee.... He came and dwelt in Capernaum, which is upon the sea coast, in the borders of Zebulon and Naphtali. (Matthew 4:12–14, KJV)

Jesus Settles in Capernaum

Then he went down to Capernaum, a town in Galilee, and on the Sabbath he taught the people. They were amazed at his teaching, because his words had authority. (Luke 4:31–32)

40

COLLISION OF KINGDOMS

Near the shores of Lake Galilee, circa AD 30

They are merely taking a casual breakfast stroll through the grain fields just outside Capernaum on this Sabbath morning. That's when Jesus first sees them approaching.[201]

It is early June, and the morning sun has just begun to ratchet up the temperature of the already-parched air. Jesus stops to wipe the sweat from His eyes with the back of His sleeve. His vision begins to clear.

A cabal of Pharisees, led by the chief among them, Malkiel,[202] spots them in the fields. The black-robed ones have been dispatched to spy on Jesus while He is abiding in the region of Galilee. They're charged with the task of delivering a full report to their overlords back in Jerusalem.[203]

After all, this Jesus of Nazareth, during the Passover feast just a few weeks back, had begun His unorthodox ministry by upsetting the money-changing tables at the Temple.[204] He needs to be watched. He *needs* to be arrested. He *must* be marginalized. But, it has to be done carefully. Skill-fully. The trick must be accomplished with an appearance of innocence. And preferably with the consent of the vast and building wave of crowds that are beginning to follow Him.

This one from Galilee has already begun to shake the powers of the unseen realm. The *dark god* has taken notice of the mysteriously powerful man who is moving so comfortably among the people. So he has begun to manipulate his human puppets into their places of attack.

Satan murmurs to himself: "Who does He think He is? Was our clash in the wilderness[205] just a few weeks back not enough for Him? Does He not know that this domain of fallen earthlings belongs to me alone? If it is war this "Son of God" wants, it is war He will have."

~

Jesus had first arrived in the region of Galilee, near Capernaum, soon after He left Nazareth, His hometown. He had first made a brief stop in Cana of Galilee, just a few short miles from Nazareth. Days later, from Cana, Jesus eventually arrived in Capernaum. After only a brief stay there, He had departed and traveled to Jerusalem to attend the upcoming Passover feast.[206] From Jerusalem, He finally returned to Capernaum, the village that would become His chief operating headquarters. It was there, from among the men of this region, that He selected His very first disciples. He had found them in the midst of their meager lives. They were from the villages and towns scattered along the shores of Lake Kinneret.[207]

For the last several weeks, Jesus had been traveling from village to village along the Galilean shoreline and preaching in their synagogues. He healed their sick and delivered those who were tormented by the demonic realm.

The news of His miraculous exploits spread like a wind-whipped prairie fire. Consequently, the people flooded the area from a huge swath of the surrounding districts of the Empire. Day after day, they came. Some arrived in small family groups, others in large caravans. They made their way from all over Galilee, Syria, the Roman cities of the Decapolis, and from Jerusalem, Judea, and the lands across the Jordan River.[208] The population of the region had already swelled by thousands. And yet, the people still came. That is why the Pharisees are now here.

The boundaries of Jesus' present ministry encompass the ancient area of two of the original twelve tribes that first inhabited these lands, Zebulun and Naphtali. Joshua brought them here after Moses had died in the wilderness. The profoundly prophetic nature of these domains is something with which the people are keenly familiar.

For this reason, the multitudes are already quoting from the scroll of Isaiah concerning Jesus' presence among them. Can this really be the longed-for Messiah for whom they have been waiting? "After all," they reason, "no one can do the things He does, unless He has been sent from Yahweh."

But their bold messianic speculations infuriate the religious elite. That renegade, John the Baptizer, started this debacle in the first place! The Baptizer had sparked the frenzy by announcing to the masses of people at the Jordan River, "Behold! The Lamb of God who takes away the sin of the world!" The religious elite of Judaism now find comfort in the fact that the relentlessly verbose desert prophet has now been taken out of commission. Herod Antipas arranged for the arrest of John and had imprisoned him only a few weeks back.[209]

But the people, especially those in the caravans, still insist on crying out the words of the prophet Isaiah. They shout the promises of the prophecy as they move from place to place, rejoicing and dancing as they worship, singing the words as they go:

The land of Zebulun and land of Naphtali, the Way of the Sea, beyond the Jordan, Galilee of the Gentiles—the people living in darkness have seen a great light; on those living in the land of the shadow of death a light has dawned![210]

As they celebrate, roars of ecstasy go up from the crowd. With tambourines banging and shofars bellowing, their worship thunders out across the otherwise serene waters of Kinneret. Echoing off the surrounding hillsides, as if answering their praise.

∽৹

The human counterparts of Satan's kingdom are just arriving at the grain-field to confront Jesus and His disciples. The procession of self-important, black-robed, religious elite waddle with wild-eyed enthusiasm toward Jesus and His men. They flail their arms in rage as they approach.

Malkiel speaks up first: "Look at this!"

Jesus glances around, as if to say, "Look at what?"

"Your disciples are desecrating the Sabbath yet *again!*" They walk right up to Jesus, huffing as they come, standing at the edges of the cornfield—their faces red with resentment.

"This is despicable! You must command your followers to *stop*—this very moment! *Cease* this lawless outrage!"[211] Malkiel's face further darkens as he strains out his angry words.

The disciples gather closer around Jesus. They stand scrutinizing this screaming cohort of Orthodox elite. As ridiculous as they might look in their dramatic display, the Pharisees still aren't finished with their sanctimonious admonishment.

"Why on earth would you instruct your followers to do such things?" they ask. "You should be ashamed to call yourself their 'Teacher!' Back in Jerusalem, even the elders are talking about how you recklessly break our Sabbath laws. They speak of how you teach others to do so as well! And now—this day, in front of our very own eyes—we have actually caught you in the act!"

Malkiel pauses for an answer, searching Jesus' face for a response. But He gives them absolutely nothing. His reaction unnerves the group of inquisitioners, especially in the awkward silence that follows.

Losing patience, Malkiel insists upon a reply.

"Well? *Answer us!* What have you to say for yourself?"

41

HEAVEN'S REPLY

As the plotting ones walk along, they are accompanied by a demonic horde.

Jesus works the grainy material back and forth in His hands with a rapid scrubbing motion. His body language indicates He might not have even heard the charges against Him—or perhaps the charges, to Him, mean nothing at all.

The studied action of His hand-scrubbing—separating the grain from the shuck—has produced a small fistful of kernels. His eyes meet those of His listeners as He discards the chaff and pops the kernels into His mouth. As their smugness oozes over the atmosphere of the moment, Jesus greets their airs with an engrossing softness showing in His face and an endearing calmness in His voice.

"Rabbi Malkiel, have you not read what David did?" Jesus asks, as He chews His meager breakfast and raises questioning eyebrows in their direction.

They bristle at His interrogation, interpreting it as audacity. Mumbling among themselves, they wonder: *Where is this conversation leading?*

Jesus waits for a response. The disciples return to casually consuming their own morning meal as they, too, wait.

It has become a form of delightful entertainment for the disciples as they observe how Jesus consistently confounds the challenges, tests, and traps of the religious elite. This process began on the day Jesus had first declared Himself to be the fulfillment of Messianic prophecy, back in Nazareth.[212] So far, no one had been able to best Him. Surely this current situation is getting ready to explode in the Pharisees' faces as well. Peter—the legendary man of mischief among the disciples—displays his famous grin, his eyes full of expectancy as he, too, awaits their response.

Seeing that the Pharisees have no immediate plan to reply, Jesus proceeds. "Surely, Rabbi, you remember when David and his companions entered the house of Eli the high priest, and of the prophet, Samuel?[213] There, the famished men asked Eli for some of the showbread to eat—something lawful only for priests to do."

The Pharisees glance at each other. They don't know exactly how to respond to this truth. If they attempt to address the charge too specifically, they risk condemning the celebrated King David, as well as the high priest, Eli, not to mention the revered prophet Samuel. This is something they can't chance. So, again they remain silent. And seethe.

"Or haven't you read in the Law," Jesus continues, "that the priests, performing their holy duty in the Temple, desecrate the Sabbath and yet they are deemed by that very same law to be innocent?"

Again, the Pharisees stand dumbfounded. They also know this statement to be a legitimate fine point of the law. A faint expression of satisfaction forms on Jesus' lips. It is barely visible...but *they* see it. And they hate Him for it.

Taking advantage of their frustrated introspection, Jesus brings an abrupt end to their haughtiness. He decides He will give them something they can discuss amongst themselves for the rest of the day.

He already knows what is in their hearts. They have not tracked Him down this morning merely to correct Him. They have shown up in the cornfield with conspiratorial intentions. They are developing a plan to remove Him as a threat. More specifically, they are determined to *kill* Him, if need be. And that day *will* come, but not yet. At this moment, they are still collecting their "evidence." He will give them a morsel of what they seek.

"And…*if you care to hear it*…I'll tell you something else," Jesus calmly and matter-of-factly proceeds. The men lift their eyes toward Him, anxious to hear His next declaration…still hoping for an egregious slip-up.

"One greater than the Temple is here among you—*right now*."[214] Several gasp as Jesus states what they perceive to be blasphemy.

"If you only understood what these words mean, 'I desire mercy, *not sacrifice*,'[215] you would not have condemned the innocent ones who stand here before you on this Sabbath day." As He speaks, Jesus motions toward the disciples standing next to Him.

"In so doing," He continues, "it is *you* who violate the Sabbath. For I tell you the truth, it is the Son of Man who is Lord of the Sabbath. It is not you or your man-made rules that are its overseers."

With that, Jesus turns and walks away. His body language declares: "I have now said all I'm going to say in this matter." Jesus and His men soon disappear like apparitions among the stalks, stalks still hanging ripe with grain.

As the ruminating Pharisees storm off, headed to the village synagogue, they can faintly hear Jesus and His disciples chuckling deep within the camouflage of the field. When Jerusalem's dark spies stop to listen, the laughter coming from the field sounds childlike—similar to the innocent bliss of those who are simply enjoying their time together.

Almost hissing as he speaks, Malkiel sputters to the others, "This ha*sss* to stop. This man, and His blasphemous teaching, will be the ruin of us all! Who does He think He is? Who is H*e* to instruct u*sss*?"

His minions huff in agreement. *Surely,* they think, *this blasphemer and His group will show up for a synagogue service sometime soon. After all, He has already been in the region's synagogues several times in the recent past. That's it! That's where we can trap Him! In our synagogue! We can set Him up there—in front of the very people who profess to adore Him! We will crush His Sabbath blasphemies on the Sabbath itself!*

As the plotting ones walk along, they are accompanied by a demonic horde. Of course, Satan's "birds of the air" are not humanly visible to them or anyone else who passes their way. The dark ones prefer to remain undetected...in the interdimensional shadows. They will simply *prod* their human subjects along, pulling the strings of their already-blackened hearts and minds, convincing them that their intentions are truly righteous.

The more the thoughts of killing Jesus mull around in the minds of the religious ones, the more the power of the plan invigorates them, and the more self-assured they become...and the more the *dark god* secures them in his grip.

42

THE SYNAGOGUE SNARE

They have a plan—or rather, what they think to be a perfect trap.

The grainfield affair has now been a week ago. But much has happened since then.[216]

Just this morning, the continuing spectacle of the Pharisees' incessant provocations moved into the Capernaum synagogue. Sabbath officially had begun at sundown the evening before.

It is now early the next morning, and the people of Capernaum are beginning to gather at the community's house of worship. Here they will recite prayers, read Scriptures, and listen to teachings from an elder. The remainder of the day will be spent in respite until sundown.

The synagogue at Capernaum is much more than just the Sabbath meeting place. It is the center of everyday village life. It is also used as a community center where public events are frequently held. During the week, the synagogue serves as the local schoolhouse and, occasionally, it is used as the town's courtroom. It is attached to the lives of Capernaum's residents in the same way as the village well from which they draw their daily life-sustaining water supply.

On this day, however, the synagogue will fill to the capacity of standing room only. It has been rumored throughout the region that *today* Jesus
and His disciples will be here. They have already been involved in several
verbal fracases with the Pharisees during the course of the last several days.
If Jesus shows up, it should prove to be a very interesting day indeed. No
one wants to miss it.

On the previous occasions of the Pharisees' confrontational meetings
with Jesus, He had thoroughly confounded them. Word of those meetings
had been spread far and wide, throughout the surrounding regions. Yet,
it was reported that His demeanor had always been remarkably calm, and
His commanding presence seemed to never fail in unnerving His chal-
lengers. And that's not to mention His *words*. His instructions dripped
with heavenly authority and supernatural wisdom. Every time He opened
His mouth to speak to the religious authorities, He set them on edge.
They had yet to be able to catch Him in a trap. But it wasn't for their lack
of trying.

As the people flow into the building making their way to their places,
the elders of the community are among them, directing the synagogue
affairs and the internal movements. Benches are aligned on three sides of
the room, and those are generally reserved for dignitaries. Malkiel and his
crew have already arrived in their usual spectacle of pomposity, and have
taken their *places of honor*. In the smaller synagogues, as are found in most
of the nearby villages, the common congregants usually sit on the floor,
on mats or carpets. But it soon becomes obvious that some protocols will
have to be set aside for this morning's service. It has been ages since this
building has contained so many occupants.

From among the esteemed elders of the people emerges Simeon, the
president of the synagogue. He is giving the final seating directions and
preparing the people for the commencement of the liturgical portion of
the services. That liturgy will be followed by the teachings of the village
rabbi, or whomever Simeon might call upon for the task. Simeon then
sets about selecting those who will have the morning's honor of reading
from the selections of the Law and the Prophets.

At the same time these customary preparations are being sorted out, Jesus and His disciples enter as a group. When they walk through the doorway, it is as if the air has been sucked out of the room. His exploits and miracles are now widely known. People point and murmur. A few begin to weep, reaching out to Him as He passes.

Simeon calls for order. The elders and Pharisees bristle at the commotion, particularly at the deference the people show this upstart Teacher among them. *Who does He think He is?*

Jesus and His group find a spot and stand together, leaning against the wall.

A man who used to be gainfully employed as a stonemason and plasterer—but now with a severely deformed right hand and arm,[217] and unable to work—is then ushered by a synagogue elder to a place on the floor just a few steps away from Jesus. The man appears to be startled, wondering why he has never been given such preferential treatment in the past. But in his heart, he is certain he knows the answer.

The chief elder, Shmuel, upon having seated the poor soul, looks up at Jesus with a faint, almost evil grin. His expression boasts that he knows something Jesus does not, and he wants Jesus to be completely aware of that fact.

Jesus' eyes meet Shmuel's until, embarrassed, the self-important man can hold the gaze no longer. Jesus looks down at the man with eyes full of compassion. He faintly returns Jesus' acknowledgment of his presence, then lowers his head. *What can he say to this miracle-worker from Nazareth?*

As the synagogue scene continues to unfold, signals of certain victory are broadcast among the elite with slight nods of heads and a certain gleam in their eyes. They have a plan; rather, they have what they actually believe to be a perfect trap. It had been arranged before they even entered the building.

The Shabbat service begins in its usual manner. The prayer leader, the *Shaliach Tzibbur,*[218] begins by leading the congregation in its holy supplications. His words are enveloped with a chanting harmonious intonation. The congregants join in at their appropriate places, with the women and children responding "*Amen!*" After that, Simeon leads the congregation in the ancient ritualistic recitation of the *Shema*—"Hear, O Israel: The LORD our God, the Lord is one...."[219]

Other prayers follow. The people know the liturgy by heart. They and their families have been reciting the main elements of it for many generations. It is as important to them as life itself. It is what unites them all, as one people.

Next comes the reading of multiple excerpts from the scrolls of the *Torah*, followed by additional readings from the *Nevi'im*—the collected writings of the biblical prophets.[220]

Each specially selected person stands to read the Hebrew passages in sections of only several verses, which are then interpreted into Aramaic summaries by the synagogue translator. This is a necessity, since not all those attending understand Hebrew. After the readings, with their corresponding paraphrases, it is time for the message to be given.

Someone who has been chosen from among them will bring a "lesson." The people wonder: *Who will be the one to preach on this Sabbath morning?*

They have no idea of the magnitude of the lesson they'll receive today.

Nor are they prepared for Yeshua of Nazareth to be the one to bring it to them.

43

REVERSING THE TRAP

"I will answer your question," Jesus replies, "but first, you must answer mine."

Those draped in black robes exchange shrewd looks.

Simeon clears his throat, signaling the commencement of the next event. Malkiel, the chief Pharisee, suddenly speaks in a booming voice, startling the crowd when he does. The crippled man lowers his head in shame. He knows what's coming.

"Tell us, *Teacher*..." Malkiel looks squarely at Jesus as he speaks from across the room. An anticipatory hush permeates the little synagogue.

When the Pharisee calls Jesus "Teacher," the speaking of that lofty title drips with disdain. The religious elite hope to diminish Jesus' popularity among the masses, and they are determined to begin that process today. Amidst the growing tension, everyone present directs their attention to the miracle worker from Nazareth.

Malkiel moves closer to Jesus as he speaks, deftly slipping through the seated crowd as he approaches. "*Tell us, Teacher*, is it lawful to heal on the Sabbath?" His voice is resonant, authoritative, invoking a sense of awe among the people.

As he finally makes his way closer to Jesus, Malkiel points with his chin toward the crippled man sitting at Jesus' feet. "What about this one?" he challenges. In humiliation, the man once again looks away from Jesus. Great drops escape from his eyes and trickle down the poor soul's cheeks.

This is what they consider to be their perfect plan, a trap from which they are certain Jesus cannot emerge unscathed. The Pharisees know that even amongst themselves they cannot agree upon the proper answer to the question. Even the great rabbis of the past have struggled with the intricate workings of this particular Sabbath matter. Their many written commentaries on the topic reflect their factional frustration.[221]

Consequently, disparate teachings have been passed on to the various synagogues throughout the Roman Empire. As a result, even their own congregations have become divided over the legalistic issue. So, whichever way Jesus answers the question, He is certain to divide the people. *Perfect! How can this plan go wrong? The ploy has to work! They now have Him in front of a crowd, and right in the middle of a synagogue worship service, of all places!*

"I will answer your question," Jesus replies, "but first, you must answer mine."

Members of the Pharisee enclave glance around the room at one another. Their expressions belie their exasperation. *Here we go again...*

The crowd gasps when Jesus offers the challenge. No one has ever spoken to the elders in this fashion before—especially not in a service. It wasn't that Jesus was rude, or even the slightest bit disrespectful. It was simply that no one had ever dared to openly question these men—ever. They are powerful men. They hold deep ties with the Sanhedrin in Jerusalem and even with dominant government officials in Rome. Everyone knows it isn't wise to cross them—everyone, apparently, except for Jesus. He seems to have no fear of their black robes and phylacteries.[222]

Jesus motions for the man with the deformity to rise. Stunned, he looks up at this preacher from Nazareth with a glimmer of hope in his eyes. Jesus takes him by his good hand and assists him to his feet. As he stands, Jesus eases His hand upon the man's shoulder and squeezes it with a grip that says, "Trust me. I've got this." He then refocuses His gaze at the gang of his inquisitors.

Malkiel has not yet responded to Jesus' challenge; he has only glowered at Him. Jesus opens His mouth to speak, directing His address toward the group of Pharisees, but also glancing around at the entire congregation.

"If any *of you* has a sheep and it falls into a pit on the Sabbath, will you not take hold of it and lift it out?" Jesus pauses. He scans the room, looking at the congregation, then continues. "Could it really be that you would value the life of a sheep—a mere animal—above that of a fellow citizen, especially one who lives among you, and who suffers so much?"

A number of the congregants are visibly agreeing with Jesus, shaking their heads in the affirmative and forming approving countenances on their faces. *Of course, we would give assistance to one of our sheep—even on the Sabbath!*

Then several of the astute among them begin to think: *Why haven't we thought of this before?* This one simple illustration settles the whole theological issue of their divisive interpretations! After all, those sheep represent their livelihood; their very existence depends upon the animals. But surely, in the greater scope of all things, a genuinely hurting man is much more valuable than a lowly sheep. *This Jesus fellow is brilliant! What a Teacher!*

Malkiel stiffens. The rest of his entourage are silent. They can already imagine where this might be going. What they had thought to be a flawless setup is, once again, taking a very bad turn.

And, what if? What if Jesus actually *were* to heal this man, right in front of everyone? They don't want to even consider the ramifications of such a spectacle. So, they remain mute, swallowing hard as they wait. Praying that what they dread the most about this moment will never happen. Their prayers are in vain.

"It seems you are having trouble formulating an answer to my question," Jesus says. "Let me make the issue sparkling clear. I will ask you again, in yet another way."

He continues, "Which is the most lawful work to perform on the Sabbath: to conduct an act of mercy, or to do evil? To save a life or to ignore it?

And if that life *is* ignored, could it not turn out that the hurting one might even be utterly destroyed in the end of it all?"

The Pharisees still stand dumbfounded. *Is Jesus actually going to perform a miracle in the midst of this congregation? Will He heal the man's hand in front of all these witnesses? Will He dare to attempt an act of such outrageous insolence in their presence? On a Sabbath? In a synagogue? If so, there will be no end to the news that will spread throughout the entire region!*

Have we been caught in our own trap?

The Pharisees have failed to consider that they might be providing Jesus the very stage He needs in order to gather even *more* followers. Several of them lean into each other's ears as they whisper their panicked concerns.

As Jesus and the man stand in front of the congregation, and as the Pharisees confer amongst themselves in conniving whispers, the people begin to weigh the gravity of the moment as they, too, murmur to those nearest them: "Will we witness another miracle today—right here in our midst—in our synagogue service?" This would be something to talk about for generations to come! As their eyes grow wider in suspense, expressions of exasperation continue to bloom upon the faces of their leaders.

Without removing His scrutiny from the Pharisees, especially the one who had issued the challenge, Jesus calls the man by name as He instructs him to show his hand to the congregation.

"Yosef, stretch out your hand, expose your arm…so that all may see."

Gasps go up from the crowd as Jesus turns His full attention to the man.

"Come on," Jesus gently coaxes, "let everyone see what the Lord has done for you today." The expression on Jesus' face makes known His genuine love for the man. Yosef sees it. He embraces it. It had been a long time since he had seen that look, from anyone.

As the man pushes forward what has been a grotesque deformity from within the folds of his sleeve, his hand and arm emerge whole. The skin is healthy and vibrant; his entire arm is as firm and muscular as it had been years earlier. He moves his fingers and makes a hard, gripping fist!

He pumps it open and shut...open and shut, with ever widening eyes of excitement. It's as if it has never been deformed! Yet, for many years, a long time before this little village had even heard of Jesus, Yosef has lived among them with a hideously shriveled and completely useless hand and arm. *How can this be? What is this that they now behold with their own eyes?*

Yosef begins to weep uncontrollably. He holds his hand before his face, gawking at it, working it back and forth, and extending his fingers in and out. His right arm is now as whole and strong as his left one! He can't believe what he sees and what he feels. *How can this be? Who is this man?* Yosef's life has been given back to him, forever transformed and restored! He weeps as though he is inconsolable, yet they are tears of joy that stream down his face. Several of his fellow citizens from Capernaum jump from their seats and encircle him with great embraces of encouragement and congratulations. Some come to get a closer look and even to touch the miraculously healed hand. This is a day none of them will forget. *Ever.*

Who is this man that can command even the fundamental elements of life to rearrange a deformed arm into a whole one? Has Yahweh somehow come among them on this day, through the presence of this Heaven-sent one?

One of the Pharisees mumbles, a little louder than intended, "Only God Himself can do such a thing! *Who is this man?*"

"Blasphemy!" comes the immediate response from the whispering lips and scrunched-up mouth of Malkiel. "You had best keep that thought to yourself, lest this man's strange power captivates you as well! He's working by the power of *demons*, not Yahweh. Surely you know this?"

At the evidence of what is before their eyes, the crowd explodes into exclamations of delight, thunderous applause, and shouts of worship. A number of them shoot to their feet, raise their hands in praise, and begin to pray aloud, thanking God for sending Yeshua of Nazareth to them.

Jesus turns to the congregation, and, with a sparkle in His eyes, declares, "As I told your Pharisees several days ago in the grainfields, 'The Sabbath was made for man...man was not made for the Sabbath, neither were they made for whatever rules and traditions that men invent in order to selfishly enhance that sacred command and their own sense of power. Indeed, the Son of Man is the only Lord of the Sabbath'!"

The continued applause that engulfs the ecstatic scene is more than the self-important elite can bear. Jesus now glances at those who challenged Him, especially Malkiel. The look on Yeshua's face seems to say: *You started this. Now, it's your move.*

In a huff, the Pharisees huddle into a seething, black-robed wad. Malkiel leads the heated discussion among them. Even the several Herodians[223] that were present join with them in their disgust. They shuffle outside the synagogue as a group, hatred simmering from every fiber of their being.

The whole affair appears to have detonated, right in their faces—and in front of the people, no less! They have to get serious now. Deadly serious. They have to do something radical before this situation gets completely out of hand and perhaps spreads to every corner of the empire. Jerusalem had sent them to confront this *Jesus fellow* and put a stop to His madness. Instead, their plan has miserably failed, maybe even fueled the continually unfolding disaster. So, together, just outside the synagogue, they come up with yet another strategy.

Their new scheme is simple. Today, they plot Jesus' *murder.*

With a unified voice, they agree the deed must be done. The miracle worker from Nazareth must die, even if they have to arrange His death themselves.[224]

But in this fairly early part of the day, they haven't seen anything yet. This day will soon grow far worse for them.

44

PLUNDERING THE STRONG MAN'S HOUSE

With a startling and authoritative command, Jesus drives out the demon.

Jesus withdraws from the synagogue. With His disciples in tow, they start down the beach road.

The crowd follows, without any urging from Jesus or His disciples. Yosef makes his way to the head of the throng. He is singing at the top of his voice, his song interrupted by moments of weeping. His life is new! He is whole! Yesterday, he had been a lowly, often ignored, and pitied man from Capernaum. Today, he is a celebrity, leading a procession of worshipers! And the man from Nazareth had merely *spoken* all of this into existence!

The people are overwhelmed by this miracle worker and master Teacher who is in the midst of their humble community. Many vow to follow Him wherever He goes—an oath that most of them will forsake as time goes on, and as the cost becomes too high. But for now, they revel in the moment.

Trailed by a growing sea of people, Jesus moves a good way down the road from the synagogue. The thoroughfare borders the glistening Lake Galilee. Jesus and His disciples head up the side of a small hill, just across the road, overlooking the lake. The Pharisees follow. A portion of the crowd does as well. The rest of the multitude remains below. From this hillside vantage point, Jesus can be heard and seen by all.

The people bring their sick to Him by the dozens. With simply a word or a touch, Jesus heals each of them. One after another, shouts of gladness rise from the crowd and reverberate through the hills, across the waters of Kinneret.

Malkiel and his group of Pharisees are beside themselves, stewing in their collective resentment. *This man has the crowds bewitched! Look how they so quickly go after Him…abandoning us!*

How can this new phenomenon be contained without causing an awful uprising? Has Jesus already become too big? There has to be a way to disrupt His ministry. Perhaps we should infiltrate it? Maybe we can develop a traitor from within the midst of His disciples? Maybe there is someone very close to Him, one we can convince to deliver this Jesus into our hands? Maybe even someone within His inner circle? How much money would that take? How much pressure and blackmail would be required to pull off such a feat?

They certainly have more planning to do; that fact is apparent. But for now, they have to deal with the matter at hand.

Demons Obey

Just then a band of people breaks through the tightly huddled crowd and presents Jesus with yet another pitiful man. He is known as Jeremiah. This one is blind and mute.

"We don't know how this happened," his friends say. "One day he could both see and speak, the next day—and until this day—he can do neither."

"This man's limitations are caused by a demonic infestation," Jesus says. "Please understand what I will tell you now…not all infirmities originate from a spiritual assault, but *this one did*. He knows what he has done. And he knows what his deeds have cost him. Yet, in his healing, Heaven will be exalted on this day." Jeremiah weeps as he reaches out to see if he can find Jesus' arm.

Grabbing the man's hand, Jesus asks, "Jeremiah, do you believe in the Son of Man?"

The man shakes his head in the affirmative and tries to mouth his muted words. A pitiful, mumbling, animal-like sound is all he can make. At this, the crowd murmurs amongst themselves, and their murmuring moves like a giant wave washing over them. *What will this miracle worker do in this kind of case? What in the world* can *He do?*

In the next instant, with a startling shout that shocks them all, Jesus commands the demon, "Leave this man! *Leave him now!*"

Immediately, the blind and mute man praises the Lord of Heaven with his newly opened mouth. "I can see! I can see! I can really see!"

He snaps his head around and scans the crowd. "I tell you the truth! I can see all of you!" The crowd stands there, staring. They don't know what to say. Can he really *see* them? He certainly can speak—of that there is no doubt. But has he truly received his sight…*instantly*? To be able to now speak *is* incredible, to be sure! But…to "see" as well? That is just too hard to believe!

The man can see their doubt. He points at them, quickly describing some of their clothing and other personal features. The people standing there are now the ones who are dumbstruck. The command Jesus has over this demonic infestation is within the reach of His voice alone! He merely spoke, and the demon left the man! They have never seen such raw power and authority. Even as they celebrate what they have seen, they are still unnerved by it all.

"Jeremiah has had his sight restored as a sign to you," Jesus says to the crowd. "And his tongue was loosed as yet another great lesson! When a man can no longer see, then suddenly sees—when he can no longer speak, but can instantly speak—he finally beholds the true Kingdom of God. And as a result, he begins to declare the praise of the Lord Almighty, the Creator of everything! He uses his tongue for the glory of the Kingdom work!"

Who is this one who speaks to them as though He Himself has come down from Heaven?

The healed man is at Jesus' feet, sobbing, while Jesus continues with the lesson. "I say unto you…for those who think they can 'see' but refuse to see the truth standing right before them…*they* are the blind ones! As a result, their praise, which should have been given to the Lord of Heaven, is now taken from them. They have become mute in the presence of His glory."

Jesus looks at Jeremiah, bends down, and whispers close in his ear, "Go. Sin no more, lest something worse befalls you next time." Jesus cups the man's face on both sides, brings his head to His own, and kisses his forehead. Jeremiah sobs, clutching Jesus' hands. He finally stands to his feet and raises his hands towards the heavens, giving praise to God. *He is free!*

At that, a roar goes up from the crowd. The people shout at the top of their voices, "Surely this is the Son of David!"

The more the masses magnify Jesus, the more determined Malkiel and his group are to try to defame Him in front of His admirers. "*Stop! Stop your praise of this deranged fellow!*" Malkiel blurts out toward the crowd, waving his hands in the air like a madman. "It is only by Beelzebub, *the prince of demons,* that He drives out demons! He is not to be trusted. He's working with the devil himself! It will be to your peril to continue to follow this evil man!"

"You are not even close to the truth of the matter!" Jesus rebukes. "Think about what you are claiming, Rabbi Malkiel. Did I not just say that you would do this very thing? Did I not just proclaim that you would refuse to give glory to God? Instead, you glorify the prince of demons!"

The Pharisees stand with a look of exasperated unbelief upon their countenances. *Who does Jesus think He is, to teach and correct us—and right in front of the crowds—yet again? And in this shocking manner? Will His insolence never end?*

"I tell you the truth," Jesus presses on, "every kingdom divided against itself will eventually be destroyed. And even a house divided against itself will not stand. Therefore, if Satan drives out Satan, then he is divided against himself."

Again, they are dumbfounded by the Nazarene's challenge.

Jesus keeps speaking. "Therefore, if I am driving out demons by Beelzebub, then tell me…by whom do your own people drive them out? What name do *they* invoke? What power do they possess? *Whose authority is it?*"

The Pharisees simply remain there, some with clinched fists, others with eyes growing wilder with barely contained rage.

"Apparently you cannot answer the question," Jesus responds, as their faces redden.

"So then, if it happens to be by the Spirit of God that I am driving out demons, then *you should know*—that is, if you have true spiritual discernment."

"We should know *what?*" Malkiel demands.

Jesus replies, "You should know—Malkiel—that the Kingdom of God has come into your very presence, right here. *Today.* In the sight and hearing of all these witnesses." Jesus motions with His arm sweeping the crowd, yet He never takes His eyes off Malkiel. "And because of this, you should have joined with the others and given God the glory for what you were privileged to see here this day. But you have not.

"And consider this truth," Jesus continues. "How can anyone enter a strong man's house and carry off his possessions unless he first incapacitates that strong man? Only then can the strong man's house be plundered."

The Pharisees are again without words.

"It is for this very purpose that I have come into the world," Jesus declares. "I have come to wreck the house of the evil one—and of those who serve him."

Several of the Pharisees wince at His words. *Is He accusing us?*

Jesus says to them, as His eyes sweep across the group of Pharisees, "I'm surprised! You are the great teachers of Israel, yet you don't even know these basic spiritual truths?" Some in the crowd of onlookers and followers chuckle.

At this, the elites open their mouths to rebuke Jesus. Their ever-darkening faces betray their thoughts and what their next words will most likely be. However, Jesus never gives them the chance to speak. Instead,

He goes on with His teaching. He turns His back on the Pharisees and faces the crowd.

"Whoever is not with me is against me, and whoever does not gather with me scatters," He says. "And so I tell you the truth, every type of slander can be pardoned before the Father, but blasphemy against the Holy Spirit will not be forgiven." Jesus pauses to let that striking declaration settle within his listeners' minds.

"Anyone who speaks a word against the Son of Man will be forgiven." Jesus then motions behind Him, over His shoulder, in the direction of the Pharisees. "But anyone who speaks against the Holy Spirit will not be forgiven, either in this age or in the age to come."

Something is happening among the crowd. An awakening is taking place. The people are beginning to understand the greater depths of what Jesus is telling them. The revelation of it can be seen upon their faces.

This *Jesus*—He is so very different! Never have they heard such authority, mixed with this intensity of freshness and love…and *for them*! He is uncompromising in His delivery, and, at the same time, He is possessed of an unction from On High. Furthermore, what He speaks makes sense!

This man's message is focused on a personal relationship with the Creator of their souls. His teaching isn't about keeping man-made religious rules and rituals. This is a message of hope. It is a message of *life*—real life—the way it is meant to be lived.

But Jesus isn't finished. He still has much more to reveal.

45

THE UNVEILING

A few moments ago, while Jesus was still talking to those inside the house,
His mother and brothers had arrived on the scene.

Jesus thunders out His next words, making certain that everyone who
has gathered on that hillside hear them. "Make a tree good, and its
fruit will be good, or make a tree bad, and its fruit will be bad, for a tree is
recognized by its fruit."

A bad tree, offering up its fruit—and claiming its rotten produce to be
good? The minds of the people harken back to the Garden of Eden. Jesus
is pointing to the Genesis account! He is speaking of trees and fruit, and
good versus evil![225]

Can this Jesus from Nazareth actually be the long-awaited "Seed" that
will crush the head of the enemy? Is He claiming to be the Messiah? Is
that what He is doing? Is He trying to tell them something by using such
speech?

Then, looking at the Pharisees, Jesus once again pierces the veil. He
pulls off the mask of evil that lurks behind that shroud, the unseen malev-
olent spirits that envelope the black-robed ones standing before Him.

"You brood of vipers!" Jesus exclaims, pointing directly at the Pharisees. Now it is Jesus' face that is reddening…in righteous anger.

The crowd freezes. The one from Nazareth continues to reach back to the account of the Garden of Eden and the beginning of all evil.[226] The people murmur to one another: "Leveling a charge like this, in the face of the religious elite, and in front of such a crowd, will not bode well for Jesus."

But Jesus isn't finished. He knows the murderous thoughts in the hearts of the evil men who are presently cutting Him to pieces with their dagger eyes. He knows they have been secretly plotting His death, for He knows the thoughts and secrets of all men.[227]

Jesus hammers them again. "Your masquerade is exposed! How can you who are evil say anything good? For the mouth speaks what is truly in the heart. A good man brings good things out of the good stored up in him, and an evil man brings evil things out of the evil stored up in him. But I tell you, everyone will have to give account on the Day of Judgment for every empty word they have spoken, and of every murderous thought they have nurtured!"

Jesus turns from Malkiel and his cohorts and begins the descent from the hillside. Upon reaching the road, He starts back toward Capernaum, the inner circle of His disciples at His side. The crowds follow. So do the Pharisees. They will, in one way or another, spy upon Jesus for the rest of His earthly life and ministry. They are resolute in their plan to destroy Him.

As they enter the village, the occupants who were unable to make the trek into the surrounding countryside swamp Him with their presence. Jesus takes His time as He works His way through the crowd, praying, touching, and healing as He goes.

Yeshua has now arrived home—at least to the home of His ministry headquarters, Peter's house, in Capernaum.[228]

They make it to the front door, still wading through the crowds, and go inside. At Jesus' urging, those who can comfortably fit are allowed to enter, directed by His disciples.

Some hang inside from the opened windows, like children at a sporting event peering over the barricades. Some in the crowd even go up to the roof and look down through openings in the slats, not wanting to be left out of witnessing the spectacle of another potential miracle being performed. Still others fill the property and the dusty street in front of the house. Just now, a respectful hush sweeps over those outside. No one wants to miss a thing. They want to hear every word that Jesus is teaching.

Malkiel steps forward, understanding that they might lose the crowd completely if cooler heads among them do not prevail. He is one of only several of the Pharisee clan who has actually made it inside the house.

Stepping through the midst of the indoor crowd and coming face to face with Jesus, he whispers, "Teacher, I know we've had our differences. And for my part in them, I apologize. But…could you just show us a sign, *perhaps?*" His arms are opened wide, and he has a childlike countenance. He is almost begging Jesus to succumb to his simple request, one that Malkiel implies can settle the whole matter right then and there.

"Maybe there's something you can do, proving once and for all that you are a man who has indeed been sent directly from God. Perhaps then some of the doubters among us can be placated. Perhaps a sign? Just *one?* *Please?* For the sake of peace."

"Malkiel," Jesus answers, "it is a wicked and adulterous generation that asks for a sign, my friend. Especially in the presence of the multitude of signs that have already been given. Miracle after miracle has been done before your group on this very day alone, as well as throughout the weeks before. What more would you desire?" Jesus pauses, then runs through a litany…

"One of Capernaum's own centurions had his servant's paralysis healed, at just a *word.* News of that healing has spread throughout the region."

The Pharisees bristle at the thought of a despised Roman officer receiving any kind of blessing from Heaven. They had all heard of the healing, and they are still incensed by it.

"My own disciple, Peter, has previously had a house full of people descend upon the tranquility of his residence," Jesus goes on. "That crowd saw, with their own eyes, many who were delivered from the demonic clutches of the kingdom of darkness. They saw a great number of others who were sick delivered from illnesses with only a spoken command; some of your own group witnessed these things."

After a brief pause, with no response from Malkiel, Jesus continues.

"That's not to mention the instant healing of Peter's own mother-in-law, who is today a living witness. She was delivered from a deadly, raging fever. Once news of that simple act of heavenly kindness spread throughout the town, it brought the burgeoning crowd to Peter's home within an hour. And, today, look! Here we are yet again…another house full! And here you are, standing right in the middle of Peter's home, demanding *more* signs?"

There is another awkward pause of silence. Hardly a sound is made from the crowd.

"Poor Peter!" Jesus remarks with a gleam in His eyes. "These are not the only times his home has been overwhelmed! Sometime back, we were teaching at this very house and a man who was paralyzed was actually lowered down through that roof!" Jesus points at the ceiling, to the very spot.

"He was lying on his mat when they lowered him by cords tied at each corner. His own friends had brought him here, right here where you're standing! And because of the crowds—even some of your own were there, *again*—they couldn't get the poor man through the door, or even through the windows! With another command from Heaven, he was also healed; he picked up his mat, and went out dancing! He went right through the crowd. Have you asked *them* about signs, Malkiel?"

Malkiel stands there, speechless. He is aware of the reports of all these matters. And, this is his concern. This is why the massive crowds are following Jesus, and are continually growing in numbers! This is why the Sanhedrin has assigned him to spy upon Jesus and catch Him in a trap, if possible. Instead, the trap they have laid has backfired on them, hor-rendously, and it has happened on this very day! In the synagogue, of all places!

"Malkiel," Jesus addresses the still-silent teacher. "Here is the truth of the matter. The dead have been raised, lepers are healed, the blind can see, the crippled are restored, and demons are driven out with shrieks. Yet you ask for more signs? Something still *greater*? Nothing has been done in dark corners, my friend. Nothing has been done in secret. My miracles speak for themselves. They have been done before the eyes of multitudes. It seems you are the only one who's still demanding a sign as proof." Jesus lowers His eyes, waiting for a response. Malkiel has yet to speak.

"Yet you did not *see* any of these miracles. At least not with your spiri-tual eyes. Apparently, you did not wish to *see* them in that way." Jesus stands, looking into the man's eyes—into his soul.

"So, therefore, no sign will be given for you on this day. Or any time soon."

Jesus turns as though He is going to walk away. But then He stops. He once again faces the elder Pharisee. "*Except*, Malkiel…except for the sign of the prophet Jonah. There truly is a greater sign that you'll soon see."

Jesus surges forward with His teaching. "For as Jonah was three days and three nights in the belly of a huge fish, so the Son of Man will be three days and three nights in the heart of the earth. That will be a sign you'll find a bit harder to forget, and to ignore. *You'll see.*"

What is the meaning of this strange teaching? Malkiel wonders. Yet again, the embarrassed Pharisee is at a loss for words. He remains silent.

Jesus turns His back to Malkiel and directs His words to the gathered crowd. "Hear, and understand, this truth! When an impure spirit comes out of a person, it goes through arid places seeking rest and does not find it. Then it says, 'I will return to the house I left.' When it arrives, it finds the house unoccupied, swept clean and put in order. Then it goes and takes with it seven other spirits more wicked than itself, and they go in and live there. And the final condition of that person is worse than the first. That is how it will be with this wicked generation.

"When miracles from my Father's throne are done before your eyes, in that moment, your soul has been given the opportunity to be swept clean. However, if those miracles are rejected, if my Father's grace is spurned, then your condition will be worse than before. Rejection of what Heaven offers only emboldens the kingdom of darkness."[229]

A few moments ago, while Jesus had still been talking to those inside the house, His mother and brothers had arrived on the scene. They are standing just outside; they have come to try to convince Jesus to leave this place. They fear for His safety, *and not without cause.*

They have received word of Jesus' vibrant challenges against the religious ruling class. They have even heard the spreading rumors about a plot to assassinate Him. Not only have they become fearful that harm might come to Jesus as a result of His straightforwardness, but some among the outer members of the family fear He might have actually become unstable.[230]

Someone in the crowd speaks up. "Teacher! Your mother and brothers are outside. They want you to come outside so they might have a private moment in your presence."

Jesus responds, "Who is my mother, and who are my brothers?"[231]

Knowing the intention of His own unbelieving relatives,[232] He points to His disciples and other gathered followers, and says, "Here are my mother and my brothers. For whoever does the will of my Father in Heaven is my true brother and sister, and my true mother."

Jesus knows the evil one has persuaded even members of His own family to question His motives. He had known this moment would come. Satan had gone right for His heart.

But Jesus also knows that even though this battle is well underway, the worst is yet to come. It will culminate at a Roman flogging post and a cruel crucifixion beam. But perhaps the worst pain of all will be the utter rejection and the jeering crowd that will watch Him die…and celebrate as He gasps for one final breath.

But today, there is still work to be done.

There is another message the people need to hear. Perhaps it is the most important message of the day. It will be a message specifically for them, and it will also be a communication for the generation right around the corner, during the days of the early church. Likewise, His teaching will also ring true for every generation from this day forward, especially those living in the very last days.

46

THE HERESY HUNTERS

The children squeal and frolic in the midst of the crowd, chasing each other like a bouncing litter of carefree puppies.

It is late afternoon. Jesus and His disciples have just left Peter's house. They are headed to the seashore.

The sun isn't far from beginning its descent. That fiery primordial orb will soon melt into the mountains…the ancient stony sentinels that have encircled and guarded the lake for thousands of years. Today, these very same mountains will, once again, be witnesses to the booming voice of their Creator.

It has been another scorching day. But, mercifully, the late-afternoon breeze is just beginning to bring its refreshment. Drawing in a deep breath of the Galilean air, Jesus closes His eyes and lifts His face heavenward, savoring the falling coolness that wafts across His brow.

There is still a little daylight before the last light of Sabbath will erode into a heavy dusk. However, it is enough time to teach an important lesson to the seaside congregation, a crowd that continues to blossom in size along the shores of Kinneret.

The flow of longing souls—so desperately poor in spirit—persist in searching Him out and following Him almost everywhere He goes. They come hungering for the righteous words that He will impart to them and the stunning miracles He might continue to work in their midst—not to mention the fact that the authority of Heaven's throne itself seems to be attached to every word He utters.

The gathering masses have not, in the entirety of their relatively simple existence, enjoyed the presence of anyone among them as much as they do with this One. Today has been the most memorable Sabbath day of their lifetime. They certainly have *never* witnessed anything like what they saw this morning, in their own synagogue, and this afternoon on the hillside just outside of Capernaum, and at Peter's house.

Now the crowds are here, mingling on the beach and boiling over with enthusiasm. They have come to the shoreline, still pouring out of the middling lakeside villages, as well as the outlying regions and their settlements, because *this* is where *He* is. And this is where they want to be right now, more than anywhere else.[233]

The men come first, leading the crowds and families. The women and children follow. *Ah, yes!* The children…the laughter and infectious emanations of the purity of childhood that flow from those little ones. It is a lovely thing to behold. Wherever they cluster, they stir up an atmosphere of innocent havoc.

Bless their hearts, Jesus thinks. The children squeal and frolic in the midst of the crowd, chasing each other like a bouncing litter of carefree puppies. Those precious little ones have no awareness of the evil that lurks among them.

It is just as well they don't yet know the depth of their utterly depraved world and even the true state of their own fallen existence. They will, soon enough, discover all of that on their own. But woe unto the one through whom that evil knowledge flows! His demise will be horrible—and eternal. And, in the relative scope of all eternity, that end will be coming soon. That's why Jesus is here. This is His divine mission.

For now, though, Jesus sits in a boat, enjoying the serenity of the moment. Seagulls circle overhead and gossip among themselves midflight as they hope to find one last morsel at the closing of the day.

Only a few moments earlier, the vessel had been jostled from the shore and anchored with just enough distance separating Jesus from the growing crowd. The boat sat swashing in rhythm with the subtle lake breeze, cradling its Heaven-sent cargo.

Several of Jesus' closest disciples were with Him in the boat. Peter was busy preparing the bow of the vessel as a makeshift speaking platform. The others were adjusting the anchoring so that it would remain sturdy as Jesus stood and preached to the throng on the beach.

The rest of the disciples had stayed on the shore, attempting to put in place some type of order among the people as they also ministered to their personal needs. They offered bits of food and ladles of water, a word of prayer, an encouraging word, or a hug. It had been a long, hot day. But the people simply refused to leave Jesus' irresistible presence.

Jesus had positioned Himself on the bow of the Galilean fishing vessel and looked out over the multitude, shielding His eyes from the slowly descending ball of fire that reflected its celestial glory upon the lake's surface. *Yes.* Satan's human emissaries were still there. He spotted them immediately. They had been skulking among the people all day long.

And here they are again—*the Pharisees.* Like exasperating flies that buzz around one's face without mercy, they hover together, tucked amongst the crowd. Jesus' eyes pierce their souls…*beyond their souls*…into another dimension. It is a dimension of profane and suffocating darkness, unseen by the crowd, enveloping them, nonetheless.[234]

Of course, the Pharisees are clothed in their unmistakable ecclesiastical garb.[235] The striking adornment has been draped upon their bodies for the purpose of setting themselves apart from everyone else. From head to toe, they are wrapped in a flowing outer garment, layered with another important addition—the *tallit.*[236]

Often embellished with phylacteries strapped to their heads and wrists, along with flowing tassels on the hems of their robes, these men serve as a constant reminder to the people that God's laws are supreme.

The daily practice of the regulations, as interpreted by the "Teachers," are to be honored above everything else in life. This, they proclaim, is the only hope the people will ever have of being made "right" with their Creator.

There is scarcely a village within the Judean countryside that doesn't have its own collection of Pharisees among them, or at least those who visit regularly. As they move among the people, their clerical uniforms command attention, invoking a sense of awe and respect.

They are the self-appointed *keepers* of the Law—the ensurers of righteousness and the hunters of heresy and blasphemy. And now a new "Teacher" is among the people. Jesus' every word will be dissected and scrutinized by these ecclesiastical surgeons of orthodoxy. Their findings will be discussed at length and reported to their elders, and eventually to the Sanhedrin Council itself…back in Jerusalem.

But for now, *the keepers* have positioned themselves amongst the people who stand upon the otherwise serene seashore. They have chosen their perches so they not only can hear every word that Jesus will utter, but, just as importantly, so they might also observe the reactions of the crowd as He speaks. They need to understand exactly what they are up against.

The black-robed ones looked like human-shaped birds of prey roosting in the rotted branches of a dying tree, peering down upon the people below as though they are mere carrion. But by now, they have convinced themselves that they are on a Heaven-appointed mission. After all, the sanctity of the Law is at stake…and so are *their* reputations and coveted positions of authority.

The Pharisees' attention is steeled upon the one standing in the bow of the boat. The Teacher is obviously preparing to speak, again, to the quickly gathering flock.

Jesus raises a hand. A hush washes over the crowd.

His voice thunders into the early evening atmosphere: *"Hear these words! Take them to heart! Ponder them in your soul! Do you have the ears to hear?"*

Nothing but the occasional yelp of a seagull can be heard. The people are awestruck, yet again. What will the Teacher say next?

"A certain farmer went out to sow his seed. And as he was scattering the seed, some fell along the path, and the birds of the air came and ate it up…"

He emphasizes the words "birds of the air," then pauses. He closes His eyes. When He opens them again, He looks directly at the Pharisees.

Actually, Jesus isn't looking *at* them—not in the way one might otherwise perceive a look. He is looking *through* them, and beyond—down through the ages. His multidimensional vision pierces several realms of reality. At the very same time, He is also peering into the vile, unseen realm that envelops the black-robed ones.[237] He sees the unclean spirits standing at their sides, invisible to those who only think they can "see."[238]

Then He turns His focus back upon the crowds. He possesses a certain, unique glint in His eyes as He readies Himself to continue His message.

As the Pharisees glare at Jesus, understanding that, somehow, He is speaking about them, they think: *There's that look again! The same one we saw in the grain fields a week ago, and in the synagogue earlier this morning!*

They hold their collective breath…

PART TWELVE

The Long Road

Scriptural Backdrop:

The Crowds

Meanwhile, when a crowd of many thousands had gathered, so that they were trampling on one another, Jesus began to speak first to his disciples, saying: "Be on your guard against the yeast of the Pharisees, which is hypocrisy. There is nothing concealed that will not be disclosed, or hidden that will not be made known. What you have said in the dark will be heard in the daylight, and what you have whispered in the ear in the inner rooms will be proclaimed from the roofs." (Luke 12:1–3)

The Portal

Then Jesus went through the towns and villages, teaching as he made his way to Jerusalem. Someone asked him, "Lord, are only a few people going to be saved?" He said to them, "Make every effort to enter through the narrow door, because many, I tell you, will try to enter and will not be able to. Once the owner of the house gets up and closes the door, you will stand outside knocking and pleading, 'Sir, open the door for us.' But he will answer, 'I don't know you or where you come from.'" (Luke 13:22–25)

The Cost

Large crowds were traveling with Jesus, and turning to them he said: "If anyone comes to me and does not hate father and mother, wife and children, brothers and sisters—yes, even their own life—such a person cannot be my disciple. And whoever does not carry their cross and follow me cannot be my disciple." (Luke 14:25–27)

47

THE FINAL JOURNEY

Near the Jordan River highway, more than two years from the Capernaum synagogue healing episode, circa AD 33

After three years of public ministry, Yeshua now has only a few short weeks to live.

Even though it is the beginning of spring, the Mediterranean sun is already unseasonably warm. There isn't a comforting cloud of shade in the sky to be seen. It will be a hot day, to be sure. But there is work to be done.

Almost 2,400 years have passed since the Flood. Yahweh, the Creator of every living thing, is standing in the midst of His own creation. Surreptitiously clothed in the flesh of humanity, He is currently on the last leg of His journey, headed to a cross. The grueling sacrificial process of setting everything aright is quickly closing in on Him. At times, the thought of the ordeal awaiting Him at the end of the road is suffocating. Yet, He knows it is coming soon. So, He presses on....

It has been almost three years since Jesus began His earthly ministry. Presently, He and His burgeoning entourage—the twelve disciples of His inner circle as well as the crowds that constantly followed after them—are moving among the villages of the Jordan River Valley. They have come from the north of Judea, down through Galilee, along the region of Samaria.[239]

Following the main road between the various hamlets of civilization, they will eventually arrive at Jericho several weeks from now. From there, they will ascend to Jerusalem one last time. The entire trip will take weeks and culminate with a brutal disfigurement of Yeshua's body, wrought under a Roman soldier's humiliating scourge. Then He will be finished off with the slamming of three thick spikes through His wrists and feet. *Pa-Pinggg! Pa-Pinggg! Pa-Pinggg!*

Jesus often hears the sound…ringing in His head, especially at night. But, for the moment at hand, He steels Himself *and presses on.* This is why He has come.

Yeshua's traveling group comes to a halt on the outskirts of yet another village. The blazing sun beats down from directly overhead, forcing rivulets of sweat to pour down His face. As He wipes them with the back of His sleeve, Peter ambles up to Him with a waterskin.

"Master, drink this," he says. "It's been a long day, and it's only halfway through."

Jesus grins, slips the container from Peter's hands, and swigs down a couple of refreshing gulps.

"I have a feeling it's about to be even longer," Peter adds, jerking his head in the direction of the village's main entrance and rolling his eyes.

A cohort of the village's Pharisees are making their way towards them. They don't look happy. They never do, especially when Jesus shows up among the throngs.

Jesus grips Peter's shoulder. Chuckling, He says, "We've seen that sight many times before, my good friend. These are always such fun *conversations,* wouldn't you agree?"

Peter shrugs his shoulders and snorts. "You mean *confrontations,* don't you?" Peter is also a subtle master of instigation. He seems to be frequently in the process of searching out heated "conversations."

Before Jesus can acknowledge Peter's remark, the Pharisees are upon them. *"Teacher! Teacher!"* the leader of the ecclesiastical parade shouts.

"Please. Give us a hearing! If you would be so gracious. *Please.* We only ask for a moment or two of your time."

Jesus nods His permission and motions with His hand for the approaching men to continue. A "moment or two" often means an "hour or two" with this bunch. But Jesus will oblige them, yet again.

"My name is Baruch,"[240] the speaker declares as they arrive. He motions toward the others with him. "We're the ones who minister the Word of *Hashem*[241] among the people of the villages of this region."

"Yes, Baruch, I remember you," Jesus says. "And I'm more than familiar with your work." He slightly chuckles, with a knowing glint in His eye.

He likes Baruch. He has spoken with him before, a couple of years back. The elder Pharisee had seemed, at that time, to have been sincerely searching out the truth of Jesus' Kingdom teachings.

Jesus stands waiting for the inquiries that are certain to come.

This group of Pharisees doesn't disappoint.

48

GIVE US A HINT!

He lowers His hand and glances back at the Pharisee.
"It's all there in in your Scriptures."

---

aruch speaks on behalf of the group. "We've heard of your teachings concerning the coming Kingdom of God," he says. "We are, as you might imagine, most interested to now, personally, learn of your deepest thoughts on the matter—"

Jesus slightly nods, indicating that Baruch should proceed. The Pharisee clears his throat, attempting to compose himself.

"Well…I suppose what we would like to know is…exactly *when* is the Kingdom of God going to come? We've waited so long! We can almost feel its approach. It's thick in the air! It seems that we're living in undeniably prophetic times. We all agree, there's a prescient heaviness about our days, like during few other times in our remembered past. It's as though something is getting ready to *snap*. Do you feel it, too?"

He searches Jesus' face for a reaction. The others indicate by their body language that they agree with their leader. "Please, Teacher, what do *you* say about this?" Baruch's voice holds a sense of urgency.

Jesus answers, "The coming of the Kingdom of God is not something that can always be observed with explosions of obvious revelations—not in the context of everyday life, anyway."

He steps a bit closer to the Pharisee. "Because it's in the middle of each day's living and each generation's passing that the Word of God and the declarations of the ancient prophets are continually unfolding. Most of the time, it's in the little things, Baruch."

"Please!" Baruch appeals. "Explain more!"

Jesus accommodates. "The coming of Messiah was foretold in the Scriptures, of course. And those Scriptures promised that He would come first unto His own people."

Baruch thoughtfully shakes his head. He seems to be engaged. So far, so good.

"Messiah's exact and initial place of revealing was foretold as well. It was to be in Bethlehem, and at a very specific place in Bethlehem." Jesus continues, "The divine miracles that He would minister were also foreseen by the most revered of prophets. Those miracles were to be wonders that could only be explained by the fact that Messiah had indeed arrived upon the earth, directly from the throne of God. Yet, at the same time, He would also come unto His own creation through very specific generations of humanity itself. This is why He would be known as the Messiah of Heaven, but also as the Son of David."

Jesus looks up at a circling vulture, shading His squinting eyes with a cupped hand. He speaks again, still looking at the bird. "Messiah's humble earthly beginnings were clearly revealed to you as well. Even the final work that He would come to accomplish was laid out through the prophets Daniel, Zechariah, and Isaiah, as well as by King David."[242]

He lowers His hand and glances back at the Pharisee. "It's all there in your Scriptures."

Baruch is speechless, as are those with him. Some of those revelations are also matters of heated debate among their various Orthodox factions.

Their lack of response quickly grows to a blossoming discomfort.

Who is this One, to think that He can teach us—especially in such matters of well-known controversy?

But Jesus knows their thoughts. Turning to Baruch's entourage, He quizzes them further. "Do you have a hard time pondering these things?"

He pauses a few seconds, then continues before they can answer. "People will not be able to accurately say, 'Here it is!' or 'There it is!' because of any one specific instance. When God's Kingdom first appears in your midst, you'll be required to possess a very special, and deeply spiritual, discernment to identify that presence. Many things will be happening at once—some little, some bigger. It is a keen spiritual discernment that you'll need in order to see it and correctly tie it together. It's a sensitivity that comes from touching the throne of God through your uninhibited love for your Creator."

Jesus scans the faces of His disciples, then looks back to the Pharisees. "God's work is to be accomplished this way for now, in order to remain veiled from the sight of the evil one. Only those with eyes to see will be able to truly recognize it when it happens."

"Can you show it to us, Teacher?" Baruch pleads. "We have those eyes *to see*! We'd love to see it now! Is that even possible?"

Jesus leans into Baruch and murmurs, for his ears only, "The Kingdom of God is in *your midst* right now my friend. It is right before your eyes."[243]

With that, Jesus steps back from Baruch and simply stands there for a moment, begging the man's soul *to see*. But there is no indication that the elder Pharisee understands the revelation. *Not yet.*

Jesus continues speaking to them as a group. "After this age has rejected what it has seen," He says, "the Kingdom of God will return again, but not to *this* generation. It will come in a future one."

Baruch's mouth falls open. His eyes widen. Before the Pharisee can express his thoughts, Jesus turns to survey the crowd gathered behind Him. Multitudes had been following Him before He even arrived outside this little village. He peers down the path ahead, deep in thought.

Jesus knows an exceedingly dark day awaits Him…just down that ancient roadway.

But not quite yet. That dreadful moment will come at its appointed time.

Right now, however, there is still work to be done. Always…work to be done.

49

JUST LIKE THIS

The Pharisees take note of the compelling sway Jesus has over the people.

Jesus motions for His inner circle of disciples to draw closer.

He talks to the Twelve in such a manner that Baruch and his entourage can also hear. "The time is coming when you, too, will long to see one of the days of the Son of Man, but you will not see it. People will tell you, 'There He is!' or 'Here He is!' But do not believe them.

"I'm very serious when I tell you this. Do not go running off after them. For the Son of Man in His day will be like the lightning that flashes and then lights up the sky from one end to the other. No one will miss Him! But first He must suffer many things and be rejected by this generation."

Baruch speaks up. "Are you saying we have already missed the Messiah? Are you telling us that our generation has forfeited His blessings and somehow overlooked His appearance?" Those with him begin to mutter among themselves, whispering words of growing resentment.

"I tell you the truth, Baruch," Jesus replies, "this generation is in fact largely missing the entire event, *yes*. Again, it's all right there, open before you. It really couldn't be any plainer. The Word of God is *living*, and it's actually coming to pass before your eyes. And the Son of Man Himself will eventually be lifted up, right in front of you. You won't be able to miss it. It will be a sight the world will never forget."

"But...*but*—" Baruch struggles for his next words, his frustration growing more obvious.

When he has gathered his thoughts, the elder Pharisee continues, his eyes narrowing, "Are you then asserting that the people of our own day have actually *seen* the Messiah, but failed to recognize Him? And that, somehow, He has already been 'lifted up,' as you say? *How is this even possible?*"

Baruch moves closer to Jesus, a hint of indignation in his voice. "Surely our high priest would have recognized Him. Certainly our elders would know the Messiah. How could it be that Messiah would not have first gone straight to our elders at the Temple and reported to them? After all, it is we who are Messiah's forerunners, His divine messengers, His heralds. Why wouldn't He have come to *us* from the beginning?"[244]

"It is the same in every generation my friend," Jesus responds. "Yahweh is always moving; He's continuously working. He's forever confirming the ancient prophecies by pushing them right along through every epoch of time. But one has to properly put together the full picture of His Word in order to *see* it happening and to correctly *understand* the prophecies. Messiah doesn't 'report' to any man, Baruch. He does not move in the direction or the manner in which man's 'teachers' presume to have determined for Him."

This further elucidation appears to genuinely grip Baruch's heart. Jesus can sense wheels of meditation grinding away deep within his soul.

"You see," Jesus says, "the world is moving toward a great and terrible day of judgment. It's still in the distance, but it *is* coming. God *will have* His Paradise restored. The evil one will not prevail in the end. In the meantime, Yahweh is patient, holding out His offer of salvation to all. Each generation is held responsible for what it does with God's movement among them—"

"These are hard sayings, Teacher!" Baruch interrupts. He looks at his feet, shaking his head in disbelief. "I don't understand how an entire generation could miss the warnings of God's Word, especially the prophetic promises."

"Oh…but they do!" Jesus rejoins. "And largely, *they have*. And it's happened even in the most unlikely of times!"

"It's like this," Jesus says, as He turns toward the crowd. "*Just as it was* in the days of Noah, *so also will it be* at the final coming, in the days of the return of the Son of Man." The crowd snaps to attention at these words.

"Think about those days of old!" Jesus goes on. "People were eating, drinking, marrying and being given in marriage, right up to the very day Noah entered the ark. But they were also immersed in all manner of wickedness, thinking that God was not watching their vile affairs! They spurned their love for their Creator, and even intimately consorted with the fallen ones! Then, right in the midst of everyday life, like a thief in the night, the Flood came and destroyed them all!"

Jesus pauses as the crowds gasp at these difficult reminders of the folly of past generations, then He speaks up again. "In Noah's day, the people didn't seem to expect what was coming upon them…until it was entirely too late."

Jesus looks away, searching for another platform from which to speak. He sees a large boulder with a flattened top and climbs upon it. From here, the crowd is sure to hear His next words:

"But that generation was without excuse! They had been warned! Yahweh never brings judgment without first issuing a merciful warning. Yet, they refused to see the utter vileness and corruption in which they dwelt, and to which they had yoked themselves. They declined to even acknowledge the enormous ark standing in the field at Noah's house. It was there for all the world to see! And, *see it* they did! But rather than rejoice at the sight of the massive wooden vessel of their potential salvation, they mocked it! They loathed its presence. It was an object of embarrassment and shame to them!"

Jesus pauses to scan the faces in the crowd. "That gigantic boat was God's vehicle of deliverance, erected and lifted up high, for all to behold.

It had been built by a master carpenter. A man of God. And it was available for *any* who would come. In it, men and women would have found safety. But no one came, except Noah, his own family, and the animals that God brought to Noah."

The crowd is amazed by these words. Only the whispering sounds of the breeze and the occasional screech of a gliding hawk looking for his next meal waft against their eardrums. Other than that, all ears and eyes are directed toward Jesus.

The Pharisees again take note of the compelling sway Jesus has over the people. He has *always* held that power, wherever and whenever He speaks. The Jewish elite despise Him for it.

See how the people love Him!

Who is this man?

"And it was the same in the days of Lot," Jesus says. Once again, He wipes the sweat from His eyes and cheeks before going on:

"In the wicked cities of Sodom and Gomorrah, the people were also eating and drinking, buying and selling, planting and building—just like they had done during the days of Noah before them. But the very day Lot and his family left Sodom, spirited away by angels, fire and sulfur rained down from heaven and destroyed them all. So it will be again, in the last days. It will be just like that."

The listeners understand these marvelous scriptural accounts. They have studied them in their synagogues. They have read the sacred stories to their children and discussed them over meals and in family prayer times. But what in the world do those pieces of ancient history have to do with *them* and *their* current generation—a time filled with all the technological wonders of the ages? Will these same kinds of horrible things really come to pass upon them as well?

Then, Jesus startles His listeners with yet another sudden exclamation. "*It will be just like this* on the day the Son of Man is revealed! On that day, no one who is on the housetop with their possessions inside should go down to get them! Likewise, no one in the field should go back for anything. *Remember Lot's wife!* Whoever tries to keep their life will lose it, and whoever loses their life will preserve it. I tell you, on that night, two people will be in one bed; one will be taken and the other left. Two women will be grinding grain together; one will be taken and the other will be left!"

"Where will these things take place, Lord?" someone shouts from the crowd.

Jesus bellows back, "They will happen *wherever* it is necessary for them to happen! And *whenever* Yahweh chooses!"

He steps down from His boulder perch, the last words of His public message having concluded for the day.

Once on the road again, Jesus walks toward the village with His disciples close on His heels. He makes no grand announcement, nor does He give any particular instructions. He simply starts walking. The crowds move along the road behind Him as one huge mass of humanity. They want—*they need*—to hear more.

Jesus keeps to His private teaching, however. "It's just like the birds of the air," He explains to the dozen closest to Him. "You understand, don't you? Where there is a dead body, there the vultures will also gather. Therefore, wherever the wicked are, those who have marked themselves for eternal ruin because of their rebellious hearts—they, too, shall be found out by the judgments of God. The stench of their vileness reaches the nostrils of Heaven."

The huge, black, scavenger birds circle them again, just overhead. It is as if the revolting things are following them. Jesus looks up at the birds and says to His disciples, "In the same way that a carcass cannot hide from a vulture, neither can a world of evil hide from its righteous Creator. That thoroughly foul generation is on its way, my brothers. Just as surely as it appeared in Noah's day, it is coming once again. *But, it is not yet the time.*"

Just then, He stops in the middle of the road, seeming to peer into the distant future.

Jesus resumes talking after a few moments of eerie silence. "And when *that day* arrives, it shall indeed come…like a roaring flood."

50

THE SELECTION

It is an entrance fit for a conquering king.
But the Jewish elite label the event as outright blasphemy.

Jesus and His disciples spend several more weeks in the Jordan Valley, moving among the hamlets, then eventually ministering for another few days in the region of Jericho, just down the mountain from Jerusalem.

The crowds follow them. They watch and they wait, hoping to witness another miracle and desiring to hear more about the coming Kingdom. Most are sincere seekers, hearts full of earnest expectation. Others are spies. *Always, there are the spies.* And traitors.

Passover is approaching. The host of pilgrims, including Baruch and his crew, will soon be on the road to Jerusalem in order to celebrate. Jesus gathers up His disciples and starts out again. Leaving Jericho, they go up through the narrow valley that leads to Jerusalem.

As they start along the way, the disciples inquire, "Lord, why did you tell Baruch that the Kingdom of God is among them now?"

"You've been uniquely blessed, my friends," Jesus replies. "You don't need to look for the coming of the Kingdom in marvelous signs, because its King is presently right before you, living in your midst. But the display of power they vainly seek will one day become visible to all. The whole earth will see it…and will mourn when it happens. But God's people will not need to stumble around in the dark to find the signs of the coming Kingdom. When the signs begin to appear, they will be vividly apparent to my sheep, those who hear my voice and who have the eyes to see. Of this I can assure you."

As they walk, Jesus reminds them, "As I have told you before, we're going up to Jerusalem. There the Son of Man will be delivered over to the chief priests and the teachers of the law. They will condemn Him to death and hand Him over to the Gentiles to be mocked and flogged… and crucified."

The disciples stare at Him, disturbed in their spirits. Why does He insist on speaking this way?

"But, on the third day," Jesus promises, "He will be raised to life."

Knowing their anxious thoughts, He offers comfort: "I know you don't fully understand what I'm saying right now. You're wondering why I'm telling you such hard things. But remember. I've told you this ahead of time so that when they come to pass, you'll remember, and then you'll know that *I am He*."

~⁊

Just like in the Jordan River Valley, Jesus is once again shadowed by the crowds of pilgrims drawn to the Holy City either by the coming Passover or by their curiosity about this Jesus who is also headed that way. Most in the procession desire to discover exactly what part the prophet from Nazareth will play in the festivities. Throughout the multitude, there is an atmosphere of feverish expectation. They expect that Yeshua might at last announce Himself as the Christ and claim His Kingdom—even the Twelve still don't understand the full measure of who Jesus really is and what He has come to do.[245]

The disciples, following Jesus along the way, have just now arrived at the village of Bethany on the summit of the Mount of Olives, a short walk from Jerusalem. It is early Friday, now just six days before the Passover.[246]

They remain at Bethany for the Sabbath and spend most of that day together. As Saturday evening falls, they sit with Jesus on the hillside overlooking Jerusalem and the Temple Mount, admiring the glimmering orangish, golden sun as it slips below the horizon.

The next day, at dawn of the first day of the week, the group makes their way to the city. They cross the Kidron Valley and enter Jerusalem through the East Gate, with Jesus riding on the back of the foal of a donkey that belongs to a friend. The crowds overwhelm the entrance pathways as the news washes over the city: "*Yeshua is entering Jerusalem!*" At the gate, the mass of humanity grows so enormous that it attracts the agitated attention of the religious elite, as well as that of the Roman soldiers and Temple guards.

Jesus' entry becomes a spectacle of pageantry, thoroughly unnerving those who are already plotting His death. Palm branches and articles of clothing are strewn into the street in front of the donkey's path so that He might pass over them.

It is an entrance fit for a conquering king. But the Jewish elite label the event as outright blasphemy. And, as far as the Romans are concerned, the spectacle could be the makings of a coming insurrection. Scrutinizing eyes follow His every move.

On that day, the crowd at the gate represents all of humanity. Of course, there are beggars, as always. Insanely rich people are present as well, attracted by the attendance of the prophet and miracle worker. People from every race, culture, and walk of life mingle…children, young adults, middle-aged folks, elderly—all are there in massive numbers, a sea of integrated humanity.

Those of royalty, and from the households of royalty, are also there. Businessmen, prostitutes, merchants, traders, thieves, soldiers, and law enforcement officials are crammed together in the belly of the great crowd. Freedmen, citizens of Rome, slaves, indentured servants, and homeless people pack into the throng, too.

Certainly, the religious are present. From every denomination of Judaism, they come, as well as the Roman and Greek pagans—not to mention those who believe in no god at all.

And on this day, at this precise moment—without even making a conscious decision to do so—the various representatives of humanity begin to choose sides. Every reaction one might imagine is on display, aimed squarely at the one riding the donkey.

The scene morphs into a logistical nightmare as the crowds move along the way as one, trying to get a closer look, to touch Him, or to have Him acknowledge their presence with just a glance. Cries of "Hallelujah!" sporadically rise to the heavens and bounce off the great walls of the city, echoing down the Kidron Valley and throughout the surrounding terrain. Plots of murder are muttered through mouths that are twisted sideways as they speak. Their diabolically influenced words are accompanied by self-congratulating slaps on backs.

But, this is why He has come. Not for the accolades and adoration of the crowds. *No*…He has come so the people can *choose*. He has come here on this day, and in this manner, *on purpose*.

He is here to fulfill the sound of the repeated crack of a whip. He has arrived so that thick, long spikes will slam through His flesh, muscle, tendon, and bones. He has come to lay down His life—even for those who hate Him. He has come to hold open the door of the "ark" for as long as possible…because there is yet another *certain day* to come.

Another ear-splitting wave of "Hallelujah!" hurtles through the Passover crowd. More weeping. More shouting. More promises of allegiance, sworn with solemn oaths…vows that most intend to keep, but will not.

More whispered threats. More plotting.

This opportunity must not go to waste! Perhaps now we can ensnare Him in a trap. We can shut down this whole operation—this "church" of which He continually speaks. We will slay their shepherd.

And the sheep will scatter.[247]

51

EVENING ON THE MOUNT

As Jesus sits upon a tabletop ledge of rock jutting out of the mountainside, the disciples quietly, reverently, slip to His side and sit down.

For those first few days, the city is abuzz because of Jesus' presence.

They are intense days, filled with intrigue. Conspiracies are still developing. And an unknown betrayer has been diabolically manipulated and placed right in the midst of the disciples.

Deals have to be made. Important secret meetings must be held. Payoffs still need to exchange hands.

There are crowds to instruct. Disciples to prepare. False teaching to set straight. Friends to make. Enemies to arise, from deep within the bowels of the dark shadows of the unseen realm. A few more miracles are still to be wrought. Money-changers' tables still need to be overturned.

And, most importantly, there are still believing souls to be collected into the Kingdom's harvest.

Jesus has only a few more days to live. It is late in the afternoon on Monday. It is sweltering in the Temple courts. Yet, the people continue to flow into the city in great droves. It has been an exhausting day as well, one of unrelenting confrontation.

At the end of it, Jesus retires once again to the Mount of Olives. It is there where He and His disciples will spend every single night of His last week on earth. If the disciples could have only fathomed what they would eventually be forced to endure in just a few short days, perhaps, by now, they would have already absconded.

As Jesus sits upon a tabletop ledge of rock jutting out of the mountainside, the disciples quietly, reverently, slip to His side and sit down. Another day is coming to an end. The men comment upon the serenity of the moment, and they especially note the magnificent beauty of the Temple below them, as they had done earlier that evening, on their way back to the Mount of Olives. Jesus had interrupted their wonderment by assuring them that, soon, the structure they were admiring would no longer exist at all.

"Tell us Lord," a forlorn Peter had inquired, "when will all these things actually happen…and what will be the sign of your coming, and of the end of the age?"

Jesus had paused, then, without directly addressing His pronouncement about the Temple's destruction, He instead spoke of the signs of His final return.

"Watch out that no one deceives you, my brothers," He had said. "Many will come in my name claiming, 'I am the Messiah,' and will deceive many. There will be a constant global atmosphere of wars and rumors of wars, but see to it that you are not alarmed. Such things must happen, but the end is still to come. Nations will rise up against nations, and kingdoms against kingdoms, all over the world. There will be famines and earthquakes in various places. All these are the beginning of birth pains showing the mother that her child is soon to be born. These signs will indicate that the arrival of the Son of Man is very near as well."

Jesus had resumed laying out the list of last-days indicators. His words were ominous, even frightening at times. But the disciples were captivated by each one.

"I can tell you something else about those days," He said. "It will be a defining characteristic that will be unmistakable by the generation that will eventually see the coming of the Son of Man. At least, those with *eyes to see* will understand it."

John spoke up, "Tell us, Teacher!"

"Here it is, my friends," Jesus announced. "In the generation that is yet to come, this gospel of the Kingdom, the one of which you are now the forerunners...it will be in the midst of being preached to all the nations, throughout all the world, into areas yet to be discovered. In those days, and in that unique generation—that's when the end will come."[248]

"What will happen *then*?" Philip entreated. Won't that be *Heaven on earth* in those days? If the whole world has received the gospel, surely they'll be pierced to their hearts and souls. Surely they'll long for your rule and reign, just like we do."

"No, Philip," Jesus replied. "Just the opposite will be true. Sadly, the world will grow angrier in its rebellion. They will hate me, and they will hate my Father. The love of most will grow cold. They will despise God's Word. They will take indignant offense at every word of truth spoken to them. They will run after false prophets and false teachers, those who will tell them only what they want to hear. In the coming days, they will hate *you*—in the very same way they now hate me. You'll see." He looked directly at each one of them as He spoke those last words.

Observing the Temple Mount with eyes full of sorrow, He continued. "And they will hate those of *that* generation as well. In fact, a time of great persecution will erupt all over the world. It will be like never before, since from the beginning. In that age, many of those who believe my Word will be delivered up to the authorities on account of my name. Some will be put in prison. Others will be killed. Others will flee to the mountains."

Jesus paused and scratched in the dirt with a stick He had broken off earlier. Then He looked up again, surveying the group in front of Him. He could see they were perplexed at His hard sayings. He continued, pointing the stick at the men, sweeping it from one end to the other, as He spoke.

"Then," He said, "After all these things have come to pass, the sign of the Son of Man will appear in Heaven. And then all the peoples of the earth will mourn when they see the Son of Man coming on the clouds of Heaven, with power and great glory. And He will send his angels with a loud trumpet call, and they will gather His elect from the four winds, from one end of the heavens to the other."

When He had finished, the disciples remarked among themselves: "Just like Lot! The angels of Yahweh rescued Lot and his family just before God poured out His wrath on those great yet perverse cities!"

"Now, also learn this lesson from the fig tree—" Jesus continued.

These words commanded the disciples' attention. They remembered that Jesus, that same morning, had actually condemned a fig tree on their way into the city. He had merely spoken to it, as if it were a person. Then they had watched the tree wither and die right before their eyes.[249]

Jesus pressed on with His lesson. "As soon as its twigs get tender and its leaves burst forth again," He said, "you know that summer is near. Even so, when a person sees all these things, they know it's near, right at the door. Truly I tell you, the generation of that day will certainly not pass away until all these things will have come to pass—every single one of them. Heaven and earth will pass away, but my words will never pass away."

The disciples looked around at each other. Did Jesus just say what they thought He said? Was He predicting the resurrection of the nation of Israel in the last days? Was this mysterious utterance yet another vital clue concerning the arrival of His Kingdom?[250]

"But about that day or hour no one knows," Jesus said, "not even the angels in Heaven, only the Father." Once again, Jesus took in His friends' attentive faces, pausing as He glanced at Judas.

Then, before the disciples could settle that thought in their minds... He did it again. He invoked the name of Noah, just as He had done weeks before, down in the Jordan River Valley.

"As it was in the days of Noah," He said, "so it will be at the coming of the Son of Man. For in the days before the Flood, people were eating and drinking, marrying and giving in marriage, right up to the day Noah entered the ark; and they knew nothing about what would happen until the Flood came and took them all away. That is how it will be at the coming of the Son of Man."

As evening fell on the Mount of Olives and Jesus had slipped away to retire for the night, the disciples continued discussing the evening's teachings.

"The clue about the 'days of Noah' must be extremely important!" they murmured amongst themselves.

Peter spoke up, "Twice in a matter of weeks Jesus has emphasized this point. Could the world really grow that vile again? How could it be worse than it is right now?"

If they had only known…

For tonight, however, they will rest well. They prepare for their evening slumber by promising each other that they will stay by Jesus' side through thick or thin. They will never leave Him. They will never deny Him.

Most of them will not keep that promise.

Within moments, they drift off into blissful slumber. In so doing, they become a living metaphor of a prophetic generation yet to come.

PART THIRTEEN

Heaven's Sorrow

Scriptural Backdrop:

The Last Supper

One of the Twelve—the one called Judas Iscariot—went to the chief priests and asked, "What are you willing to give me if I deliver him over to you?" So they counted out for him thirty pieces of silver.

From then on Judas watched for an opportunity to hand him over. On the first day of the Festival of Unleavened Bread, the disciples came to Jesus and asked, "Where do you want us to make preparations for you to eat the Passover?" He replied, "Go into the city to a certain man and tell him, 'The Teacher says: My appointed time is near. I am going to celebrate the Passover with my disciples at your house.'" So the disciples did as Jesus had directed them and prepared the Passover. When evening came, Jesus was reclining at the table with the Twelve. And while they were eating, he said, "Truly I tell you, one of you will betray me." They were very sad and began to say to him one after the other, "Surely you don't mean me, Lord?" ((Matthew 26:14–22)

One Last Garden

Then Jesus went with his disciples to a place called Gethsemane, and he said to them, "Sit here while I go over there and pray." He took Peter and the two sons of Zebedee along with him, and he began to be sorrowful and troubled. Then he said to them, "My soul is overwhelmed with sorrow to the point of death. Stay here and keep watch with me." Going a little farther, he fell with his face to the ground and prayed, "My Father, if it is possible, may this cup be taken from me. Yet not as I will, but as you will." (Matthew 26:36–39)

To Calvary

Then the governor's soldiers took Jesus into the Praetorium and gathered the whole company of soldiers around him. They stripped him and put a scarlet robe on him, and then twisted together a crown of thorns and set it on his head. They put a staff in his right hand. Then they knelt in front of him and mocked him. "Hail, king of the Jews!" they said. They spit on him, and took the staff and struck him on the head again and again. After they had mocked him, they took off the robe and put his own clothes on him. Then they led him away to crucify him. (Matthew 27:27–31)

52

ONE LAST NAIL

Passover Eve, circa AD 30

The vultures have arrived. It seems they are always the first to show up.

They appear to hang upon invisible strings overhead, dangling in their airy comfort like big, black butterflies on a springtime breath, floating and gliding on the updrafts. But, unlike butterflies, these are not carefree creatures of delicate beauty. They are ravenous and gluttonous meat eaters. As they navigate their lofty orbits, they search out the aroma of death they so crave…greedily inhaling the scents embedded in the rising air.

Pa-Pinggg! Pa-Pinggg! Pa-Pinggg!

Earlier, those mournful, iron-laden announcements had reverberated throughout the surrounding hillsides. By now, it has been hours ago since the last spike was driven.

The executioners really don't need the nails to hold the one in the middle to that rough beam of wood. The nails, the cross, the whips, the insults—these are exactly why He has come.

Other *vultures* are there that day as well. Human ones. Dressed in black, flowing, ecclesiastical robes. Surrounded by sycophants.

Some of the robed ones taunt the man in the middle. "If you truly are the Son of God, show us your authority from Heaven!" they challenge.

261

"Look at Him! He claims to save others, but He can't even save Himself? Come down from that cross! Deliver yourself!"

The blaze of the quickly warming sun drills down upon Jesus without the slightest bit of mercy. Like a worm under a magnifying glass, He squirms under its searing heat…He has no escape from it.

Sweat and blood stream down His face, pouring salty, sizzling torture into His eyes. It is impossible to wipe Himself free of the relentless liquid fire. On top of all this, the flesh of His entire body, including portions of His face, hang down in mangled, bloodied strips and gnarled, rotting slivers.

That's what has attracted the flies. Screaming hordes of them. In a buzzing cloud, they rise as one and hover over the three, like some sort of specter…a demonic black haze. Then the living, swarming cloud eventually settles down again upon the impaled and foul-smelling human bodies. Don't the flies know how loud they are? Does their own thunderous sound not drive them mad?

The miserable men are helpless to swat them away as the miniature flying demons wield their spears of unyielding torture, prodding and piercing into their eyes, noses, and ears. The people watch in morbid fascination as the flies worry the gaping wounds and oozing orifices of the pitiful crucified ones.

But, even in the midst of His suffering…Jesus prays.

Father. Forgive these people. They know not what they do.

━◦

The nightmare He is now living had actually begun to converge hours ago. While the night had still been in the most sinister hours of its darkness, the Temple guards had snatched Yeshua out of the Garden of Gethsemane. Shortly after His arrest, the disciples had fled into the cover of the foggy obscurity—expecting their own incarcerations to be awaiting them, right around the corner. They appeared to have simply melted into the night…like ghosts. All that could be heard were their muffled, hurried footsteps…growing fainter each second as they scurried away like mice.

Jesus had been whisked away to the travesty of an illegal "hearing" at the home of Caiaphas.[251] The high priest's quarters were located in downtown Jerusalem, close to the area of the Temple Mount. While He was alone in that tribunal, most of Jerusalem was still asleep. No one came to His defense.[252] Yeshua stood bound before His accusers, like a lamb led to slaughter.[253]

But He wasn't a helpless lamb. Far from it. Actually, He was purposely compliant. He was right where He wanted to be.[254] Right in front of the high priest and the Sanhedrin Tribunal stood the prophetically foretold Lamb of God. They still seemed to have no clue of the identity of the One upon whom they were gazing.[255]

After more than an hour of judicial pounding from the Sanhedrin, all of eternity's forward motion hung upon one last profound question—and one *longed-for* answer. Jesus would not disappoint them. He would give them the answer they needed. It was the response He *had waited* to give.

That question would fall from the quivering, angry lips of the high priest himself. An exasperated Caiaphas now screeched into the face of Jesus, "Tell us plainly! Are you the Christ—the Son of the Highest God?" Caiaphas took a deep breath, awaiting the response.

There it was again. How many times had Jesus heard that same question, and out of the mouths of so many different people? "If you are the Son of God...tell us!" In the past, He had refused to give the answer. Today, however, that fact would change.

Jesus raised his head to look at Caiaphas. "*I am.*[256] And from now on you will see the Son of Man sitting at the right hand of the Lord God Almighty, and returning with the clouds of Heaven's witnesses with Him."[257]

There was then a faint sparkle of light behind the throne of Caiaphas. Jesus alone saw Nachash with his gnarled hand upon the high priest's shoulder—taunting, and arrogantly glaring in His direction.[258]

At long last! The pitiful and delusional "Son of God" has played right into my hands! If nothing else could be used to bring about His death, this one particular idiotic claim surely will!

The confession Jesus had just pronounced was the so-called *blasphemous* statement Caiaphas had hoped for. Upon Jesus' claim of equality with God, the Sanhedrin could appeal to the Roman officials for the death penalty. After all, if they didn't kill Him quickly, this one could attract crowds of over ten thousand in one place! They had seen it done before. He could very well start a national insurrection!

The Romans shouldn't be too hard to convince, now that they had this admission from His own lips. Now they could be rid of this troublemaker once and for all. Only then could they begin to regain their own prominence among the people—a standing that had been almost destroyed by this Jesus of Nazareth and His traveling "magic show."

That morning, the council had delivered Jesus before a thrown-together hearing with the Roman governor. They laid out their demands for His immediate death. The frenzied crowd, outside Pilate's headquarters, had been worked into a fury by well-positioned Sanhedrin operatives who mingled among the people. Over and over again, the operatives had screamed "Crucify Him! Crucify Him!" until the whole mob cried out the demand, seemingly with one loud voice of agreement.

Pilate positioned himself before the people as though he possessed no choice in the matter, even making a public spectacle of washing his hands as a feigned act of innocence.

Wishing to appease the crowd and prevent an unfortunate uprising, upon Pilate's orders, Jesus had been stripped to His barest undergarments and strapped by His hands to an iron pillar that had been buried in the cement outside the Praetorium, on the far side of the portico. Yeshua's back had been bent over and stretched taught, so as to bare the greatest width of it to the Roman scourge…and to receive the fullest force of the breath-stopping blows from the leather straps.[259]

The priests had implored the governor to lash Him openly, in their presence, and in the sight of the angry mobs they had already whipped into a murderous frenzy. Pilate, to pacify them, consented, contrary to his expressed preference, hoping that the gruesome punishment of the scourge would excite the pity of the Jews and perhaps prevent Yeshua's crucifixion. That, however, was not to be the case. Nothing short of a long, torturous death would satisfy them.[260]

Jesus being thus thrashed within moments of being able to take His last breath, and His flesh being laid open from head to feet, the Scriptures—and His own prophecies—had now been perfectly fulfilled.[261]

After the brutal flogging, the governor had Him taken back into the Praetorium. There, He was surrounded by the whole company of soldiers. They put a scarlet robe on Him, then twisted together a crown of thorns and shoved it down hard upon His head, the sharp barbs plunging deep into His scalp. Rivulets of blood poured down His face.

After further derision, as He wore their makeshift crown, they placed a staff in His right hand. They knelt in front of Him and mocked, "Hail, to the king of the Jews!"

They jettisoned their spit at Him, shooting it out of their mouths until the slimy sputum drizzled down His face and into His beard, where it matted into putrid knots. They took the staff from His hand and repeatedly struck Him on the head with it, until several times He momentarily saw nothing but black, almost passing in and out of consciousness.

"Prophesy for us!" they taunted. "Tell us! Which one of us struck you?" They shook their heads in repulsion when Jesus refused to play into the hands of their twisted morbidity. "Humph!" they grunted. "A prophet, indeed! More like a shyster, if you ask us!"

After they finished their mocking, they took off the robe and shoved His clothes back upon His now mutilated body. Then they led Him to the "Place of the Skull," forcing Him to carry the thick crucifixion beam upon His own shoulders and back.

Upon arriving at Golgotha, His hands and feet had been pinioned upon the spar with iron spikes, and then the timber was raised...with its writhing victim attached. It took a specialized team of Roman soldiers to accomplish the feat. They were highly skilled at what they did; they should have been—they had done it thousands of times before.

To those soldiers, it was a mere routine, an imperial duty. But, at that moment, around Heaven's throne, the entire affair was a heart-rending travesty.

But, it was a necessary one.

The *First Kingdom* had ordained it before the foundation of the earth.

And now, all of Heaven looked upon the spectacle.

And they wept.

53

THE MARIONETTES

The *foul one* will be back, though. Yeshua is certain of it.

And so it is that Jesus now hangs before the crowd like a prized trophy. He has been crucified between two common thieves while the clouds of ridiculously buzzing flies torment them all. Practically unrecognizable as a human being, He dangles there, on the nails. His moaning, mangled visage is etched against the reddish-hued sky, bloodied by the evil of the vileness on display for the people who stand here.

Every nerve in His body screams in searing agony—and the day has only begun. The torture will greatly intensify as the hours cruelly slither along and the sun grows hotter. He is living the nightmare He had foreseen back at the Garden of Gethsemane. There will not be one iota of relief until it is finished.

Wait! There he is!

Just now, Jesus spots him…Beelzebub, the *lord of the flies*.[262]

Satan, the interdimensional hunter—*the prince of this fallen world*— moves among the crowds again—a dark, foul figure. He is unseen by those of the earthly realm. They have no spiritually discerning "eyes to see." But he is certainly there.

Jesus catches several glimpses of Heaven's traitor—in those scant moments when His eyes occasionally refocus through the bloodied veneer of the searing streams of pain that *drip-drip-dribble* through His eyes.[263]

When their gazes meet, the pompous Nachash leers at Him, his upper lip curling as he stares. Satan glances up at the circling vultures, then looks back down at Jesus and smirks again.

His diabolical plan is coming together just as he has calculated. Satan rubs his hands together and, looking up toward the heavens, mumbles, "Look what I have done to you! If this really is your 'Son'—well, you failed! I have killed the Son of Heaven! Soon, your throne will be mine!"[264]

Nachash drifts across the ground, invisible to the human crowd, arriving behind a particular man standing amongst them—a dignified member of the Jewish ruling class. That priest also stands next to Baruch, who has an unsettling feeling of regret about what he is witnessing. The ancient serpent lays his hand upon the esteemed priest's shoulder. The elderly cleric has no idea what just happened to him from the realm of darkness.

Instantly, like a marionette having its strings pulled, the priest cries out, "Save yourself! Come down from that cross—*if you are the Son of God*! Work a miracle for us now!" His arms fling upward, his fists ball toward the heavens in an irrational rage. Baruch looks at Him in disbelief. How could He be so insensitive and grossly uncaring at such a pitiful moment as this?

Others in the crowd join the cacophony, arrogantly hooting in agreement, unknowingly directed by the unseen maestro. Mocking, cajoling, and cursing pour forth, aimed at Yeshua hanging there in His indescribable misery.

"Yes! Come down from the cross! If you can! If you dare! Show us your power!"

Baruch remains silent, heart-stricken, as he glances around witnessing the vicious spirit that seems to have overtaken the crowd.

In that moment of apparent triumph, Nachash eases back through a brief, folding shimmer that has just parted the atmosphere, and he is gone again. No one had seen his arrival. No one sees his exit.

Except Jesus.

The *foul one* will be back, though. Yeshua is certain of it. His arrogance won't allow him to miss much of this demonic exhibition. After all, it is a spectacle that he himself arranged...

Or so he thinks.

54

THE LAST TEMPTATION

Their blood-darkened, contorted faces expose the demonic rage
that burrows deep within the caverns of their covetous hearts.

A muffled agony emanates from the lips of the one in the middle. His grunting request is barely discernable.

"I thirst..."

The crowd moves closer. Jacob is still among them from earlier that morning. So is Baruch.

"What's He's trying to say now?"

"And...by the way—where are His disciples?"

"Only one of them is here. Just a youngster. We think his name is John. But the others...they aren't anywhere to be seen!"

"We heard, just a few moments ago, that they ran for their lives!"

"Cowards!"

One of the soldiers lifts a sponge impaled on a hyssop branch to His lips. Tasting that the graciously offered relief contains a bit of common painkiller, He turns His head and refuses further refreshment.

The pathetic visage of Jesus' flesh-mangled form is now completely encircled by the mob. They stand there, just in front of the soldiers who

271

are holding them back from the cross. He was beaten beyond recognition before the Romans even nailed Him there.

Just days before, as He had made His way into Jerusalem on the back of a donkey, many in this same crowd had welcomed Jesus as the possible Messiah. They had scattered palm branches and even articles of their own clothing in His path…welcoming Him, worshiping Him.

But today…they hate Him. The fickleness of humanity's fallen nature has overwhelmed them.

"He had to die. Doesn't everybody understand that?"

The Sanhedrin, together with the Roman governor, had seen to the affair. After all, the event was orchestrated through a perfectly legal decree. It simply had to be done. Life with Jesus in their midst had become… well…*too dangerous.* So the government must be obeyed. *It was the right thing to do—perhaps even the* godly *thing to do. Right?*

Somebody had to pay. *Better Him than us.*

Clenched fists are lifted up in anger and raised toward His face in defiance.

"He claimed He could save others!" some in the crowd cry out.

Several teachers of the law join in. "But look at Him now! He can't even save Himself! Let the Lord deliver Him, since He trusts in Him!"

They wait for a response, but Jesus gives them nothing.

"If you are the Son of God, then save yourself! Save yourself…and come down off that cross!"

Their rage-darkened, contorted faces expose the demonic fury burrowed deep within the caverns of their covetous hearts. And…their shrill invectives are familiar ones. These are the very same temptations that had been railed at Him in the wilderness at the very beginning of His ministry. They are the equivalent words, simply screamed from different mouths. The same dark god is behind them all.

"Liar!" "Fraud!" "Trickster!" They lash out again…and again.

The pack of religious elites stands at the back edges of the crowd gathered in front of the crucified one. Filled with arrogance and deluded visions of self-importance, they can't help the smirks upon their faces.

But, they are also relieved, in an evil sort of manner. Soon, this insufferable, insolent, agitating "Teacher" will be gone from their lives, and they can get on with their normal and so very important lives. They can now go back to the way it used to be. With *them, not Him,* commanding the crowds.

The voice coming from the roughly hewn cross shouts again. He looks up into the blackening sky and cries out—

"Father!"

"He speaks again! Listen!"

A smothering hush envelops the crowd.

Jesus then repeats what He said earlier that day, not long after the spikes had been driven and His body had been raised toward the heavens: "*Forgive them! They don't know what they are doing!*"

"What is this? In His dying moments this crucified one is praying for 'our' forgiveness?"

At first, there is deep contemplation, then a growing realization that soon morphs into a panicked doubt.

"Who is this? Have we perhaps made a mistake? Is this thing turning out to be a terrible blunder, something we can never undo?"

Faint sounds of sniffling begin to ripple through the crowd. It is as if this spirit of self-doubt has come down upon them all…at the very same moment.

Jesus looks down from the cross. He sees the faces through swollen eyes, stinging with salty sweat…and tears.

Baruch stands ashamed.

He is ashamed that he did not speak up in defense of Jesus when he had the chance. He is gravely embarrassed as he feels the depths of his own guilt, now more apparent to him than ever. He grows increasingly mortified that this event is even underway in the first place, and he is infuriated with himself for voluntarily choosing to witness this horrifying spectacle.

He thinks: *Everything about this is truly a travesty!*

It didn't have to come to this…

55

THAT SOUND!

That had been hours ago. Six long, merciless hours ago.

It is now the final three hours of Jesus' earthly life. The sky has darkened beyond anyone's attempt to explain the spectacle.

Baruch had actually arrived on the scene even before the first nail was driven. He was there when the two thieves were first spiked to their beams of death, then lifted up to be placed on each side of Him. Their animal-like shrieking had been pitiful. Horrific to hear. Excruciating to watch. A sound and sight that would haunt him until his dying days.

But Baruch had stayed. And because he remained there, he was present when the nails were first slammed into Jesus' hands. In fact, he was just a few yards away when it happened. He kept watching until the last one was driven into His feet, one foot placed on top of the other to accommodate that one final spike.

As that last blow rang out, it had unnerved him.

That sound! That *awful* sound!

That last clash of metal against metal had been so different! It was an intonation clearly distinct from the other two, as if it was a glancing blow, instead of full-on. It was hard to explain, but it seemed to have the ring of a message to it. That last spike may as well have been driven through Baruch's heart. He heard it echoing off the towering stone walls of Jerusalem and distantly reverberating through the valley below.

But that had been hours earlier. On the other hand, only moments ago, Jesus had promised one of the two dying men a soon entry into Paradise. The thief, now repentant, was calling Jesus "Lord."

But right now, in *this* very moment, Jesus' eyes catch those of Baruch.

What's this? Is Jesus looking directly at me? Did He just smile at me? Or, is my mind playing tricks on me?

Dropping his head to avoid Jesus' eyes, Baruch sees the men. Roman soldiers, casting lots for Jesus' clothing...under the cross. He is immediately revolted by what he sees. *These despicable heathens!* He spits into the dirt below his feet as he mumbles the words under his breath.

The circling scavenger birds—now a mixed cluster of vultures, crows, and ravens—screech their maddening protests of hunger—nonstop. They are waiting for something to die. *Anything.*

Even in the ensuing hours, the crowd continues to grow. Practically everyone in Jerusalem has heard that the Romans and the Jewish elders are in the process of killing the miracle-worker from Galilee. But few publicly protest the event, lest their own lives be put in danger.

The mockers start up their reviling taunts again. "Look at Him! He says He's the King of Israel! Can you believe it? What delusions of grandeur!"

Others join in. "Well then, let Him come down from the cross!" they challenge. "That's what a true king would do! Where are the *king's* troops?" They cackle as they enjoy each other's barbs aimed at the man in the middle.

Additional onlookers become tangled in the demonically induced frenzy of the moment. "If He would just deliver Himself, maybe then we would believe in Him! He claims to trust in God. So...let God rescue Him!"

By now, they mindlessly echo the expected jeer. They had heard the mantra for the better part of the day. It is as if they are being enticed to repeat the words by some unseen power, a cosmic conductor, an interdimensional entity.

In truth, their mocking words had actually been prophesied one thousand years before this day. King David had seen this day in a vision, and he had faithfully recorded what he had seen and heard.[265]

Now, Jesus shouts out again—louder than before.

"My God! My God! Why have you forsaken me?"

Waa…wait! Why does Jesus say this? What can He mean?

Then something bizarre happens.

In that moment, the centurion looks up in apparent shock. He removes his helmet and drops to the ground, landing on his knees under the feet of Jesus. The two look at each other for a brief moment as Jesus' head falls to His chest. Although many miss the intimacy of the exchange, Baruch sees it. He stands dumbfounded as he watches. So does Jacob.

Jesus mutters something to the Roman officer—only slightly moving His lips, barely able to speak. No one in the belly of the crowd can possibly hear exactly what Jesus says to the man. But the huge soldier begins to weep, lowering his head in apparent remorse. Grieving in his soul…his wide, armor-covered shoulders heaving—something primordially deep has demoralized him.

The next words the centurion utters stun those close enough to hear. His words are articulated through quivering lips: "Surely, this man is the Son of God!"

Baruch feels his agony as well. He is certain that others are experiencing a similar emotion. *Such guilt. Such remorse. Such a crime!*

In that moment, an ancient psalm explodes into the old Pharisee's consciousness.

That's it!

It is David's psalm that Jesus has started to speak! Its opening words resound through Baruch's head: "My God. My God. Why have you forsaken me?"

This is the first verse of that passage!

Baruch's mind races through the stanzas of that psalm. Is there a key he is missing? Has Jesus just given another mystical clue? Baruch has known this particular thousand-year-old psalm by heart since he was a boy, but now it is living and breathing, right in front of him! He begins to murmur the verses as he stands, stupefied, in front of Jesus.

All who see me mock me; they hurl insults, shaking their heads. "He trusts in the Lord," they say, "let the Lord rescue him. Let the Lord deliver him, since he delights in him."

My mouth is dried up like a potsherd, and my tongue sticks to the roof of my mouth; you lay me in the dust of death.

Dogs surround me, a pack of villains encircles me; they pierce my hands and my feet.

All my bones are on display; people stare and gloat over me.

They divide my clothes among them and cast lots for my garment.[266]

My God!
This can't be happening!

56

HOW CAN IT BE?

Has the truth of it, *the whole plan,* been right before him all along?

In a few more moments, Jesus will be dead.

No one knows this fact except Him. Actually, He knows the *exact* moment when it will occur. He knows the instant His last breath will leave His human lungs. He will speak it, and it will happen.

As the knot of guilt that is currently clogging his throat almost strangles him, Baruch suddenly remembers what the "Teacher" revealed that day in the village several weeks back, when Jesus and His disciples had stopped to address the group's questions about the coming Kingdom of God.

He had asked Jesus if it were really possible for an entire generation to miss the Messiah when He actually did arrive. Jesus had leaned in and whispered in his ear, "The Kingdom of God is in your midst right now, my friend."

Then Jesus had said something else that day, weeks ago. "I tell you the truth, Baruch," He said. "This generation is, in fact, largely missing the entire event, *yes*. Again, it's all right there, open before you, in your Scriptures. It really couldn't be any plainer. The Word of God is *living*, right before your eyes. And, like the serpent in the wilderness, it will eventually be lifted up, right in front of you. When it happens, you won't be able to miss it."

Baruch's memories are interrupted by a sound. An awful sound.

Jesus grunts as He pushes Himself up. The rumbling moan comes from deep within His heaving chest.

The sound that Yeshua makes is cavernous, guttural, and laden with excruciation.

The dying man gathers what appears to be the last of His remaining reserve of strength. With wild eyes, Jesus strains against the tormenting spike that has been driven into the top of His feet. He pushes up on it and winces in the agony caused by His action.

He quickly gasps for one final breath. His lungs fill with the pungent air that presses in upon Him. He heaves out the last breath His earthbound lungs will ever hold…and shouts at the top of His weakening voice.

"It!"

"Is!"

"Finished!"

Instantly, His head drops to His chest. He never takes another breath.

But how can this be? How can someone actually "call into existence" the exact second at which they will die? This is impossible!

Unless…

Most of the throng stands dumbfounded at the announcement of the one who has just seemingly willed the very moment of His own death.

How does this seemingly impossible moment they have just witnessed square with the centurion's declaration moments ago? Didn't he implicate *them* in His death? *Surely, we would never dream of crucifying the genuine Son of God! How dare He!*

Yet, how can they respond to this heartfelt charge leveled against them by a Roman military officer—one who could easily place any one of them upon a similar wooden beam of death and torture?

The Sanhedrin mob responds to the centurion's decree and Jesus' stunning last words by storming from among the midst of the crowd…

unspoken outrage oozing from their countenances. The black line of robes leaving the crowd snakes its way through the mob muttering amongst themselves.

That arrogant, Gentile pig of a Roman soldier! How dare he proclaim this delusional blasphemer they have just crucified to be the Son of God! Will this continual sacrilegious refrain ever end?

Another unseen presence is there as well. He has never left. *This is his day.* At least, that is what he imagines it to be...*until* this precise instant arrives. And in this moment, a stifling uneasiness wraps around him, like an irritating woolen blanket worn in the middle of a summer day.

For the first time, the ancient serpent isn't quite so certain of himself. Has this event actually been preordained by Elohim? If that is true, how has he missed the clues? Has the truth of it, *the whole plan*, been right before him all along? But...a crucified Savior? How can *that* be? A cold shiver courses through his body. He glances over at the men who have been gambling for Jesus' tunic. He thinks of the very words that he himself injected into their muddled minds, only to dutifully spew forth from their demonically enslaved mouths: "He saved others; let Him save Himself if He is the Son of God!"

This doesn't make any sense, Nachash thinks. After all, *he* orchestrated this event himself! Didn't he? The scourging, the mocking, the hammer, the nails! The traitor! Yes, the traitor—*his idea! Right?*

But, if this is not really *his* doing...then whose is it? *What will happen next?* What does this mean for his plans of securing the throne of Elohim as his very own? At least a dozen unanswered questions churn through his twisted mind of depraved delusions. But, thus far, the most obvious answers to each of his questions only point to his potential demise.

As the creeping sense of dread catches up with itself, Nachash balls his fists and fumes. His fury grows into a consuming rage. He will *not* be defeated! This is *his* kingdom!

The atmosphere fizzles, then folds in on itself—right where Nachash has been standing.

Upon hearing those last three words of Yeshua and watching his colleagues slink away from the scene, Baruch now discerns the message of that echoing last nail he heard earlier that day: *Three* dying men. *Three* unnecessary nails buried in the flesh of the Man in the middle.

Three painfully uttered last words. The world will never be the same.

Divine judgment is on its way. Humanity will not be found guiltless for what has happened here this day!

It's their fault! Baruch points to the Romans as he spins around facing them. *It is your fault!* He turns again and motions, with an outstretched index finger, to the quickly absconding religious elite. *This is my fault!* He punches himself in his chest with a balled-up fist and weeps bitterly. He drops to his knees, because he is too weak to stand. When he has composed himself enough to speak, Baruch looks up at the lifeless form of Jesus hanging there. He calls out to Him.

"Lord! Please remember me also, when you come into your Kingdom! I understand it now! *I do!*" The old Pharisee holds a look of unexplained joy, as his quickly watering eyes well up as he speaks. A liquid warmth washes over him, calming him, soothing him, assuring him. He is unashamed...he is supernaturally strengthened.

At last, he understands.

But there is still another "three" on its way. Just three short days from now, the planet will be spiritually knocked off kilter, yet again. When it happens, Baruch will be floored by it. His life and ministry will be eternally transformed in the turbulent wake of the resultant shaking.

From among the Orthodox elite, he will become one of the first true, born-again believers in Yeshua.[267]

57

THE REVENANT

The body of the mysterious man in the middle has vanished.

After three full nights, and early on the morning of the third day, Nachash possesses the answer he has long sought. Jesus had actually given life to Himself. No one could pull off a feat like that except Elohim. It was at that moment Satan knew what the title "Son of God" meant. Nachash has been duped. He had gambled everything on his crucifixion plan—and lost. But, unbeknownst to him, the whole ordeal had never really been *his* plan. It was Heaven's plan...from the very beginning.

Not long after Jesus exclaimed His last words on the cross—and with special permission from Pontius Pilate—Jesus' tortured, mangled corpse is collected from the crucifixion beam by Joseph of Arimathea, a secret disciple of Jesus,[268] and interred in his own private garden tomb not far from Golgotha. Joseph is accompanied by Nicodemus, a chief rabbi of the Pharisee class, also a disciple of Jesus.[269] Ironically, Joseph and Nicodemus are wealthy and respected members of the Sanhedrin Council—the same religious body that had appealed to Rome to have Jesus put to death. But these two men would have no part in passing that decree upon Him.

On the day after the crucifixion, at the urging of the high priest and upon the orders of Pontius Pilate, Roman guards are placed at the site of the borrowed crypt. The Sanhedrin officials lobbied for this particular safeguard because of Jesus' well-known claims that He would "rise from the dead" on the third day.[270]

In spite of the enormous efforts of Rome and the Jewish rulers to prevent such a spectacle, *on precisely the third day* following the crucifixion, the tomb is indeed empty. The body of the mysterious man in the middle has simply vanished, apparently into thin air, and no one seems to have a clue where it might be.

The entrance to the tomb, a several-ton rolling stone, is standing open, mockingly displaying its emptiness…an accomplishment that could have only been worked by a company of strong men.[271] On this morning, however, the feat had been achieved by a singular and brilliantly shining divine being sent from God's throne. At His appearance, through a folding in the atmosphere, as though he has simply walked through an unseen doorway, the soldiers had fainted into the dirt…and eventually fled.[272]

Despite the diligent search conducted by Roman officials and the Jewish religious elite, and all the enemies of Jesus working together—His body is never found.

❧

The worst nightmare of the Sanhedrin Council and Rome has burst to life, right before their eyes. *How can this be? What else can go wrong? Can this fiasco grow any worse?*

Tellingly, throughout the four Gospels that would be written by Matthew, Mark, Luke, and John, from the time of Jesus' resurrection on, Satan's name will not be mentioned again. Those eyewitness accounts will not include any reports of Satan launching a direct attack upon the divine Son of God, not even during His forty days upon the earth after the resurrection.[273]

Instead, Satan will later focus his attacks upon the believers—*the Church*—the remaining army that Jesus will raise up against the serpent's stolen valor.[274] They will be the new "Body of Christ," the new "Temple of God."[275] Satan, in an eternal fit of rage, will make them pay for brandishing that name.

But, perhaps there is still time. Maybe, Satan thinks…just maybe…my kingdom can yet be salvaged.

If history has proven anything at all, it is that Satan's conceit and grandiose tenacity knows no boundaries. Thus, the closing chapters of history's saga of diabolical pummeling continues. But not much longer.

In those early days, neither the enemies of God nor the faithful followers of Jesus can imagine the birth of the Church that will occur within the next fifty days after the resurrection event. Neither can they fathom the world-changing power that will ultimately follow the more than two thousand years of the subsequent preaching of the gospel of Jesus Christ.

Nor can they believe that the resurrection of Jesus Christ will literally change the calendars of the world…and will create, as well as violently upheave, empires yet to come.

This singular, rather obscure event has just changed the entire planet… forever.

PART FOURTEEN

Not Yet Ascended

Scriptural Backdrop:

"You are Israel's teacher," said Jesus [to Nicodemus], "and do you not understand these things? Very truly I tell you, we speak of what we know, and we testify to what we have seen, but still you people do not accept our testimony. I have spoken to you of earthly things and you do not believe; how then will you believe if I speak of heavenly things?

"No one has ever gone into heaven except the one who came from heaven—the Son of Man. Just as Moses lifted up the snake in the wilderness, so the Son of Man must be lifted up, that everyone who believes may have eternal life in him." (John 3:10–15; emphasis added)

58

RETURN TO EDEN

They were headed to another dimension of reality.

This seems like a good place to temporarily step away from our immersive narrative for a few brief chapters and stop to unravel another scriptural mystery—one that is related to the resurrection of Jesus and a seemingly difficult passage for a number of students of God's Word. Yet, once it is understood in its proper context, we discover that it goes directly to the theme of our entire study…the intricate, interdimensional nature of Yahweh's glorious creation that surrounds us all.

According to John's account, the resurrected Jesus pronounced an amazing assertion to Mary Magdalene on that morning:

Jesus said:

Do not hold on to me, for I have not yet ascended to the Father.
Go instead to my brothers and tell them, "I am ascending to my
Father." (John 20: 17)

What did Jesus mean when He said He hadn't "yet ascended to the Father?" Of course, we know from the Scriptures that He did, in fact, ascend into Heaven some forty days later. But if He truly had not yet entered the Father's presence in any way whatsoever at the time He spoke those words to Mary, then where *did* Jesus go during those three days?

Of course, you already know the answer to that question. We're talking about multiple dimensions again. Not only that, but the Scriptures tell us to which of the exact dimensions He traveled. Now it's only a matter of squaring that truth with the rest of Scripture, so we can fill in the entire picture.

Jesus spoke the beautiful words of promise to the dying thief who had placed his trust in Him on that fateful, barbarically miserable afternoon. Jesus was clear: "Today, we're going back to the Garden! To Paradise! Through an interdimensional portal, *behind the veil*, to the Garden that has always been there."[276]

They were headed to another dimension of reality, bound for an unseen realm—a place that can only be entered when accompanied by Jesus Christ. He is the only door—the only portal—the only gate, the only way. Yeshua had called the place "Paradise."

But, we still have to ask, "Wouldn't going to Paradise be the same as going into the presence of the Father?" The answer to that question lies in the following biblical truths.

Let's connect these stunning dimensional dots, starting at the beginning.

59

THE ISLAND OF PARADISE

In relating the account of the rich man and Lazarus,
Jesus established the fact of a literal Paradise.

Following is a conceptualization that might help make the mystery we're examining a bit clearer.

Think of Eden as an island of Paradise that exists in another dimension, yet in the realm of a true physical nature. In the middle of that glorious island is an indescribably beautiful mountain.

On top of the island's mountain is a lush garden. A life-giving river of crystal-clear water flows from the base of the mountain. Also, on top of the mountain is a place of glorious holiness—the Temple of Yahweh. But human admittance to the inner sanctum of the Temple is not yet available.

Huge swaths of the book of Hebrews were given to declare and illustrate these biblical—and genuinely interdimensional—truths. As you have a look at only four such passages, out of many, notice how many times you run into the concepts of dimensions, portals into those dimensions, and the assertions of what happened when Jesus entered those domains— after His crucifixion, resurrection, and ascension. I have highlighted those important pronouncements.

Now the main point of what we are saying is this: We do have such a high priest, who sat down at the right hand of the throne of the Majesty in heaven, and who serves in the sanctuary, the **true tabernacle** set up by the Lord, **not by a mere human being.** (Hebrews 8:1–2; emphasis added)

The priests serve at a sanctuary that is **a copy and shadow** of what **is in heaven.** (Hebrews 8:5; emphasis added)

But when Christ came as high priest of the good things that are now already here, **he went through** the greater and **more perfect tabernacle** that is **not made with human** hands, that is to say, **is not a part of this creation.** He did not enter by means of the blood of goats and calves; but he entered the Most Holy Place once for all **by his own blood,** thus obtaining eternal redemption. (Hebrews 9:11–12; emphasis added)

It was necessary, then, for **the copies** of the heavenly things to be purified with these sacrifices, but **the heavenly things themselves** with better sacrifices than these. For Christ did not enter a sanctuary made with human hands that was **only a copy of the true one;** he **entered heaven itself, now to appear for us** in God's presence. (Hebrews 9:23–24; emphasis added)

Therefore, brothers and sisters, since we have confidence **to enter the Most Holy Place** by **the blood of Jesus, by a new and living way opened for us through the curtain,** that is, **his body.** (Hebrews 10:19–20; emphasis added)

Wow! There are an awful lot of "interdimensional revelations" there, wouldn't you say?

The bottom line is this. In order for fallen humanity to come into the holy presence of Yahweh's glory within the true Temple—even a redeemed human who is now on the island of Paradise through faith—they must come through the blood of the Son of Sacrifice. Before Jesus' offering on Calvary's cross, that access was denied.

When Jesus accompanied the crucified thief to the "island of Paradise"—as He promised He would—He, at that particular time, did not go up the Holy Mount and enter the Temple of Yahweh. The opening of the Temple to the residents of Paradise would not happen until the day of Jesus' ascension. On that glorious day, He would present His blood in Heaven's Temple, thus unlocking the entrance to the throne of the Father.

This is exactly what the thousands of years of the wilderness Tabernacle and the Jerusalem Temple, along with their prescribed rituals of sacrifice, had symbolized. Jesus would eventually fulfill the role of the ultimate Great High Priest. However, He had no need to offer a blood sacrifice for His own sin, because He is the sinless Son of God (Hebrews 9:11–15) who also gave Himself as the final offering (Genesis 22:8).

Now, observe the biblical "timeline" concerning all we've laid out thus far.

Through the Veil

In the beginning of Jesus' earthly ministry, He had declared, "No one has gone into heaven, except the one who has come down from heaven" (John 3:13).

He said this to Nicodemus, the Pharisee who had come to Jesus at night so that he might seek further clarification about His teachings.

Jesus had spoken the absolute truth to Nicodemus—only He had come from God's throne room. No mortal had ever set foot in that place since the Garden Fall—*not yet.*

But, in a little over three years from that nighttime meeting with Nicodemus, Jesus would change everything. He alone would open the veil to the real Temple—the genuine one, in Paradise, the one that had *always* been.

The Scriptures are clear. We know that Daniel had experienced a *vision* of the holy presence of Yahweh upon His throne (Daniel 7). Even Isaiah "saw the glory of it" through a vision (Isaiah 6). Moses had come near His holy presence in the burning-bush experience (Exodus 3:1–17). And Abraham had spoken to Yahweh in a physical, flesh-and-blood human form (Genesis 18).

But no one had ever gone into Paradise and then ascended the holy mountain of God in order to enter the literal and physical presence of the Great I Am—to behold Him and know Him as He is—*no one* (Exodus 33:20; John 1:18).

In the Middle of Jesus' Ministry

As another important illustration of the dimensional divisions beyond the earthly realm, Jesus told about the rich man who had died outside of faith in Yahweh. He had gone through life in total self-absorption, ignoring God's sovereignty over his life.[277]

As a result of his faithless life, the rich man went to Hell, or prison, when he died. Yet, while in Hell, he was totally aware of himself, and he was in physical torment. He was also aware of what he had missed out on by not being in Paradise.

The rich man recognized someone he knew quite well from his days upon the earth: Lazarus, who was living in a state of *Paradise blessing* because he had been faithful toward the ways of God. But the rich man had, all his life, mistreated and even looked down upon Lazarus.

Abraham informed the rich man that a great and unscalable chasm existed between Paradise and Hell's prison, and Lazarus was in Abraham's Bosom because he had been a man of great faith. The early Jews understood Abraham's Bosom to mean Paradise, or more importantly—the interdimensionally separated Garden of Eden.[278]

In relating the account of the rich man and Lazarus, Jesus established the fact of a literal Paradise, as well as the reality of a literal Hell—the prison/waiting place for the coming judgment. Jesus also acknowledged that after our physical/earthly departure by death, there is no "second chance."[279] Sadly, the rich man knew that fully well. But for him, it was far too late.

Near the End of Jesus' Earthly Ministry

Jesus fulfilled every messianic prophecy of the Old Testament concerning His First Coming, ultimately delivering Himself to Calvary's cross.[280] He spilled His own blood as divine payment for fallen humanity's sin nature, the penalty required by the Garden Fall. At His last earthly breath, Jesus entered Paradise, where Lazarus, Abraham, and all the saints of old were waiting. The thief from the cross would soon follow, on the promise of Jesus' word.

In that moment of earthly departure, even as Nicodemus and Joseph were placing His body in the borrowed garden tomb, Jesus had already entered through the myriad dimensions of the unseen realm. He could do this because He was the sovereign *Creator* of those realms. All things, and all dimensions, were created by Him and for Him, and nothing that was made was made without Him, and in Him all things hold together.[281]

As Jesus entered those dimensions, He presented Himself to the realm of Hell itself (i.e., the rich man's waiting cell) as a testimony of His glory and His ultimate victory over Satan.

> He was put to death in the body, but made alive in the Spirit. After being made alive, he went and made proclamation to the imprisoned spirits. (1 Peter 3:18–19)

He also presented himself to the "island of Paradise" in the presence of all who had previously left this world in faith—those who were looking forward to the eventual coming of Messiah's redemption.

This was the day for which Paradise had been waiting.

60

FORTY DAYS

As in the case of Paul, John also physically entered the heavenly Temple of God.

After His resurrection, Jesus would present Himself alive in the presence of many hundreds of His followers.[282] He would also perform other divine miracles to verify to the earthly, as well as to the demonic, realms of authority that the long-awaited Christ had indeed risen, and that He had forfeited none of His divine power and glory.[283]

Jesus also demonstrated to the demonic realm and the principalities of the earth that He is the undisputed victor, and that the Genesis 3:15 prophecy was being completed. The divine Seed had arrived to crush the head of the serpent.[284]

During those forty days, Jesus thumbed His nose at Satan, making a spectacle of Nachash, saying to the entire demonic realm and their fallen prince: "You lost. And soon...*you will be gods of nothing.*"

Having canceled the charge of our legal indebtedness, which stood against us and condemned us; he has taken it away, nailing it to the cross. And having disarmed the powers and authorities, he made a public spectacle of them, triumphing over them by the cross. (Colossians 2:14–15)

After the Ascension

On the Mount of Olives, Jesus returned to the right hand of the Father, from whence He had originally come. This is the event He was speaking of when he told Mary that He had not yet ascended to the Father. Now, however, even this last important detail would be completed.

Upon His ascension, Jesus returned to Paradise and entered the Holy of Holies in the Temple in Heaven—the *real* Temple.[285] It is there where Jesus would present His blood.[286] He had fulfilled the role of the true Great High Priest.[287] The holy place had been opened, and we can, now, approach the throne of our Creator in boldness, through the blood of Jesus.[288]

Paul in Paradise

The Apostle Paul died in AD 67, but sometime before his death, he was physically taken up to Paradise. It was not a vision, or a dream, or an angelic visitation—Paul was *there*, in the Temple of Paradise. He informed his readers that he was caught up to the Third Heaven, into the presence of Yahweh Himself.[289] Paul was in Heaven's Temple, in the literal presence of the Creator of the Universe.[290] He was only there because Jesus had previously opened the way!

In the Third Heaven, at the throne of God, Paul was given the end-time revelations of the Rapture, the Antichrist, the last-days apostasy, the sounding of the last trumpet, the coming great deception, the return of Jesus Christ, the demonic outpouring of the last days, and more. Paul revealed each of those truths in his letters—which are now the New Testament Scriptures—to the various churches of that day. He assured them that they could not even begin to comprehend what lay ahead for those who are under the blood of Jesus Christ. He had seen it, and it was absolutely indescribable.

However, as it is written:

What no eye has seen, what no ear has heard, and what no human mind has conceived—the things God has prepared for those who love him. (1 Corinthians 2:9)

From that point forward, Paul preferred to be absent from the earthly dimension of reality and to be "present with the Lord," living in Paradise.[291]

John in Paradise

Sometime in the AD 90s, about three decades after Paul's experience, the Apostle John—one of the pastors of the first church and subsequently a renowned pastor in Ephesus—was also caught up to Paradise.[292] In that interdimensional experience, John was given the fullest revelation of end-time events that had ever been passed down to mortal man.

As in the case of the Apostle Paul, John also physically entered the heavenly Temple of God. He gazed upon the Holy Creator. John saw the Lamb in the middle of the throne. And he saw the Divine Council: the holy cherubim, the thrones around the thrones, and the ten thousand times ten thousand angels of the heavenly host (Revelation 4–5).[293]

The reason John and Paul could be allowed physical access into the holy presence of the Ancient of Days was because the divine portal had been opened by the blood of Jesus Christ. They had literally stood in the *Garden of God*—and were, thankfully, allowed to come back and testify of its reality.

Paul would eventually enter Paradise again...as he closed his eyes, waiting on the sword of Nero's soldier to fall upon his neck. He had fought the fight, finished the race, and—most importantly—kept the faith.

John still had a few more years to go before it was his "time." The Lord wasn't ready to call him home yet.

But, that day was drawing closer.

PART FIFTEEN

The Revelator

Scriptural Backdrop:

I, John, your brother and companion in the suffering and kingdom and patient endurance that are ours in Jesus, was on the island of Patmos because of the word of God and the testimony of Jesus. On the Lord's Day I was in the Spirit, and I heard behind me a loud voice like a trumpet, which said: "Write on a scroll what you see and send it to the seven churches: to Ephesus, Smyrna, Pergamum, Thyatira, Sardis, Philadelphia and Laodicea." (Revelation 1:9–11)

John: A Brief Historical Overview

John first began his ministry as a disciple of John the Baptist (John 1:35).

He was one of the first six disciples called by Jesus in His early ministry in the province of Judea (John 1:37–51).

John originally had a home in Jerusalem, and was acquainted with many people of that city. To that home he took Mary, the mother of Jesus, whom the crucified Savior entrusted to his care (John 19:26, 27).

We find in historical documents of the second century [according to Melito of Sardis[294]], the common teaching that Mary, the mother of Jesus, is associated with the Mt. of Olives in later tradition, including her own tomb near that of her son, and that she "went out every day" to pray at the tomb of Christ, and at Golgotha—which implies that Golgotha was in close proximity to the Mt. of Olives.[295]

John was the youngest of the apostles, and survived them all.

Peter, James and John were the only witnesses of the raising of the Daughter of Jairus. All three also witnessed the Transfiguration, and these same three witnessed the Agony in Gethsemane more closely than the other Apostles did. Jesus sent only John and Peter into the city to make the preparation for the final Passover meal (the Last Supper) [Luke 22:Ɛ].

At the meal itself, the "disciple whom Jesus loved" [John] sat next to Jesus. It was customary to recline on couches at meals, and this disciple leaned on Jesus. After the arrest of Jesus, Peter and the "other disciple" (according to tradition, John) followed him into the palace of the high-priest.[296]

John alone among the Apostles remained near Jesus at the foot of the cross on Calvary alongside myrrh bearers and numerous other women; following the instruction of Jesus from the Cross, John took Mary, the mother of Jesus, into his care as the last legacy of Jesus. [John 19:25–27] After Jesus' Ascension and the descent of the Holy Spirit at Pentecost, John, together with Peter, took a prominent part in the founding and guidance of the church.[297]

He was with Peter at the healing of the lame man at Solomon's Porch in the Temple [Acts 3:1 et seq.] and he was also thrown into prison with Peter.[Acts 4:3] He went with Peter to visit the newly converted believers in Samaria.[Acts 8:14].[298]

After the reference to the pillar apostles in Galatians 2:9, in which John is named by Paul, silence falls on the life of John, and we know nothing of his life and activity **until we read of his banishment to Patmos.** There we meet those references of the elderly apostle at Ephesus, which occur in the Christian literature of the 2nd century.[299] (Emphasis added)

From: The Prescription of Heretics-Tertullian

According to Tertullian,[300] John, the bishop of the church of Ephesus, was banished to Patmos, sometime after being plunged into boiling oil in Rome and suffering nothing from it. It is said that "all in the audience of the Colosseum were converted to Christianity upon witnessing this miracle." This event would have occurred in the late 1st century, during the reign of the Emperor Domitian, who was known for his persecution of Christians.[301]

61

TARGETED

The Roman city of Ephesus, in the province of Asia Minor, circa AD 90

We now return to our immersive narrative. The scene opens with John the Revelator answering to the Roman authorities for his "obstinacy." He has refused to worship Emperor Domitian in an officially ordered, and open, display of allegiance.

The judicial chamber is elegantly appointed. Everything about the place testifies of the sheer power and technological prowess of the Roman Empire of the first-century *anno Domini*.[302]

The courtroom gallery is packed with Ephesian citizens, mostly because of the presence of one particular man. The humble, smallish, and elderly man is a prominent resident of Ephesus, especially within certain religious circles. He is the only surviving member of Jesus' original twelve disciples. But today, he is in desperate trouble with the Roman legal authorities.

One by one, the current docket of the criminal rabble is paraded before the judge. His Honor, an appointee of Rome, is prominently elevated, peering down from on high at the lowly throng. The *cognitio extra ordinem*—a special investigation ordered by the governor—has been completed.

The gang of the variously accused has been ushered into the room, wearing clanging chains. Court attorneys and prosecutors scuttle about from client to client, chattering procedures and promises to them in hushed tones.

At the magistrate's order, the elderly little Jew shuffles to the front of the judge's bench. A legal advocate accompanies him. Two guards stand at either side. After ten full minutes of his attorney's pleas for acquittal and then a petition for mercy, the magistrate indicates that sentencing will be pronounced.

"You, John, pastor of the church at Ephesus, are hereby sentenced to be exiled to the Island of Patmos." Murmurs of delighted agreement erupt from some in the courtroom. John remains silent, as required. He faces his judgment with honor, yet a sadness envelops him.

Exile? How in the world will my congregation survive? What is to be my destiny for the Kingdom work now? How can my life be made useful any longer, for the sake of the gospel? His head throbs with the questions he can't seem to answer. His eyes well up with tears.

The room becomes silent again. A few in the gallery nervously clear their throats. The judge continues as he adjusts the collar of his robe.

"On this venerated day, in the reign of our dear Emperor Domitian, *Dominus et Deus*, I sentence you on the grounds of your proven crimes against good Roman society, a society that you have so consistently spurned and so smugly disdained by your appalling disrespect and sacrilege against the throne! It is done, and ordered! *That is all!*"

The gavel falls with a deafening crack.

"Guards!" the judge orders. "Take him into custody!"

The men approach John with heavy chains and iron shackles. As they draw near, the old man slowly lifts his head and willingly extends his arms for the restraints. *The Lord will provide*, he thinks. *Somehow.*

He follows them to his assigned spot and falls back into the rickety chair. He folds his hands, lowers his head, and silently prays. His hands tremble, the chains rattling as they do. Hot tears splatter to the floor at his feet. His court-appointed lawyer now ignores him and scurries over to the next client.

62

BLASPHEMY

Many had simply succumbed to the humiliation, rationalizing that there really is no harm in humoring the foolish Romans who think their emperor is a god.

John, the acclaimed gospel preacher of Ephesus, had been accused of being an anti-emperor worship activist. Being the most prominent figure of his cultic Jewish-Christian group, as the Romans called it, he had been specifically targeted by the authorities.

John's frequent protests concerning the abjectly pagan ritual had been noticed by Rome itself. Domitian had become enraged by John's reputed influence over a sizable segment of the Ephesian citizenry. Banishment was a common punishment used during the Imperial Period for a number of offenses. Among such offenses were the practices of magic and astrology. Prophecy was viewed by the Romans as belonging to the same category.[303] John's "offenses" as a Christian were considered to be numerous, wanton, and dangerous to the empire.

Earlier, for months, and unbeknownst to John and his congregations, government-appointed spies had been dispatched to Ephesus. John's arrest had been ordered directly from the emperor's throne. They had determined that this disrespectful throng of disgusting Christians had to be stopped. John's case would make a good example, and a formidable warning to the Christian community that followed his illegal teachings and practices.

The worst punishment reserved for criminals who were not sentenced to death was to strip them of their civil rights and banish them to some remote or isolated corner of the empire. The Roman Empire had long ago designated the rocky, forlorn island of Patmos, forty miles off the coast of Asia Minor, as one such spot of utter seclusion. A banishment sentence was dreaded by many people of John's day, often even more than a death sentence—and the Romans knew it.

John had been accused of refusing to sacrifice a pig and obstinately declining to lay a worship tax of gold coins upon the altar of the imperial cult—the worship of Domitian. To refuse to participate in the forced pagan ritual was a capital crime, punishable by death or exile, a banishment that could sometimes last the rest of the convicted one's natural life.

Emperor Titus Flavius Caesar Domitianus Augustus saw himself as the new Caesar Augustus, an enlightened autocrat predestined to direct the Roman Empire into a new era of civilized luminosity. The year was AD 95. Religious, military, and cultural propaganda fostered a growing and frenzied cult of personality surrounding Rome's newest god.

By nominating himself to be a perpetual censor, Domitian set out to redirect the public and private morals of the entire culture over which he now presided. As a consequence, the emperor was popular with the vast majority of the Roman people, especially the military. His senate, however, was terrified of his unbridled power.

Domitian, relishing the authority he now wielded, became the first Roman emperor to demand to be addressed as *Dominus et Deus*—"Master and God." He ensured that those who produced libelous writings, especially writings specifically directed against him, were severely punished. As a result, large numbers of Jews and Christians suffered miserably under his tyranny.

The huge edifice of his sacrificial altar was located just to the south of the town square in Ephesus. The ornate building had become the first temple of the imperial cult erected in the Roman province of Anatolia. Many Jews and Christians had simply succumbed to the humiliation of the presence of this abomination, rationalizing that there really is no harm in humoring the foolish Romans who think their emperor is a god.

The fact is a large number of Christians had flatly compromised; furthermore, they had actually grown quite comfortable in their conciliation. John had tried to awaken them from their spiritual stupor and blasphemous practices.

Now he will pay for his unswerving commitment to the purity of the gospel of Jesus Christ. And no one has come to his defense—especially those who were convicted in their souls that the old preacher had been correct, and courageous, in his biblical stance.

Now, he is alone.

"The truth is...why should I be exempt?" John mumbles softly to himself. "After all, every one of my brother apostles is now gone.... I am the only one left. Peter, James, and Matthew, each of them paid the ultimate price. Why not me as well? Why should I live to be such an old man?"

A faint smile forms at the corners of his mouth. He remembers the words of Jesus, spoken decades earlier, "What if I decide that John should live until I come again?"

But the next pronouncement of a sentence rips at John's heart. The prisoner's name is Prochorus. He is John's fiery young disciple who had stood with him in the defiant protest of the repulsive emperor worship.

They had been arrested on the same day and held in the same cell awaiting this day of sentencing. They had clearly known the dangers of their actions, and John possessed no reservations about his own protests. But now...he watches in sorrow as Prochorus is shuffled before the judge's bench.

"Guilty!" The gavel crashes. The judge continues his pronouncement with an austere voice. "You have followed your teacher's perverse and superstitious ways—now you may follow him to Patmos...perhaps for the rest of your natural life!"

The judge shoots a wicked glance in John's direction. "See, old man, what you have wrought upon this religiously manipulated life?" he accuses. "How many more innocents will you destroy by your insolence? How much more anguish would you have willfully brought to your congregation?

"We simply will not tolerate, in this great city, a misguided religious insurrection against our dear emperor—not in Ephesus! *Dominus et Deus* will be honored among us! And I intend to lead the way. Perhaps others of your kind will learn the lesson of your sentence. Done and ordered!"

Oh, God, have I done the right thing? John prays in agony, silently. Never before has he been uncertain of his own actions. But now, a young man's future is over—forever. John's zeal has cost the boy dearly.

John feels a dash of reassurance when Prochorus turns from his sentencing, looks his old pastor squarely in the face—and shoots a glancing grin in his direction. The guards fasten Prochorus' shackles and prepare him for delivery to Patmos. *Unless the Lord intervenes,* John thinks, *we will never return to civilization. We may as well be dead to Ephesus, and to our families and friends. Life, as we have known it, is over.*

He jumps, startled as the judge's gavel once again crashes down upon the desk, concurrent with his ominous exclamation.

"Next!"

63

TO THE SEVEN CHURCHES

"I write this personal note to accompany the scroll of the Revelation, which I have received directly from our Lord Jesus Christ."

Within days of their sentencing, John and Prochorus arrive on Patmos along with a shipload of other unfortunates.[304] First-century Patmos, with its natural protective harbor, is a strategic island on the sea lane from Ephesus to Rome. Patmos is also an important quarry for the Roman Empire as well as the home of banishment to numerous political and religious prisoners. The island is rocky and certainly has the feel of isolation; however, it is anything but desolate. Besides the mammoth stone building that serves as the main edifice for the officials who oversee the mining work of the island, Patmos also contains several outlying fishing and agricultural villages, a hippodrome for horse racing, and at least three pagan temples. As such, there is quite a large population here among which John and Prochorus can work, live out their remaining lives, and even minister.[305]

However, for John and Prochorus, the first few weeks on the island are almost unbearable. They have no idea if, or when, they might ever be allowed to return to their families, their church, and their friends back at

Ephesus. The cruel uncertainty of that fact is maddening. But John and his young protégé soon assimilate. They have to; there is no other choice. To attempt an escape from their lawfully executed sentence would mean certain death, and perhaps increased persecution leveled upon their families even after their demise. They understand that this remote place must now become their life's new mission field. The desperate souls on this island need the Lord as much as anyone else. They will simply have to adjust, be faithful where they are, and make the best of what days remain of their lives.

To his great joy, within the first few months on the island, John leads several to salvation in Jesus Christ. He even finds a secluded cave among the rocky cliffs that he frequents for his own personal times of worship. And, through his secretary Prochorus, he spends much of his time writing. He writes of his past. He writes of his times with Jesus. He chronicles the life, ministry, death, and resurrection of Jesus. He records these accounts for the benefit of those on the island, and also with the hope that perhaps someday he might be able to convince someone to get his writings off the island and into the hands of the believers back in Ephesus. Perhaps he might even be able to deliver his letters and writings personally.

But weeks turn into months; months pass into more than a year. By now, Prochorus has resigned himself to the fact that they probably won't ever leave the island. John is beginning to be of the same mind. So the two of them continue to work the mines and agricultural fields by day—and minister as often as they can by night. From their labors, they are able to find a humble home to rent. And, not surprisingly, under God's anointing, John eventually grows to become trusted by several of the island's chief Roman authorities.

How ironic, John thinks. *I was banished to this place for preaching the gospel and refusing to worship the emperor. But here, I am allowed to share the gospel, and rarely is the emperor's name even mentioned. God's ways certainly are not our ways.*

And it is here, on Patmos, on a certain Lord's Day of worship, alone in his secluded cave of refuge, where John receives a startling message from

Heaven's throne. That eternal and divine message is initiated by the resurrected Jesus Himself. It is a missive that will change the way the church will look at itself throughout the thousands of years to come. For anyone who knows the Word of God at all, this book will be used to measure the prophetic times during each successive generation. John has no idea of the ultimate impact of his assignment at the time he receives it. All he knows is that he has been instructed to "write what you see," and he is obedient to that command.

After the writings have been supernaturally communicated to him, he has to get them delivered to those whom the Lord has instructed. But in what frame of mind will they receive it? Will they believe its message, or will they think he has gone mad in his banishment? It doesn't matter. He has to send it.

So, John musters his strength, steels his resolve…and writes:
To the seven churches of Asia Minor.[306]

I, John, write this personal note to accompany the scroll of the Revelation, which I have received directly from our Lord Jesus Christ while on the island of Patmos, suffering for my unflinching stand on behalf of our Lord, and His Holy Word.

Truly our resurrected Lord has visited me! I speak the absolute truth to you in this matter—I am not lying, nor have I gone mad. Please relate this letter, in full, to all of our brothers and sisters, scattered throughout the world, beginning with the seven churches to which I make my initial delivery.

It was on a Lord's Day, a few months after my arrival upon Patmos, when the most amazing thing happened to me. It was a Sunday, as the Romans call it, the first day of the week. I stumbled into a small cave I had discovered only a few weeks earlier. This location has become, for me, a place of rest, seclusion, and prayer.

On that particular Sunday, I made my way there to meditate upon the Word of our Lord and to pray. I looked around the dimly lit void, took a deep breath, and started to kneel so that I could lean against the wall. But, all of a sudden, I was stopped. An alarming, deeply resonant noise erupted behind me. The commotion sounded as if it had come from within the cave's shadowy depths. Suddenly, the voice of it was everywhere. It was booming and splendid—it was inside and, at the same time, outside, like the sound of a shofar blasting through the hills of Judea. Then the voice evolved into intelligible words.

"Write!" the voice asserted. "Write in a book, what you will see. You will see things that speak to your own day. And, John, you will speak to things you will be shown about the distant future. Send your book to the seven churches of Asia Minor."

My body began to tremble uncontrollably. I hesitated to turn and gaze upon the source of the proclamation. Was it the Lord? I was certain I recognized the voice of our Lord. Had He come to Patmos? Had He come to me? Had He come to deliver us? I took another deep breath. I gathered my nerves and slowly turned. And there He stood! Among a set of seven dazzlingly beautiful golden lampstands!

He was clothed in pure, unadulterated, brilliant light. The radiance of His glory filled the cavern. The air sparkled with flecks of shimmering luminosity. His face was as bright as the sun itself, yet visible and recognizable, and bathed with love. In His right hand He held what appeared to be seven small stars, spheres of burning, white-hot, incandescent substance.

I fell at His feet as though I were a dead man. I was wholly overwhelmed. I buried my face in the dusty floor of the cave. He laid His hand upon my shoulder. I felt a surge of hot energy burst through my body. I sensed an overwhelming peace enveloping me. I have never before felt such love.

"Do not be afraid John, my dear John, the one whom I love," He said to me. "I am the first and the last, and the living One; and I was dead, and behold, I am alive forevermore, and I hold the keys of death and of Hades."

Then, He lifted my head with His hands and looked at me with "that look" —a look that only He can give! I burst into sobs of joy as He tightened His loving grip on my shoulder. "Write, therefore, the things which you will see," He continued, "and the things which are, and the things which shall take place after these things. As for the mystery of the seven stars, which you saw in my right hand, and the seven golden lampstands: the seven stars are the angels of the seven churches, and the seven lampstands are the seven churches."

At once I was in the Spirit. I felt somehow transported. Exactly how, I know not. But I can tell you *where*. I stepped through a thin, billowing veil of earthly atmosphere—as though it were a mere curtain—blown open by the breath of God Himself. The scenery of this worldly life around me simply rolled back like a scroll—and I stepped through it and away from it. I was in another world…yet only one mere step from the world I had just left. I was in this perfect place in the twinkling of an eye, and I was once again enveloped in light-bathed, irresistible love. There is nothing like it in this earthly existence!

Our brother Paul was right. Truly he, too, just as he told us, was caught up to Paradise—the Third Heaven. The mind cannot comprehend the glory of that place. The ear has never heard the sounds that I heard. I have no words other than these with which to describe the matter.

I do not have time in this letter to relate all that I experienced. What I was ordered to write, I have written in the scroll, which you now possess. The seven letters that accompany this scroll must be delivered at your earliest possible convenience to the respective churches. This is an important task. I know not how the thing will be accomplished on your part, but I am certain that it will be faithfully carried out under your watch. Our Lord has commanded it.

I have seen the future! I have been in the throne room of God.

I am utterly overwhelmed by what I have experienced. It was not a dream; it was not even a mere vision. *I was there.* I breathed its air. I felt its tranquility. I smelled its aromas, saw its indescribable colors. And I spoke with angelic beings!

I have done my best, with the simple, earthly words that I possess, to describe what I have seen. In some cases, I was given specific words and names; I felt as though they might have been distinctive clues, given by our Lord for a future generation. In other cases, I was only allowed to observe the scenes before my eyes, merely glimpses and foretastes of things yet to come, and I was told to write what I saw, using my own words…moved along by the Holy Spirit.

And then I saw a mighty angel proclaiming in a loud voice, "Who is worthy to break the seals and open the scroll?" But no one in heaven or on earth or under the earth could open the scroll or even look inside it. I wept and wept because no one was found who was worthy to open the scroll or to even take a peek inside it! Then one of the elders said to me, "Do not weep, John! Behold! The Lion of the tribe of Judah, the Root of David, has triumphed! He is able to open the scroll."[307]

Then I looked and heard the voice of uncountable angels! Numbering thousands upon thousands, and ten thousand times ten thousand! They encircled the throne and the living creatures and the elders. In a loud voice they were singing: "Worthy is the Lamb, who was slain, to receive power and wealth and wisdom and strength and honor and glory and praise!"[308]

It was at that time that the Scroll of the Ages was opened in my presence. I beheld magnificent things! I saw futuristic machines of war that could crush our mighty Roman legions as though they were mere ants. Some of the machines, though they looked like living things, crawled along the ground. Others flew through the air, in swarms, like locusts. And they appeared to contain men within them.

I saw their terrifying faces! Fire issued forth from the mouths and tails of these things...whatever they were. They proved to be of great torment to the throngs that challenged them. I saw disease, famine, and pestilence of pandemic proportions. These plagues swept the earth at blinding speed, invoking great fear among all the nations. Lawlessness began to prevail. Truth was thrown to the ground, and God's people, those who followed the Lamb of God, were persecuted, belittled, and despised all over the earth! It's all in the scroll. You'll understand as the Spirit of God gives you wisdom. And so will the generations that follow.

Then I saw a mountain of fire rising out of the sea. I saw stars falling from the heavens, and demonic forces bearing down upon the earth like a vise. I saw a thousand streams of fiery Hell gushing from the earth. Men were in torment because of the opening of the Abyss.

I saw the abomination that causes desolation. It will soon stand in God's *true Temple* of the last days. It is an unspeakable horror. Domitian is a foreshadowing of the Antichrist; this I now know. But he is not the one of whom our Lord spoke. There is one who will yet come, in the very last days. I have seen him. I beheld his countenance but was prohibited from publishing a detailed description. He will make our ferocious Domitian appear as a benevolent and gentle father!

The one who is to come will be the embodiment of the vilest type of evil. Unimaginable wickedness. But the people—those that are not sealed with the Holy Spirit of God—will not recognize this fact until it's far too late. He will bring about an unfathomable delusion that sweeps the planet. The lie of that delusion is unspeakable—it is unimaginable. It is the master of all masquerades! I have seen it. I feel faint even speaking of it.

Men's hearts will indeed fail them in those days, just like our Lord foretold. I saw it in the vision! Horrifying fear will eventually grip the entire world!

I saw the end of days. I saw the Great Throne of Judgment. I saw the New Heaven and the New Earth. I saw it all! I speak the truth.

Forgive my rambling.

Please be vigilant in your handling and delivery of this material. We are conveying the words of God for many generations to come. It is a task that has engulfed me with its enormity. I pray that God will help us to fully accomplish it.

Prochorus sends his greetings. He is well. Pray for us.

Give my greetings and my love to the saints.

May the Lord bless you and keep you...forever.

Your faithful and fellow servant of the Lord Jesus Christ

—John

After making arrangements with John's newfound governmental friends on the island, his Revelation is delivered back home to Ephesus and the other six churches.

Then, on September 18, AD 96, following almost two full years after John's initial banishment, Emperor Domitian is assassinated in a palace conspiracy involving members of the Praetorian Guard and several of his freedmen. On that same day, a high-ranking government official under Emperors Nero, Vespasian, and Domitian—the widely respected consulate named Nerva—is declared emperor by the Roman Senate. As the new ruler of the Roman Empire, he vows to restore liberties that were curtailed during the autocratic government of Domitian. Consequently, Nerva releases all who were on trial for high treason and restores them back to their original homes.[309]

Thus, the sentences of Domitian are officially annulled. The Roman Senate decrees the return of those in exile, as well as the restoration of their property. The Apostle John, after his lengthy languishing on Patmos, finally returns home to Ephesus along with Prochorus.[310]

But this certainly isn't the end of John's story.

Part Sixteen

Home at Last

Scriptural Backdrop:

The Apostle John—His Death

John is said by most scholars to have lived to an extremely old age, dying a natural death at Ephesus sometime after AD 98—during the reign of Trajan.[311]

John's traditional tomb is located in the former basilica of Saint John at Selçuk, a small town in the vicinity of Ephesus, in the modern nation of Turkey.[312]

64

SERENITY

John, the beloved disciple, is ninety-four years old, circa AD 100

John, the son of Zebedee—one of the *Sons of Thunder*—is slipping away. Soon, he will leave behind this earthly dimension of existence.

His breathing is noticeably labored—even more so than just an hour ago. And his chest feels like it has one of Alexander the Great's famed war elephants standing upon it. *So...this is what it feels like to die?*

But why shouldn't it be this way? John chuckles to himself. After all, he is now approaching his mid-nineties, and it is almost the turn of another century.

He is surrounded by loved ones, though he can barely see them through his dimming eyes. Even though he can't always make out their specific words, he can still hear them speaking and laughing. That is enough for him at the moment, just to know they are there, as he lies in his bed.

Warm blankets have been snuggled around him, and a crackling fire in the fireplace creates a ballet of dancing shadows across the room. A familiar warmth envelops him. It is calming, peaceful, and penetrating to the depths of his soul. What more can a dying man ask for?

He has experienced this same presence of serenity several times before, even in his darkest moments of despair and grief—especially when he survived being thrown into a vat of boiling oil, then banished to Patmos for refusing to offer an altar sacrifice in honor of Emperor Domitian.[313] Mercifully, those horrifying days had ended, and he had been allowed to return home.[314]

But for now, John is fairly comfortable. It won't be long. He can feel it. He is more certain of that truth than he is of life itself.

In fact, for the vast majority of his existence upon this earth, this is what he has been living for—his instantaneous moment of passing back to the divine realm, into the presence of his Creator. He will soon be in that hidden dimension, eating the fruits of its joy and bliss, feasting upon the tree of life. He already knows what he is going to see when he arrives, and he can't wait to get there.

Please, Lord, take me soon…bring me home.

Caught Up

Some thirty years earlier, the Apostle Paul had also witnessed the reality of Paradise.[315] He, too, had been caught up to the throne room of Elohim. From that day forward, Paul had longed to be "absent from the body and present with the Lord." Yes, Brother Paul *knew*.

John has a look of sheer pleasure upon his face when he thinks of these wondrous things. Even though he has faithfully preached the great truths that the risen Yeshua gave to Paul as a result of his catching up, John has no idea that before his own life is over, he too will be summoned into the Lord's literal presence. He cannot have dreamed that he also will enter Paradise—and that he too will return to the earthly realm to tell of his experience, just like Paul did.

Not only will John return, but he will also come back with a scroll—the scroll of the *Revelation*. And, at the command of Yeshua Himself, John will faithfully disperse that scroll among seven very specific churches. Those churches are located in a region that will prove to be central to the very last days, before Yeshua's return.[316]

The Portal

During his foray into that unseen realm, John had been whisked into the distant future, thousands of years from his own day. Dimension after dimension of the progression of time had flown before his eyes. He had been taken to a "high mountain"[317] and shown things that were beyond his comprehension, yet he was told: "Write what you have seen."

He had obediently written. The indescribable imagery, letter by letter, flowed from his pen, guided by the hand of the Holy Spirit. There was no other way to define the phenomenon. Not only had he somehow traveled through time, deep into the future, but to this very day he has often smelled the air of the eras through which he passed. He has heard the sounds of each passing age of humanity, growing more riotous and metallic as the pages of the calendar flip by—like leaves blowing on a blustery fall afternoon.

John had not experienced a mere vision. No—it had *not* been a dream. He had actually been there, in the flesh, from the throne room of God all the way into the halls of the Antichrist's kingdom lair.

John now understands what Jesus meant when He assured the disciples that He alone was the door, the gate, and the only portal through which the believer can enter. John had been through that entryway to the future. He had traversed time itself. There had been no dimensional barriers standing in his way after entering through the "door" of Jesus.

But, even in the midst of the tumult of these final days, John has also witnessed the amazing patience and endurance on the part of the saints who are faithfully advancing the gospel of Jesus Christ. They are the only ones who understand what life is really all about, and where everything is ultimately heading. In the end, he has seen them greatly rewarded for their faith and for their witness, as they are devotedly advancing the kingdom work...

Even in the days of global chaos and lawlessness.

65

THE VERY LAST

John saw the New Earth—that old and fallen dimensional layer of
reality—at the command of Yahweh supernaturally fold into another.

ost terrifying of all was when John had beheld the rise of the appalling Beast that is to come. He had seen the son of perdition seated
upon the throne of his lustful desire. He was high and lifted up, and
was blindly worshiped by the inhabitants of the earth. The demonically
beguiled world had no idea this mesmerizing man was actually possessed
by Satan himself. This was the dragon's "Christ," his diabolical counterfeit
of Heaven's Son. For a brief while, this fallen *elohim* will possess his long-
coveted kingdom.

Then John foresaw the final days of the wrath of Yahweh. He saw, in
an instant, the sky rolled up like a scroll and the dimension of the divine
realm of *Elohim* exposed to the planet. The stars of the skies appeared
to fall from the sky as they shot toward the earth at supersonic speed.
The entire spectacle had burst into global view at the sound of celestial
trumpets.

The ominous, blood-curdling blasts of those angelic shofars had filled
the heavens, echoing throughout the earth. People who had formerly

cursed the God of Heaven scattered like panicked insects. The inhabitants of the earth cried out for the mountains to fall upon them. John heard their anguished pleas for mercy, but their entreaties came far too late. The wrath of the Lamb was upon them, and there was no place to hide.[318]

The Great White Throne

After this, John saw the gleaming white throne of Yahweh's final judgment upon Satan's doomed kingdom and all that belonged to it. The prisons of death and Hell had been opened. The condemned of the ages were brought forward. They stood as a multitude, as far as the eye could see. He watched as the books were opened. And he heard the collective groans of humanity as the pages were read aloud. There was no escape from the condemnation of their purposed rejection of the Lamb of God.[319]

And John witnessed Satan, along with the Beast, the False Prophet, and the disobedient angels being thrown into the Lake of Fire. The kings of the earth were appalled to see the final end of this one who, for eons, had so easily controlled and manipulated them. He was gone from their midst forever, cast into an impenetrable dimension of alternative existence, never to return…never to be remembered again.[320]

John saw the New Earth—that old and fallen dimensional layer of reality—at the command of Yahweh supernaturally fold into another. From this point forward, there would be no more pain, no more crying, no more death. The old order of things would instantly pass away. Everything would be revealed as sparkling new. Paradise, previously hidden from fallen humanity, but *there* all along, would become the home of redeemed humanity. The restitution of all things would arrive, just as Jesus promised.

John saw it all. He had seen it in real time, and in the flesh. He had been physically present—there, in the future.

However, there was a price to pay for what he had been shown. Much of what he witnessed ceaselessly haunted him from that day forward—vexing his righteous soul, just like so many of the prophets before him.[321]

Until now. In the last few moments, an unspeakable tranquility has swept over him. He has never felt anything like it before. That's when he knows...

Soon, he will be by Jesus' side once more.

66

THE GLORY

The room, and everything that fills it, melts away behind him,
almost as though it never existed.

The old man shivers as a sudden chill courses through his body. Alexander's elephant grows heavier upon his breast. John's breathing becomes shallower, more labored.

He groans aloud, in a gargled whisper. "How much longer, O Lord?"

His thoughts are interrupted as someone places another log in the fireplace. The flames sputter back to life and spew forth a rush of warmth. The room once again fills with a lovely golden glow, punctuated by a soothing, crackling sound. A cool rag is placed on his forehead. The tears are wiped from his cheeks by a gentle hand.

John remembers the amazing days of Messiah.

Those sweet memories ambulate through the creases of his mind and into the depths of his soul. *God was actually with us in those days! What a thought! Our Creator! In the flesh...walking with us...like it must have been in the Garden!*

How can it be that he, John, had been born for such a time as this? How can it be that the Creator of the universe had actually chosen *him* to walk by His side during those amazing and prophetic days? But this is truly the substance of *real* life…the way it was meant to be from the beginning. If the world could only understand this boundless, liberating, and wonderful truth.

Yeshua had tapped a small group to be His inner circle. But how could John have known that day at the Jordon River what the rest of his days would eventually entail? From the faithful exploits of that small group, however, the world would never again be the same. And now, John has become the last living one from among Jesus' inner circle. The rest of them have been martyred for their faith.[322]

Why am I the only one who will leave this world lying upon the bed of old age? But then, John remembers what Yeshua had said to Peter after the resurrection event, as they had walked the shores of Galilee together: "If I want John to remain until I return, what is that to you? You follow me!"[323]

Great dribbles of salty tears trickle down his face as the memories flood his mind. A slight smile forms on his lips. He opens his eyes wide as if they had suddenly beheld great windows of excited revelations. He glances about the room, which grows silent as its occupants notice the sudden change in John's demeanor.

As his family and friends gather around him, John announces in a raspy whisper, "The music! The singing! It's magnificent! I see them! I…"

He exhales a great sigh as his eyelids gently flutter together, shuttering out the sights of his former earthly existence. John is gone from this world.

Paradise

In that very next instant, in the twinkling of an eye, and in a spontaneous burst of an intensely dazzling light, a shimmering golden veil is lifted. Only John can see it. The room, and everything that fills it, melts away behind him, almost as though it has never existed. He is presently enveloped in a covering of divine luminance—bathing him in unspeakable ecstasy—and music! Exquisite, rapturous, angelic music…*and singing*!

He holds out his hands and marvels at what he sees. His ninety-plus years of earthly life are melting away as he is beginning to change! Wrinkles and frailness are being replaced by youth and vigor! His entire body is transforming right before his eyes! His very being is enveloped in a supernatural renewal. His eyes and ears work as though his younger days are instantaneously returned to him. It is happening! It all seems so natural—so *blissful!*

Just then, he hears a familiar voice. It is the voice he has desperately longed to hear.

"John! Come here! Well done my friend! Here—take my hand."

John walks through the open veil. He takes hold of the strong and outstretched hand. A blast of air hits him in the face, like a cool, utterly delightful ocean breeze. The smell of it is invigorating! He feels more alive at this moment than he has ever been! He is vibrant, and at complete peace—and he is whole.

He is on *the other side.* And, he knows it! The entire experience is as peaceful and natural as if he has just walked through the front door of his own home, as he had done in ages past. But, this time, his "home" is wrapped in rapturous glory…and peace.

The light suddenly separates, as if a great and magnificent door has been flung open before him. Behind the folds of unparalleled beauty and brilliance, John beholds a face…a familiar and welcomed face.

He falls to his knees and weeps, sobbing uncontrollably. His cries are not the sounds of a broken man or a man in agony. Far from it! His tears are in response to his reborn state, the purest ecstasy he has ever experienced.

Just then, John feels that strong and wonderful hand in his—as the other hand firmly grips his shoulder, gently squeezing, in the same way a father would comfort his child. Then he feels the embrace for which he has been yearning—the embrace of the Master—his dearest Friend. *His Life.*

John—the disciple whom Jesus loves—is in Paradise.

He has come home, where he is meant to be…at last.

No more suffering. No more pain. No more death. All things are being made new…right before his eyes.

Forever.

PART SEVENTEEN

Final Glimpse

You were shown these things so that you might know that the LORD is God; besides him there is no other. (Deuteronomy 4:35)

67

IT IS FINISHED

Understanding these truths is inexpressibly revelatory.

---

pray that the journey you've just taken has given added insight to life, death, and eternity—as well as our place in the midst of it. At this point, there's really no denying the fact that our world is multidimensional, not only in space, but most likely in *time* as well[324]—as I've tried to illustrate in the immersive portions of this book. In fact, it appears that, according to the Bible and science, our entire existence is multidimensional. On top of that, the eternity to come and our place in it, is—you guessed it—multidimensional! The Word of God assures us that this is exactly how Yahweh designed the universe from the very beginning, when the sons of God shouted for joy as they witnessed it bursting forth into all of its splendorous existence. On that day, they stood and worshiped Him and sang in awe because of the ineffable grandeur of it all.[325]

It's all there, right up to the very last words—those last chapters in Revelation—promising the ultimate dimensional shift of *all* dimensional shifts, and the revealing of Paradise!

Then I saw "a new heaven and a new earth," for the first heaven and the first earth had passed away, and there was no longer any sea. I saw the Holy City, the New Jerusalem, coming down out of heaven from God, prepared as a bride beautifully dressed for her husband.

And I heard a loud voice from the throne saying, "Look! God's dwelling place is now among the people, and he will dwell with them. They will be his people, and God himself will be with them and be their God. 'He will wipe every tear from their eyes.

There will be no more death or mourning or crying or pain, for the old order of things has passed away." He who was seated on the throne said, "I am making everything new!" Then he said, "Write this down, for these words are trustworthy and true." (Revelation 21:1–5)

Eden Restored[326]

Then the angel showed me the river of the water of life, as clear as crystal, flowing from the throne of God and of the Lamb down the middle of the great street of the city. On each side of the river stood the tree of life, bearing twelve crops of fruit, yielding its fruit every month. And the leaves of the tree are for the healing of the nations. No longer will there be any curse.

The throne of God and of the Lamb will be in the city, and his servants will serve him. They will see his face, and his name will be on their foreheads. There will be no more night. They will not need the light of a lamp or the light of the sun, for the Lord God will give them light. And they will reign for ever and ever. (Revelation 22:1–5)

We have this assurance because we know that our Lord Himself holds the keys to *all* the portals of everything that exists. He is the *door*, He is the *gateway* to every single dimension of reality—seen or unseen, known or unknown, space and time—because He alone created them. He alone is *the Way.*[327]

> For in [Jesus Christ] all things were created: things in heaven and on earth, visible and invisible, whether thrones or powers or rulers or authorities; all things have been created through him and for him. He is before all things, and in him all things hold together. (Colossians 1:16–17)

Understanding these truths is inexpressibly revelatory. They help us keep our biblical perspective intact, especially as we're trying to faithfully make our way through this fallen, earthbound existence.

Through these divine disclosures, we are bathed in courage, strength, wisdom, hope…and a Holy Spirit-steeled confidence that enables us to face the vile filth of Satan's quickly encroaching last-days outrage.

68

THE PROPHETIC NATURE OF OUR DAY

It is our responsibility to correctly handle the Word of Truth
and faithfully take our stand upon that Word.

When a singular generation[328] of humanity lives to see just one or two prominent biblical prophecies of the last days being fulfilled in the midst of their lifetimes—that is, indeed, a significant indication of where that generation is located within the timeline of prophetic history. But what do we say about a generation that lives, in real time, through *multiple* prophecies—ancient biblical declarations that are bursting forth all around them?

Well...*we* are that generation! The prescient occurrences of our day are historically unparalleled. The sad fact is that most of today's slumbering church doesn't even comprehend what should have been so apparent to them all along. Consider the following stunning fact that's documented in a Bible Gateway interview with George Barna, the internationally renowned researcher and pollster of all things religious:

> The first national survey of the worldview of Americans conducted
> by the Cultural Research Center at Arizona Christian University

shows that although seven out of ten consider themselves to be Christian, only 6% actually possess a biblical worldview.[329]

Think of it! In today's world, even in the United States of America, the "largest Christian nation" the planet has ever seen, far less than 10 percent of all who claim to be "God's people" actually believe and live by the foundational basics of what it means to be a true child of God. That includes understanding how biblical prophecy truly unfolds and how to know where our place in that unfolding rests. This, too, is a definitive global marker of the very last days, a marker that has occurred only in our historical generation. The Scriptures very pointedly speak to the doctrinal falling away and the pervasive pollution of biblical truth in the days just before the return of the Lord Jesus Christ.[330]

How It Happens

As a stark illustration of how God's people often flatly miss prophecy unfolding, consider the eternally significant blunder of the first-century religious leaders. Those "deeply religious ones"—along with the accomplices of Rome—nailed the Son of God to a cross. They did this outside the city of God, just outside the Temple of God, and they did it *in the name of God!* As they walked away from the cross that day, they slapped each other on the backs and celebrated what had just happened, thinking they somehow had done God and Rome a really big favor. All of that transpired even while Yeshua was in their physical presence working miracles, signs, and wonders that had long before been prophesied to accompany the arrival of God's genuine Messiah.

How in the world could they have missed something like *that?* The answer to the question is multifold. And it's not pretty.

One of the biggest factors of their blindness was that *they had another agenda.* It was an ancient agenda of selfishness and envy. And Jesus called them out on it regularly. His teachings and ministry exploits didn't square up with their "rabbinical" talking points or the "religiously correct" doctrine of their generation. Yeshua deeply disturbed their influence over the people and their self-empowering ecclesiastical network. So…they purposely ignored what was right before their eyes. They simply changed the narrative. They covered over the truth of what Jesus was revealing by couching it in fake news reports (blatantly false allegations that were presented as absolute truth), nefarious and accusatory *labeling*, and a never-ending string of diabolically deceptive language. Sound familiar?

Never doubt it: Satan, and the world system over which he rules, does indeed possess an underlying anti-Christ agenda. The cultures of our planet are now flooded with lies and obfuscation…as well as deranged minds and delusional political correctness. These are all part of Satan's process to veil the truth of God's plan from us. To top it all off, the National Institutes of Health are even reporting that a global epidemic of the fear of death is now sweeping the planet, causing a dramatic rise in mental disease.[331]

In the midst of the ensuing madness, it's our God-given responsibility to correctly handle the Word of truth and faithfully take our stand upon that Word, regardless of how the world labels us for doing so. This is the only way we can be assured that we are standing on the eternal foundation…built upon the rock. And it's the only way we will eternally impact the fallen world around us.[332]

The "Falling Chain" Effect

But, there's still another way God's people overlook what He's actually doing. Consider this illustration. Genuine, prophetic events run in a line, like a string of dominoes arranged to begin falling in a certain pattern. The continually falling chain only comes to life after the first plank is toppled over. Then, the uninterrupted tipping of the tiles ripples right through every generation, until the last of countless other dominoes plops down and the chain ends. All this is taking place regardless of whether or not a specific generation along the way recognizes the prophetic events when they occur. Again, I remind you of the Sanhedrin leadership in the time of Messiah being among them in the flesh.

Consider a couple of other biblical/historical examples—like when Caesar Augustus issued a decree ordering all citizens to travel to their towns of origin, thus putting Mary and Joseph in Bethlehem. With that imperial diktat, the eternally significant chain of our own salvation began. The first domino toppled. It culminated at the empty tomb. Then...*plop!*

Or, what about that one, precise, preordained spark of an instant when Jesus cried out, "It is finished!"? The message of His divine cry effectively proclaimed that God's plan of personal salvation was coming to fruition, and everything would begin to cascade toward restoring that which was corrupted in Eden. Once that "word" fell from Heaven's lips, the prophetic conglomeration that followed was activated. With that cry also came an interdimensional call to battle. In that singular moment, the demonic powers were freshly awakened and have been actively fighting against the decree...right up to, and in the midst of, the events of our own lifetime. Those dominoes that toppled two thousand years ago are directly impacting our lives *today*, along with the intricate geopolitics of our world!

And don't forget when Yahweh decreed, in the Garden of Eden more than six thousand years ago, as recorded in Genesis 3:15: "From the womb of a woman will come a seed, and even though you'll bruise His heel, He will *crush your head*" (emphasis added).

From God's first speaking that prophecy over Satan until Jesus was on the cross accomplishing the promise, almost four thousand years had passed. Think of the number of expectant generations that came and went, most of whom didn't think they saw anything prophetic that pointed to God keeping that promise in their lifetimes. However, regardless of what they did or did not see, the promise *was* marching forward...to a pre-ordained ending, until the last domino fell. That's how prophecy works.

In the meantime, the people of each successive generation must choose where their allegiances will ultimately align, regardless of what they "think" they might see regarding the fulfillment of last-days biblical prophecy.

That's where *we* come into the picture. *This is our generation.* It's now our time to choose where our allegiance is grounded. It's our time to step up and make a genuine difference in the overall Kingdom mission.

Year by year, with every rotation of earth's orbit around the sun, the dominoes are falling, like it or not.[333]

69

UNTO ALL THE WORLD

We are the only generation to see all of these things happening, right before our eyes.

While I am not, and never have been, a *date-setter* regarding the biblically prophesied return of the Lord Jesus Christ, I can, without reservation, say that four of the most distinguishing and undeniable *last-days* prophecies and "falling dominoes" have already come to pass. And, they've occurred only in our generation—one in only the last few years. God declares in His Word that these three specific fulfillments would be heavenly *signs to the nations*—in the days just before the return of Jesus Christ.

The first one is the prophetic declaration that the gospel of Jesus Christ would be in the process of being unprecedentedly carried into *all the nations of the world*.[334] This declaration did not mean that the gospel of salvation would be distributed throughout the Roman Empire alone. Jesus' words speak of *the very last days*...in the time when "the end will come." He is very clear on that point. Therefore, that specific prophecy tells of *our days*, and perhaps a little beyond, and it means the preaching of the gospel will be in the process of being fulfilled throughout *the entire planet* of the *last days*. Most renowned scholars affirm this assertion.[335]

And now, for the first time since the birth of the church, that prophecy is literally being fulfilled twenty-four hours a day, every single day, without ceasing. It's as if a massive dam has burst open and is disgorging its contents upon the valley below in a disastrous flood. No other generation before us has seen such a thing take place on a global scale. Yet, even though its fulfillment is such a part of our own daily life and world events, most of the church doesn't even see it or understand the prophetic significance of what's happening right before our eyes—just like the religious elite of the first century.

- "[Jesus said to them,] And **this gospel** of the kingdom **will be preached** in **the whole world** as a **testimony to all nations**, and **then the end will come**" (Matthew 24:14; emphasis added).
- "The **end** will come **like a flood**" (Daniel 9:26; emphasis added).
- "**And there shall be a time of trouble, such as never was** since there was a nation even to that same time: and **at that time thy people shall be delivered**, every one that shall be found written in the book. And many of them that sleep in the dust of the earth shall awake, some to everlasting life, and some to shame and everlasting contempt. **And they that be wise shall shine as the brightness of the firmament; and they that turn many to righteousness as the stars for ever and ever.** But thou, O Daniel, shut up the words, and seal the book, even **to the time of the end:** many shall **run to and fro, and knowledge shall be increased**" (Daniel 12:1–4; emphasis added).

God's Countdown Clock

God's most prominent and historically undeniable countdown began a little less than a generation ago. That clock started when the nation of Israel was resurrected out of the ashes of ancient history and returned to the land…a 2,800-year-old prophecy that has burst to life only in our historical period. That supernatural event is the singular most important prophecy[336] that God told us would be revealed as His definitive sign *to the nations*…and that the end of man's wicked rule over the planet was quickly approaching.[337] Jesus declared this truth again, most specifically in His Olivet Discourse.[338]

Today, the young nation of Israel is already a top-tier leader in science and technology among all of the other hundreds of nations of the world. In 2019, it was ranked the world's fifth most innovative country by the Bloomberg Innovation Index. And, it ranks thirteenth in the world for scientific output as measured by the number of scientific publications per million citizens.[339]

The Third Sign

In addition to the global preaching of the gospel and the return of the nation of Israel, yet another miraculous event was foretold to happen in the end times. It was biblically predicted to further punctuate the stunning domino effect that would take place within the framework of the *specific* last days.

That event would be the "return" of Jerusalem to the revenant nation of Israel as its foremost city—*the capital*. And that particular segment of the *domino effect* was prophesied to create an international firestorm of events that would follow, resulting in a major international war. That war would involve the "nations of the earth" surrounding Jerusalem for the purpose of destroying it and/or recapturing it for themselves. This, of course, would first require that Israel itself would indeed "return." And only after that return would Jerusalem, somehow, become the capital again.[340]

From the time of the writing of this book, it's been less than a handful of years since Jerusalem was declared to be the official capital of Israel. Since that time, the nations of the world have gone into a literal prophetic tailspin of rage—foretold only in the Word of God. Please remember that when these prophecies were first given, there was no returned Israel in the Middle East, much less Jerusalem being its "capital," or any need for the nations of the earth to surround it and try to "take it back." Again, we are the only generation to see all of these things happening, right before our eyes. How much more proof do we need before God's people, as a whole, will understand the true prophetic nature of our times?

Even More to Come

In addition to the preceding three end-time harbingers, it's also a fact that all of the technologies necessary to fulfill *every one of the last-days prophecies* is now bursting into existence upon our very own generation. There's nothing in the Bible that even hints at some technological marvel of the future that we don't already possess, or that isn't already in the works of being brought forth…*right now*. We are also the first generation to see this phenomenon taking place.[341]

In the midst of all of these things, the spirit of Antichrist is sweeping the entire globe. A huge percentage of the world's population is very aware of this fact, even if they can't put their finger on the genuine biblical reason for it.[342] It's happening through the technologies of instantaneous, 24/7 information and communication. Never before has this been possible… only in our time has it happened.

For example, in 2020, for *the first time* since the birth of the church two thousand years ago, one could hardly find a church service to attend, in person, on that year's Resurrection Sunday. Think of it. That's the one day out of the year that represents Satan's ultimate defeat. And, on that day, in that specific year—and probably beyond—Nachash effectively shut down and drastically "weakened" the church…all over the planet, almost overnight, through a global panic over the *fear of death*.

Through that unprecedented epidemic of fear, the planet further plunged into the downward-spiraling grips of a drug-and-alcohol-addiction epidemic, an epidemic of suicide, and an epidemic of mental disease.[343] And these newest epidemics have been documented by the NIH to have been brought on as a direct result of COVID-19—a virus with a survival rate of well over 99 percent.[344] Most importantly to the prophetic scenario is the fact that through all of this, an outpouring of unprecedented global persecution against the church as a whole has since resulted.[345] This particular worldwide collision of prophetic phenomena also began *only in our historical generation.*

Only in Our Day

Surely, you've noticed how many times I have spoken of our prophetic days as being "unprecedented," and of the number of monumental "domino-falling" prophecies that have occurred "only in our generation." What is it that Satan appears to possess an intimate understanding of, yet the majority of today's anesthetized church seems to have missed—over and over again?

Now *we know.* God has shown us. He has not left us in the dark. We have the Holy Spirit of truth. He has shown us in His Word, and He speaks to us through our souls, minds, and hearts...through heavenly foretastes of what is to come.

For you know very well that the day of the Lord will come like a thief in the night. While people are saying, **"Peace and safety,"** destruction will come on them suddenly, as labor pains on a pregnant woman, and they will not escape.

But you, brothers and sisters, are not in darkness so that this day should surprise you like a thief. You are all children of the light and children of the day. We do not belong to the night or to the darkness.

So then, let us not be like others, who are asleep, but **let us be awake and sober.** For those who sleep, sleep at night, and those who get drunk, get drunk at night. But since **we belong to the day**, let us be sober, putting on faith and love as a breastplate, and the hope of salvation as a helmet.

For God did not appoint us to suffer wrath but to receive salvation through our Lord Jesus Christ. He died for us so that, whether we are awake or asleep, we may live together with him. **Therefore encourage one another** and build each other up, just as in fact you are doing. (1 Thessalonians 5:2–11; emphasis added)

Look at those last words again, from 1 Thessalonians 5: "Therefore **encourage** one another!"

We have this hope, because we have *seen* the truth of the meaning of genuine life. We've seen it through spiritual eyes and observed it with a spiritual mind...guided by the Holy Spirit of truth.

We belong to the "day," therefore we are given these divine hints of His rapidly approaching glory and victory.

70

THE CHOSEN ONES

We are the Noahs of our day...building the ark of God's salvation.

Here's the ultimate truth of the matter: *There's another world coming!*
All things will be made new. Our Creator is going to make everything *right* for His children. The entirety of what this fallen world has stolen from us will be gloriously restored—no more pain, crying, mourning, or death. The old order of things will pass away. Any sacrifices we have to make now in order to lay hold of these promises in Jesus Christ will be, in the end, eternally worth it!

In that day, our hungering and thirsting for righteousness, justice, and truth will be forever satiated. Oh, what a magnificent day that will be! In the meantime, we must remain faithful. And vigilant. And aware.

Don't give up. *Fight the fight. Finish the race. Keep the faith.*

And think of this! We are here, on this earth, during a specifically appointed time that was created just for us! God Himself determined the very days of your life—even the length of your days. He determined in which age of human history that you were to be born. And, He alone decided where *you* would live and how long you would be given to make your "eternal mark" for the glory of the coming Kingdom of God.[346]

One more thing. He also brought you and me to be here, together, in these days, at this time, and for this one great and glorious purpose: to be His representatives—His royally appointed ambassadors—and to declare His eternal glory that is soon to be revealed from Heaven! Have a look at this promise for yourself:

> **The God who made the world and everything that is in it,** since He is Lord of heaven and earth, does not dwell in temples made by hands; nor is He served by human hands, as though He needed anything, since **He Himself gives to all people life and breath and all things;** and He made from one man every nation of mankind to live on all the face of the earth, **having determined their appointed times and the boundaries of their habitation,** that they would seek God, if perhaps **they might feel around for Him and find Him,** though He is not far from each one of us; for **in Him we live and move and exist.** (Acts 17:24–28, NASB; emphasis added)[347]

Now it's *our turn* to shine for the Kingdom! We are emissaries of the glorious, life-changing gospel of Jesus Christ. This is the reason for our next breath, our next heartbeat! We are the *Noahs* of our day…building the ark of God's salvation—holding out the gospel of Jesus Christ—in front of the entire world before it's too late—before the floods of destruction descend upon the planet. We are the *Lots* of this age. As the world around us spirals into darkness, we are to hold steady and shine the light of Truth. We are the *Esthers* for our time. We will boldly confront the powers of darkness and deceit with the guidance of the Holy Spirit's wisdom, understanding that we have been raised up "for such a time as this."

Furthermore, just as Mary and Joseph were chosen by Heaven to play their parts in the Kingdom work, we now are the *chosen ones*! Like them! In every single biblical prophecy of the last days that has come about in our own lifetimes, those prophecies were *about us*, in much the same way that Micah 4 and 5 were about Mary and Joseph!

Meditate on that great biblical truth for just a moment. We are the ones carrying the precious cargo of our day, the gospel of Jesus Christ, and the warning message that the soon-coming King of Kings is on His way!

This earthly existence can be wonderful, to be sure, even in its fallen state. And life itself is so very important as well. But at the end of it all, *this life* is not the "final purpose" of everything. There's more to come—so much more! And to keep us going straight and strong in the midst of it, the Word of God assures us that as we faithfully progress, with our eyes fixed upon Jesus, from time to time we'll be given marvelous, indescribable, and amazingly refreshing *glimpses of glory*. We have not been left alone! He wants you to know He's there! He wants you to know that you are loved by Him.[348]

It is my prayer that this book has played a part in providing some of those divine glimpses for you, by illuminating them within the theater of your mind and soul.

Thank you for taking this journey with me. I am deeply honored that you have done so. If this biblical excursion has blessed you at all, please share it with others.

In the meantime—because of Yeshua, I'll see you there, on that *Day* around the throne, surrounded by the crystal sea and ten thousand times ten thousand angels shouting the praises of the Lamb of God. That's the *Day* when our faith will be made *sight!* On that *Day*, we shall see Him, and all that He has made, as it truly is!

Every bit of that glory is just behind an interdimensional barrier...a divine veil. *Even now.*

Do you *see* it?

Jesus Christ holds the key to all of it—to every single dimension of His resplendently intricate and utterly indescribable creation. You can trust Him in this! It is the central message of the entire Word of God.

A gloriously eternal life is waiting for you.

Especially for you...

In Paradise.

~o

I consider that our present sufferings are not worth comparing with the glory that will be revealed in us. The creation waits in eager expectation for the sons of God to be revealed. For the creation was subjected to frustration, not by its own choice, but by the will of the one who subjected it, in hope that the creation itself will be liberated from its bondage to decay and brought into the glorious freedom of the children of God. (Romans 8:18–21)

ABOUT THE AUTHOR

Carl Gallups has been the senior pastor of Hickory Hammock Baptist Church in Milton, Florida, since 1987. He is a graduate of the Florida Law Enforcement Officer Academy, Florida State University (BSC in criminology), and New Orleans Baptist Theological Seminary (MDiv in theology), and has served on the board of regents at the University of Mobile in Mobile, Alabama, since 2000.

He is a former decorated Florida law enforcement officer, having served under three sheriffs with two different offices, and has worked in an administrative capacity in the Central Office of the Florida Department of Corrections in Tallahassee.

Pastor Gallups is also a critically acclaimed, Amazon Top 60 bestselling author, an internationally known talk-radio host since 2002, and a regular guest on numerous television and radio programs. He is a frequent guest speaker at national prophecy and Bible conferences. He has preached the gospel of Jesus Christ on three continents and in four nations, including Peru and Israel, and all over the United States—including Hawaii and Alaska. He has also preached, on several occasions, in the Canadian provinces of British Colombia, Alberta, and Ontario.

He lives in Milton, Florida, with his beloved wife, Pam. You can find more information about him at www.carlgallups.com.

Carl's *life promise* Scripture is Romans 8:28, 31:

And we know that in all things God works for the good of those who love him, who have been called according to his purpose.... What, then, shall we say in response to these things? If God is for us, who can be against us?

THE SECOND COMING OF SATURN

by Derek P. Gilbert

Following are just a few delectable excerpts from Derek Gilbert's *Saturn's Reign*, hopefully giving you a taste of what you'll experience when you read it.

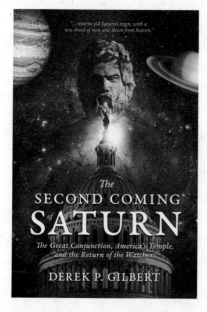

The movement of the planets and the stars across the sky do not have any influence on our lives whatsoever. But *important people believe they do*, so it's worth paying attention. We want to understand what the enemy—by which I mean fallen angels and demons who have been worshiped by pagans for thousands of years—wants them, and us, to think.

If this sounds to you like a fanciful conflation of the Bible with a hodgepodge of ancient myths and legends, you would have been among a small minority in the early church. Christians during the first few centuries after the Resurrection knew that the gods of their pagan neighbors were fallen angels and demons....

The goal of this book is to shed some light on a powerful, supernatural rebel who continues to influence the world today. We'll examine what the ancients believed about this entity and share some surprising examples of how he is still venerated.

Interested yet? Just wait!

NOTES

1. The uniqueness and exactness of this prophesied "manger's" location is revealed in a subsequent chapter of this book. Regarding the child being protected by angels, see examples at Matthew 1:20ff, 4:11; and Luke 22:41–43.

2. 1 Corinthians 2:7–8: "No, we declare God's wisdom, a mystery that has been hidden and that God destined for our glory before time began. None of the rulers of this age understood it, for if they had, they would not have crucified the Lord of glory."

3. See Numbers 2:21–24.

4. *The Biblical Illustrator*: "**The first Adam** fell from the garden into the wilderness; the **Second Adam** rose from the wilderness to the garden. **Christ began where Adam ended, and ended where Adam began**. Adam armed death with his sting; Christ has taken away the sting of death" (emphasis added).
See: John 19:41. *The Biblical Illustrator*, Studylight.org, https://www.studylight.org/commentary/john/19-41.html.

5. Revelation 13:8: "All inhabitants of the earth will worship the beast—all whose names have not been written in the Lamb's book of life, **the Lamb who was slain from the creation of the world**" (emphasis added).

6. For the distinct biblical possibility of Gethsemane's relationship (direct or indirect) to the original Garden of Eden, see the following scholarly evidences:

    1) See: Gallups, Carl. *Gods of Ground Zero: The Truth of Eden's Iniquity.* (Crane, MO: Defender, 2018) chapter 39, "Garden of Sorrows."

    2) *The Biblical Illustrator*: "The first **Adam fell from the garden** into the wilderness; the Second Adam rose from the wilderness to the garden. **Christ began where Adam ended, and ended where Adam began**. Adam armed death with his sting; Christ has taken away the sting of death" (emphasis added)." https://www.studylight.org/commentary/john/19-41.html.

3) *The Pulpit Commentary*: "John alone tells us of the "garden;" and he clearly saw the *significance of the resemblance* to the "garden" *where Christ agonized* unto death, and *was betrayed with a kiss*, and *also to the garden where the first Adam* fell from the high estate of *posse non peccare* [created without sin]" (emphasis added). https://biblehub.com/commentaries/john/19-41.htm.

4) *MacLaren's Expositions*: "We think of Eden and the first coming of death.... The grave in the garden reversed Adam's bringing of death into Eden." https://biblehub.com/commentaries/john/19-41.htm.

5) *Coffman Commentaries on the Bible*: "Thus the Second Adam slept in a garden, associating the redemption of the race with a garden, even as the fall of the first Adam had occurred in a garden." https://www.studylight.org/commentaries/eng/bcc/john-19.html.

6) *A. W. Pink's Commentary*: "Beautifully suggestive is the reference to the 'garden.' It was in a 'garden' that the first Adam sowed the seed which issued in death; so here, in a 'garden' was sown the Seed which was to bear much fruit in immortal life. In the 'new' sepulcher 'wherein was never yet man laid' we have the fulfillment of still another type: 'And a man that is clean shall gather up the ashes of the heifer (previously slain) and lay them up without the camp in a clean place' (Numbers 19:9). https://www.studylight.org/commentary/john/19-41.html.

7) Dr. Thomas Constable: "The fall of the first Adam took place in a garden; and it was in a garden that the second Adam redeemed mankind from the consequences of Adam's transgression." https://www.studylight.org/commentary/john/19-41.html.

8) *Lange's Commentary on the Holy Scriptures: Critical, Doctrinal and Homiletical*: "John 19:41. A sepulcher in a garden, to expiate Adam's sin committed in a garden." https://www.studylight.org/commentary/john/19-41.html.

9) *Peter Pett's Commentary on the Bible*: "The fact that it was in a garden reminds us that when man first sinned that too was in a garden. Now a garden was seeing the death of the second Adam, He through whose coming sacrifice the first Adam had been spared." https://www.studylight.org/commentary/john/19-41.html.

10) Dr. Ernest L. Martin (PhD): "Using **the Land of Eden** in its symbolic fashion, this meant the [Mount of Olives and the altar of the Red

Heifer Sacrifice] was situated "without **the Land of Eden**" and on **its east side.** Where was this altar situated in **relationship to the Temple?** In the time of Jesus, Jewish records show that this outer altar was **located near the southern summit of the Mount of Olives** directly east of the Temple. It was also positioned just "outside the Camp" of Israel, **which made it to be analogous to being just "outside the Land of Eden."** …at the **eastern entrance (door) to Eden"** (emphasis added).
See: Dr. Ernest L. Martin (PhD). *Secrets of Golgotha: The Lost History of Jesus' Crucifixion* (Second Edition), Academy for Scriptural; 2nd edition (June 1, 1996), Read the entire book online here: https://www.askelm.com/golgotha/Golgotha%20Chap%2000. pdf.

11) Although I am personally convinced of the great potential of it, we cannot be dogmatically certain that the Garden of Gethsemane was the exact spot of the original Garden sin. However, the spiritual connections between the Garden of Eden, the Garden of Gethsemane, and the garden area associated with Calvary (John 19:41), the Mount of Olives, and the Garden Tomb have been documented by renowned scholars for many centuries years, as are the facts of Jesus (God with us) being *betrayed* in this spot, just as He (Jesus the Creator) was *betrayed* by Satan in the Garden of Eden. For further research concerning these truths, the reader is encouraged to see following excellent resources:

12) Porat, Zev. *Unmasking the Chaldean Spirit.* (Crane, MO: Defender Publishing, publication date pending).

13) Chaffey, Tim. "The Good Shepherd and the Three Gardens," Answers in Genesis, 4/9/13, https://answersingenesis.org/jesus-christ/ resurrection/good-shepherd-three-gardens.

14) Bradharte. "The 4 Hidden Meanings of Gardens in the Bible That Will Empower You," 7/6/15, https://ccsouthbay.org/blog/ the-4-hidden-meanings-of-gardens.

15) Our Daily Bread. "Two Gardens," April 17, 2006, https://odb. org/2006/04/17/two-gardens.

7. The Mount of Olives stands 2,652 feet high, overlooking the entire city proper of Jerusalem. It's several hundred feet higher than Mt. Zion's highest peak.

Encyclopedia.com. "Mount of Olives (Olivet)," accessed 6/1/21. https://
www.encyclopedia.com/philosophy-and-religion/bible/biblical-proper-names/
mount-olives.

8. There actually *is* a huge rock in the Garden of Gethsemane. Its presence is a
fact of history, geology, and archeology, and it is currently enshrined (for better
or for worse) under the covering of the Church of All Nations, on the Mount
of Olives, at the Garden of Gethsemane. The rock is thus set apart precisely
because it has long been held by a majority of the Christian world to be the
exact spot where Jesus agonized. It is called the Rock of Agony.
See: "Church of All Nations," Wikipedia. Accessed April 12, 2021, https://
en.wikipedia.org/wiki/Church_of_All_Nations#:~:text=The%20Church%20
of%20All%20Nations,have%20prayed%20before%20his%20arrest.%20(.

9. Solomon's outrage on the Mount of Olives: "On a hill east of Jerusalem,
Solomon built a high place for Chemosh the detestable god of Moab, and for
Molek the detestable god of the Ammonites" (1 Kings 11:7–8).
Gill's Exposition of the Entire Bible: "A high place for which he ordered to be
built, or at least suffered it to be built, at the instigation of his Moabitish woman
or women, 1 Kings 11:1, this was built in the hill that is before Jerusalem;
on the mount of Olives, as Jarchi, called from hence afterwards the mount of
corruption, 2 Kings 23:15 and for Molech, the abomination of the children of
Ammon, 1 Kings 11:5."

10. *Nachash*. The Hebrew word for "serpent, or snake." It can be used of the
actual reptile, or of a person. As in "that old snake is constantly lying about
me!" In this case it is definitely used in the second manner. See Revelation 12:9
and the next note.

11. Revelation 12:9 definitively settles the matter. Satan has never "entered"
a snake. Neither did Satan cause a snake in the Garden of Eden to walk and
talk. The word "serpent" is a metaphor for Satan. So is the word "dragon,"
according to Revelation. Yet, we never find in any biblical passage where Satan
enters a literal dragon and causes it to walk and talk. Just like Jesus is called the
Lion of Judah, or the Lamb of God, yet never "became" a lion, and neither was
it a real lamb that was nailed to the cross. The notion that it was a talking snake
in the Garden of Eden is simply a matter of very poor biblical interpretation.
We call Satan a snake or a serpent in the same way we might say of a human
being: "that old serpent has slipped in among us!" or "That lying snake!" Never
would we intend to mean that a person had become a literal snake, or was
somehow inhabiting that snake.

Revelation 12:9: "The great dragon was hurled down—that ancient serpent called the devil, or Satan, who leads the whole world astray. He was hurled to the earth, and his angels with him."

For further detailed proof of this matter, please see my book *Gods of Ground Zero: The Truth of Eden's Iniquity* (Crane, MO: Defender Publishing, 2018).

12. Ezekiel 28:13–15.

13. *Yeshua* is Hebrew, rendered in English as "Jesus." *Yeshua* means "salvation."

14. Isaiah 34:4; Revelation 6:14; Hebrews 10:19–21.

15. Villines, Zawn. "Hematidrosis (sweating blood): Causes and Treatments," *Medical News Today*, 8/26/17, https://www.medicalnewstoday.com/articles/319110.php.
Also see: Web MD. "What Is Hematidrosis?" accessed 1/12/19, https://www.webmd.com/a-to-z-guides/hematidrosis-hematohidrosis#1.

16. *Bene Elohim*, Hebrew for "sons of God." Literally an angel. See Luke 22:43 for the appearance of this angel in the Garden of Gethsemane.

17. See Hebrews 10:19–21.

18. "A Roman Legion at the time of Jesus was six thousand soldiers and they were very well trained men. Therefore twelve legions of angels would have been seventy-two thousand angels. And we don't have any idea more legions He could have called. But Jesus said the Father would give Him more than twelve legions of angels; therefore, you can conclude that there were potentially many additional thousands of angels available to Jesus the night He was arrested."
Greenfield, Mike. "12 Legions of Angels," 8/18/20, https://widjiitiwin.ca/12-legions-of-angels.

19. Hebrews 4:15: "For we do not have a high priest who is unable to empathize with our weaknesses, but we have one who has been tempted in every way, just as we are—yet he did not sin."

20. While the biblical text doesn't specifically speak of the physical appearance of Satan in the Garden of Gethsemane, it is a contextual probability, and one that makes perfect theological sense for at least four reasons:

1. Satan certainly showed up in person at the wilderness temptation; why not here as well?

2. The Bible says that Satan "entered into Judas" for the purpose of getting Jesus crucified. That had been just hours before Gethsemane.

3. Judas, filled with Satan, was the one leading the way for the Temple

guard on that night. So, at least in that moment, "Satan" was indeed there.

4. Jesus was struggling with a satanic battle of temptation in that garden prayer time, like at no other time of biblically recorded temptations. He sweat drops of blood as He struggled with Satan's continual pummeling. Why else would He cry out "Not my will, but Thine!"? Therefore, for the purposes of this narrative, I have chosen to personify that temptation in the physical appearance of Satan, the ultimate adversary to the throne of God.

21. In following chapters, this assertion will be biblically and scientifically addressed.

22. Ezekiel 28:14–15: "You were anointed as a guardian cherub, for so I ordained you. You were on the holy mount of God; you walked among the fiery stones. You were blameless in your ways from the day you were created till wickedness was found in you."

23. The offers that Satan makes to Jesus here are, of course, fictional as far as the written biblical text goes. However, these are the same categories of temptations that Satan presented to Jesus in the wilderness three years back. In that temptation, the Bible says that Satan left Him for a more "opportune" time. I have placed that opportune time here, in Gethsemane—the most opportune time of all, right up to the cross.

24. Reversing the curse: The Second Adam: "But Christ has indeed been raised from the dead, the firstfruits of those who have fallen asleep. For since death came through a man, the resurrection of the dead comes also through a man. For as in Adam all die, so in Christ all will be made alive" (1 Corinthians 15:20–22).

"And so it is written, 'The first man Adam became a living being'"
The last Adam became a life-giving spirit" (1 Corinthians 15:45).

"Nevertheless death reigned from Adam to Moses, even over those who had not sinned according to the likeness of the transgression of Adam, who is a type of [Jesus] who was to come" (Romans 15:12–15).

25. *The Biblical Illustrator*: "The first Adam fell from the garden into the wilderness; the Second Adam rose from the wilderness to the garden. Christ began where Adam ended, and ended where Adam began. Adam armed death with his sting; Christ has taken away the sting of death."

See: John 19:41. "The Biblical Illustrator," Studylight.org, https://www.
studylight.org/commentary/john/19-41.html.
Ibid. "For the distinct biblical possibility of Gethsemane's relationship to the
Garden of Eden, see the following evidences."
26. Luke 22:3; also see Matthew 23:45.
27. There exists a huge body of scholarly evidence that this place called
Golgotha was located on the Mount of Olives. The Old Testament and the New
Testament actually point vividly to this location as the place. This fact opens
up all manner of additional biblical revelations and connections. Following are
four examples of scholarly attestations in this matter:

1) Dr. James Tabor: "*The basic case for the Mt. of Olives being the site of
   Jesus' crucifixion* rests on several interrelated arguments The first, and
   in my view, the most weighty, is a passage in the New Testament book
   of Hebrews (13:10–13)."
   See: Dr. James D. Tabor. "Locating Golgotha: Archeology," 2/26/16,
   https://jamestabor.com/locating-golgotha.
   Dr. James D. Tabor bio: "James D. Tabor served as Chair (2004–2014)
   of the Department of Religious Studies at the University of North
   Carolina, where he has taught since 1989. He is currently Professor of
   ancient Judaism and early Christianity. Previously he held positions
   at the University of Notre Dame and the College of William and
   Mary. He received his Ph.D. from the University of Chicago in
   1981 in Ancient Mediterranean Religions." https://jamestabor.com/
   about-dr-tabor/.

2) Dr. Douglas Jacoby: "**No need to follow the crowds.** There will be
   little need to 'compete' with the 'tour groups' down the traditional
   Via Dolorosa and inside the Church of the Holy Sepulcher, since we
   recognize that they are well over a kilometer from **the true site of the
   crucifixion, on the Mount of Olives.**"
   See: Dr. Douglas Jacoby. "The Red Heifer Sacrifice and the
   Crucifixion." (1997, Revised 2001). https://www.douglasjacoby.com/
   the-red-heifer-sacrifice-and-the-crucifixion.
   Dr. Douglas Jacoby bio: "Douglas Jacoby is a Bible teacher who
   has served as a minister on church staff for 20 years, in London,
   Birmingham, Sydney, Stockholm, Philadelphia, Indianapolis, and
   Washington, DC. He also serves as adjunct professor of theology at
   Lincoln Christian University and professor of theology in the Rocky

Mountain School of Theology and Ministry. With degrees from Drew, Harvard, and Duke, Douglas has written 35 books, recorded nearly 900 podcasts, and spoken in over 100 universities, and in over 500 cities, in 126 nations around the world. Douglas has led 25 tours to the biblical world." https://www.douglasjacoby.com/about

3) Dr. Ernest Martin: "There is no longer any doubt. **Jesus was crucified near the summit of the Mount of Olives about half a mile east of the Temple Mount**. This fact is confirmed in the New Testament in a variety of ways.... In fact...the Book of Hebrews...[was to the early church] sufficient to pinpoint the region where the crucifixion of Jesus took place."

See: Dr. Ernest L. Martin (PhD). "Secrets of Golgotha: The Lost History of Jesus' Crucifixion" (Second Edition), Academy for Scriptural; 2nd edition (June 1, 1996) 14–15. Read the entire book online here: https://www.askelm.com/golgotha/Golgotha%20Chap%2000.pdf.

Dr. Ernest Martin bio: "From 1960 to 1972, Dr. Martin taught history, theology and elementary meteorology at the Ambassador College campus in Bricket Wood, England where he became Dean of Faculty. He earned his Ph.D. at Ambassador College.

"Between 1969 and 1973, Ambassador College entered into an alliance with Hebrew University in Israel which had been negotiated by Dr. Martin. This undertaking commenced a five-year archaeological program with students from Ambassador College working on Dr. Benjamin Mazar's excavation near the Western Wall of the Temple Mount. During this period, Martin supervised 450 participating college students during summer months. The partnership was mentioned in a *Time* magazine article. ["Education: Digging for Credit". 3 September 1973—via content.time.com.].

"Following the eventual closure of the Ambassador College campus in England, Martin became Chairman of the Department of Theology at Ambassador College in Pasadena, California, in 1973. Dr. Martin was a dear friend of the famed and deeply conservative theologian, commentary writer, and **biblical scholar F. F. Bruce**." (See documentation of this fact: "Secrets of Golgotha: The Lost History of Jesus' Crucifixion," Second Edition, Chapter 29, p. 412).

4) For an outstandingly unique and extremely in-depth study of this

topic see: Messianic Rabbi Zev Porat. *Unmasking the Chaldean Spirit* (Crane, MO: Defender Publishing, publication date pending).

28. A fictional character inserted by the author into the narrative to make it a bit more personal in feel.

29. Equivalent with our noon. By ancient Hebrew reckoning, the day started with the first hour—6 a.m. Jesus was crucified at the third hour—about 9 a.m. The sixth hour would then have been three hours later...noon.

30. All three of the synoptic Gospels records the event of the supernatural nature of this heavy darkness, lasting from noon until 3 p.m. Several ancient records report this unique darkening of the sun, including writings from Phlegon, the astronomer and freedman of Adrian, cited by Origen, as well as Tertullian and Eusebius. Some even mention the accompanying earthquake cited by the New Testament as well.

Benson Commentary: "Eusebius, in his Chronicle, at the eighteenth year of Tiberius, says, 'Christ suffered this year, in which time we find in other commentaries of the heathen, these words: "There was a defection of the sun: Bithynia was shaken with an earthquake; and many houses fell down in the city of Nice." https://biblehub.com/commentaries/matthew/27-45.htm.

31. Matthew 21:5; Zechariah 9:9; Psalm 118.

32. Tiberius was the stepson of Caesar Augustus (Gaius Octavius), grand-uncle of Caligula, paternal uncle of Claudius, and great-grand-uncle of Nero. He reigned for twenty-two and a half years in Rome. His reign, after Augustus, would be the longest for the next 120 years of Roman history.

33. John 18:14.

34. John 1:46.

Pulpit Commentary: "The 'good thing' may, however, be the contrast between the unimportance of the place in the political or religious history of the people, as compared with Jerusalem, Tiberius, Jericho, Bethlehem. It is never mentioned in the Old Testament or in Josephus. Nathanael may have known its mediocrity, and have been startled by the possibility of a carpenter's son, in a spot utterly undistinguished, being the Messiah of whom their sacred writers spoke."

35. *Adonai.* The Hebrew word for Lord. In this context, the use of it was an acknowledgment of the thief's belief that Jesus was indeed Lord and Savior— the Messiah.

36. (Paradise): The second sentence of the statement that I used in this chapter does not appear in the original biblical text. It was added here for contextual

illumination. This is because the word "paradise" comes from a very specific Greek word used only three times in the New Testament (Luke 23:43; 2 Corinthians 12:4; Revelation 2:7). **Each time it means** the same—**the Garden of Eden**—which still exists behind the veil of a dimensional divide. See the following:

Thayer's Greek Lexicon ("Paradise"): "This word (NT: 3857 PARADISE—*paradeisos*) means: 'Universally, **a garden**, pleasure-ground; grove, park…that delightful region, **"the garden of Eden," in which our first parents dwelt before the fall.**' The dying Jewish thief would have been very familiar with its contextual meaning." https://biblehub.com/greek/3857.htm.

Gill's Exposition of the Scriptures: "**Verily I say unto thee**, today thou shall be **with me in paradise; 'in the garden of Eden'**; not the earthly paradise, nor the church militant, but the future place, and state of the happiness of the saints, **even heaven**, and **eternal glory**, which **the Jews frequently call by this name.** https://biblehub.com/commentaries/luke/23-43.htm.

Cambridge Bible for Schools and Colleges: "[The word "paradise" here] is used for **the Garden of Eden.**" https://biblehub.com/commentaries/luke/23-43.htm.

Pulpit Commentary: "**Paradise.** In the ordinary language used by the Jews, of the unseen world, **it signifies the 'Garden of Eden,'** or **'Abraham's bosom.'** https://biblehub.com/commentaries/luke/23-43.htm.

Ellicott's Commentary for the English Reader: "In the figurative language in which the current Jewish belief clothed its thoughts of the unseen world, **the Garden of Eden** took its place side by side with **'Abraham's bosom,'** as a synonym for the eternal blessedness of the righteous, presenting a vivid contrast to the foul horrors of Gehenna. https://biblehub.com/commentaries/luke/23-43.htm.

Benson Commentary: "The paradise of God, Revelation 2:7, **alluding** to…the **Garden of Eden**, in which **our first parents were placed**, when they were innocent. It is termed **Abraham's bosom**, in the story of Lazarus." https://biblehub.com/commentaries/luke/23-43.htm.

Vincent's Word Studies: "In Paradise. **The Garden of Eden**. In the Jewish theology, the department of Hades **where the blessed souls await the resurrection**; and therefore **equivalent to Abraham's bosom** (Luke 16:22, Luke 16:23)." https://biblehub.com/commentaries/luke/23-43.htm.

37. Ibid., ("Paradise").

38. Jesus died at exactly the ninth hour, according to the Scriptures. That hour

corresponds to our 3 p.m. It was at that hour that the last *tamid* (daily) *sacrifice* in the Temple was being completed. At the moment Jesus cried out "It is finished!" and then "willed" the moment of His death, the Lamb of God had been sacrificed—just when the *tamid* sacrifice in the Temple was also being completed.

Torah Life Ministry. "The Unique Tamid Sacrifice—Why does it Matter?" Torahlifeministry.com, 9/15/16, https://torahlifeministry.com/blog/item/185-the-unique-tamid-sacrifice-why-does-it-matter.html.

39. Concerning the immediacy of the word "today":

Pulpit Commentary: "**Not in the far-off** 'coming,' but **on that very day**... would be in closest **companionship with him...not, in some far-off time** in the midst of the awful tumult of the bloody and fiery dawn of the judgment advent, **but almost directly** in the fair garden…. There, in company **with his Lord**, would the tortured condemned find himself **in a few short hours**." https://biblehub.com/commentaries/luke/23-43.htm.

Bengel's Gnomen: "Today, is ***not to be referred (joined) to the verb, 'I say,'*** as if the robber **should have to wait for his entrance into Paradise** during I know not how long periods of time. That the words were spoken to him **on that day**, is of itself evident (without it being necessary to say so). Therefore **we must read the words thus, '*Today shalt thou be*** with Me in paradise.' Thus the power and grace of the Lord, and also His own ready **and immediate entrance into Paradise**, is **openly declared**." https://biblehub.com/commentaries/luke/23-43.htm.

40. See my book, *Gods of Ground Zero: The Truth of Eden's Iniquity* (Crane, MO: Defender Publishing, 2018), for an in-depth study of the meaning of "Paradise." A truly shocking revelation.

41. Lim, Eugene. "The Theory of Parallel Universes Is Not Just Math—It Is Science That Can Be Tested," PHYS.org, 9/3/15, https://phys.org/news/2015-09-theory-parallel-universes-maths-science.html.

42. String field theory—the scientific theory that multiple universes and dimensions truly exist. See: Siegel, Ethan. "What Every Layperson Should Know about String Theory," *Forbes*, 11/25/16, https://www.forbes.com/sites/startswithabang/2016/11/25/what-every-layperson-should-know-about-string-theory/?sh=43e1a0e15a53.

43. In physical cosmology, cosmic inflation, cosmological inflation, or just *inflation* is a theory of exponential expansion of space in the early universe.

Following the inflationary period, the universe continued to expand, but at a slower rate.
See: "First Second of the Big Bang." *How The Universe Works* 3. 2014. Discovery Science, https://en.wikipedia.org/wiki/How_the_Universe_Works#Season_3.

44. Warmflash, David. "Three Totally Mind-bending Implications of a Multidimensional Universe," *Discover Magazine*, 12/04/14, http://blogs.discovermagazine.com/crux/2014/12/04/multidimensional-universe/#.W9uSRJNKhdg.

45. Dr. Kaku holds the Henry Semat Chair and professorship in theoretical physics and a joint appointment at City College of New York and the Graduate Center of City University of New York.

46. Freudenrich, Craig, PhD. "What Are the Four Fundamental Forces of Nature?" *Science*, accessed 11/3/18, https://science.howstuffworks.com/environmental/earth/geophysics/fundamental-forces-of-nature.htm.

47. Kaku, Micho. "Nobel Prize Awarded to Two Quantum Physicists," *Big Think*, 10/10/12, https://bigthink.com/dr-kakus-universe/nobel-prize-awarded-to-two-quantum-physicists.

48. Williams, Matt. "A Universe of 10 Dimensions," 12/11/14, PHYS.org, https://phys.org/news/2014-12-universe-dimensions.html.
Also see: Glanz, J. 1997. "Strings Unknot Problems in Particle Theory, Black Holes." *Science,* 276:1969–1970.
Also see: Kestenbaum, D. 1998. "Practical Tests for an 'Untestable' Theory of Everything?" *Science,* 281:758–759.

49. CERN is the European Organization for Nuclear Research. The name CERN is derived from the acronym for the French *Conseil Européen pour la Recherche Nucléaire*, a provisional body founded in 1952 with the mandate of establishing a world-class fundamental physics research organization in Europe. https://en.wikipedia.org/wiki/CERN.

50. Ibid. Cern. "The Large Hadron Collider."

51. Milton-Barker, Adam. "How CERN Plan to Use the Large Hadron Collider to Open Portals to Other Dimensions, and Possibly Already Have." Techbubble.info, 5/4/15. https://www.techbubble.info/blog/quantum-physics/entry/how-cern-plan-to-use-the-large-hydrogen-collider-to-open-portals-to-other-dimensions.

52. Page, Lewis. "'Something May Come through' Dimensional 'Doors' at LHC," *The Register*, 10/6/09. https://www.theregister.co.uk/2009/11/06/lhc_dimensional_portals.

This Bertolucci quote was reported all over the Internet, including through *Charisma Magazine* and *Breaking Israel News*. I am not aware of any reputable source that claims Bertolucci or CERN denies the veracity of the quote.

53. Deuteronomy 32:17: "**They sacrificed to demons** that were no gods [*elohim*], to gods [*elohim*] they had never known, to new gods [*elohim*] that had come recently, whom your fathers had never dreaded." (Emphasis added)

54. Tate, Karl. "How Quantum Entanglement Works (Infographic)." Live Science, 4/8/13, https://www.livescience.com/28550-how-quantum-entanglement-works-infographic.html.

55. *Universitat Autonoma de Barcelona.* "Record Quantum Entanglement of Multiple Dimensions," PHYS.org, 3/27/14, https://phys.org/news/2014-03-quantum-entanglement-multiple-dimensions.html.

56. Kaku, Micho. "4 Things That Currently Break the Speed of Light Barrier," Big Think, 11/9/10, https://bigthink.com/dr-kakus-universe/what-travels-faster-than-the-speed-of-light.

57. Alamanou, Marina. "The Applications of Quantum Entanglement," Data Drive Investor, 6/20/29, https://www.datadriveninvestor.com/2019/06/20/quantum-entanglement.

58. Hebrews 11.

59. "They will look upon me, whom they will pierce…"
Cambridge Bible for Schools and Colleges: "The Speaker is Almighty God. … They pierced Him, literally and as the crowning act of their contumacy, in the Person of His Son upon the Cross, John 19:37. Comp. Revelation 1:7."
Pulpit Commentary: "There was a literal fulfilment of this piercing, i.e. slaying (Zechariah 13:3; Lamentations 4:9), when the Jews crucified the Messiah, him who was God and Man, and of whom, as a result of the hypostatic union, the properties of one nature are often predicated of the other. Thus Paul says that the Jews crucified 'the Lord of glory' (1 Corinthians 2:8), and bids the Ephesian elders 'feed the Church of God, which he hath purchased with his own blood'" (Acts 20:28).
For the foregoing quotes from the *Cambridge* and *Pulpit* commentaries, see: Zechariah 12:10, "Commentaries," Biblehub.com, https://biblehub.com/commentaries/zechariah/12-10.htm.

60. James Burton Coffman (May 24, 1905–June 30, 2006) was known for his exhaustive writing and study of Old Testament and New Testament Scriptures. Throughout his life, he served as a preacher, teacher, author of biblical

commentaries, and community leader. Most of his career defined him as a teacher and administrator in school systems, congregational contexts, and as a military chaplain.

61. Zechariah 12:10. *Coffman Commentaries on the Bible*, Studylight.org, https://www.studylight.org/commentary/zechariah/12-10.html.

62. Dr. Constable is the founder of Dallas Seminary's Field Education department (1970) and the Center for Biblical Studies (1973), both of which he directed for many years before assuming other responsibilities. Dr. Constable served as senior professor of Bible Exposition, Dallas Theological Seminary. https://www.logos.com/search?filters=author-15793_Author&sortBy=Relevance&limit=30&page=1&ownership=all&geographicAvailability=all.

63. Zechariah 12:10. *Expository Notes of Dr. Thomas Constable*, Studylight. org, https://www.studylight.org/commentary/zechariah/12-10.html.

64. *Cambridge Bible for Schools and Colleges*: "**The Speaker is Almighty God**… They **pierced Him, literally** [it was "literally" the Almighty, not metaphorically] and as the crowning act of their contumacy, **in the Person** [in flesh and blood] **of His Son upon the Cross**, John 19:37. Comp. Revelation 1:7. (Emphasis) Zechariah 12:10."
See: Cambridge Bible for Schools and Colleges, Biblehub.com, https://biblehub.com/commentaries/zechariah/12-10.htm.

Pulpit Commentary: "The Speaker is Jehovah. But there was *a literal fulfilment* of *this piercing*, i.e. slaying (Zechariah 13:3; Lamentations 4:9), when the Jews crucified the *Messiah*, him *who was God and Man,* and of whom, as a result of the hypostatic union [the union of the divine and human natures into one singular being—at one time], the properties *of one nature* are *often predicated of the other.*" (Emphasis added)
See: Zechariah 12:10. *Pulpit Commentary*, Biblehub.com, https://biblehub.com/commentaries/zechariah/12-10.htm.

Jamieson-Fausset-Brown Bible Commentary: "**The change of person** is **due to Jehovah-Messiah** [Yahweh in the flesh *is* Messiah, and Messiah *is* Yahweh existing with humanity in the flesh!] **speaking in His own person first**, then the prophet speaking of Him…. **The Hebrew word** is always used of **a literal piercing** (so Zechariah 13:3); **not of a metaphorical piercing.**" (Emphasis added)
See: Zechariah 12:10. *Jamieson-Fausset-Brown Bible Commentary*, Biblehub.com, https://biblehub.com/commentaries/zechariah/12-10.htm.

Gill's Exposition of the Entire Bible: "**The Messiah here** prophesied of

appears to be both God and man; a divine Person called **Jehovah, who is all along speaking in the context**, and in the text itself; for none else could pour out the spirit of grace and supplication; **and yet he must be man, to be pierced**; and the **same is spoken of, that would do the one, and suffer the other; and therefore must be the or God-man in one person**…. And as for **the change from the first person to the third**, this is **not at all unusual in Scripture**."(Emphasis added)

See: Zechariah 12:10. *Gill's Exposition of the Entire Bible*, Biblehub.com, https://biblehub.com/commentaries/zechariah/12-10.htm.

65. This apparent conundrum is called "Hypostatic union" in the realm of theological scholarship: "At no time did Jesus ever cease to be God. Although He was made fully human, there was never a point when He abrogated His divine nature (see Luke 6:5, 8). It is equally true that, after becoming incarnate, the Son has never ceased to be human. As the apostle Paul wrote, 'For there is one God, and there is one mediator between God and men, the man Christ Jesus' (1 Timothy 2:5). Jesus is not half-human and half-divine. Rather, He is *Theanthropos*, the God-man. The Lord Jesus Christ is one eternally divine Person who will forever possess two distinct yet inseparable natures: one divine and one human."

"How Can Jesus Be Both God and Man at the Same Time?" Got Questions, accessed 3/18/21, https://www.gotquestions.org/Jesus-God-man.html.

66. Below are ten striking examples of the biblical representations of multiple dimensions and how they were created by Jesus Christ, and hold together in Him.

"**For Jesus has rescued us from the dominion** [dimension] **of darkness** [the unseen realm of demonic, but physical, reality] and **brought us into the kingdom of the Son** he loves, [into another dimension altogether] in whom we have redemption, the forgiveness of sins. **The Son** is the image of the invisible God [Who came into our physical dimension in earthly flesh], the firstborn over all creation. For **in him** [Jesus, the Son] **all things were created: things in heaven and on earth, visible and invisible** [all of creation is comprised of the dimension we live in and can now see, as well as all the other dimensions of reality that we cannot yet see with our physical eyes], whether **thrones or powers** or **rulers or authorities**; **all things** [All dimensions, and *everything in them] have been created through him and for him. He is before all things, and in him all things hold* *together* [Jesus is the power that holds the multiverse of dimensions together]." (Colossians 1:13–17; emphasis added)

"Jesus answered, '**I am the way** [the door, or the portal; the interdimensional entrance] and the truth and the life. **No one comes** [goes from one dimension to the other] **to the Father** [into Paradise, where God's Kingdom genuinely exists] **except through me'** [because Jesus is the only portal to that dimension]." (John 14:6; emphasis added)

"In the past God spoke to our ancestors through the prophets at many times and in various ways, but in these last days he has spoken to us by his Son, whom he appointed heir of all things, and **through whom also he made the universe**. The Son is the radiance of God's glory and the exact representation of his being, **sustaining all things by his powerful word**." (Hebrews 1:1–3; emphasis added)

"**All things were made by Jesus**, and without Him was not anything made which was made." (John 1:3; emphasis added)

"So the Lord God **banished him from the Garden of Eden** [Paradise] to work the ground from which he had been taken. After he drove the man out, **he placed on the east side of the Garden of Eden cherubim** and a flaming sword flashing back and forth **to guard the way to the tree of life**." (Genesis 3:23–24; emphasis added)

"**I know a man** in Christ who fourteen years ago was **caught up to the third heaven**. Whether it was in the body or out of the body I do not know—God knows. And I know that this man—**whether in the body or apart from the body I do not know,** but God knows—**was caught up to paradise** and heard inexpressible things, **things that no one is permitted to tell**." (2 Corinthians 12:2-4; emphasis added)

"**Whoever has ears, let them hear** what the Spirit says to the churches. To the one who is victorious, I will give the right to eat from **the tree of life, which is in the paradise** of God." (Revelation 2:7; emphasis added)

"With all wisdom and understanding, God made known to us **the mystery of his will** according to his good pleasure, which he purposed in Christ, to be **put into effect when the times reach their** fulfillment—to **bring unity to all things in heaven and on earth under Christ**." (Ephesians 1:8–10; emphasis added)

"Then the angel showed me **the river of the water of life**, as clear as crystal, flowing **from the throne of God and of the Lamb** down the middle of the great street of the city. On each side of the river **stood the tree of life**, bearing twelve crops of fruit, yielding its fruit every month. And the leaves of the tree are for the healing of the nations. **No longer will there be any curse. The throne of God and of the Lamb will be in the city,** and **his servants will serve him. They will see his face**, and his name will be on their foreheads. There will be no more night. They will not need the light of a lamp or the light of the sun, for the Lord God will give them light. **And they will reign for ever and ever.**" (Revelation 22:1–5; emphasis added)

"After this I looked, and there **before me was a door standing open** [a dimensional portal] **in heaven.** And **the voice** I had first heard speaking to me like a trumpet said '**Come up here,** and I will show you what must take place after this.' **At once I was in the Spirit, and there before me was a throne in heaven** [*Paradise*—the same Third Heaven to which Paul was caught up] with someone sitting on it." (Revelation 4:1–2; emphasis added)

67. Main, Douglas. "Expedition Explores World's Deepest Hydrothermal Vents," LiveScience.com, 2/21/13, https://www.livescience.com/27326-deepest-vents-expedition.html.
68. 1 John 5:11; Acts 4:12; John 14:6.
69. Romans 8:29; 2 Corinthians 3:18.
70. Once again, as in the Garden of Gethsemane, the Scriptures do not directly declare that Satan showed up at the scene of the cross. I have chosen to represent the scene that way for the following reasons:

1.   We have now repeatedly demonstrated that Satan is an interdimensional being. There is no doubt that he *could have been* at the cross. And…

2.   Certainly, he would *want* to be there! He was, after all, the one who had entered Judas (Jesus' own words) in order to deliver Him to the cross. Why would he not desire to be there as well? Of course he would.

3.   We also know that Jesus could/can see through any and all of the dimensions of reality at will. He created them.

4. We see Satan "showing up" in multiple realms, for example: In Job 1, at the throne of God, and in Matthew 4 and Luke 4, in the wilderness temptation.

5. We get a potential hint that Jesus "saw" Satan manipulating Peter at Caesarea Philippi (Matthew 16:23) when Jesus looked at Peter, yet seemingly called him "Satan." Jesus used almost the very same words He used with Peter when addressing Satan himself in the wilderness (Matthew 4:10). Observe the two instances:
"Then Jesus says to him, 'Get you away, Satan!' (Matthew 4:10; Berean Literal Bible).
"Jesus turned and said to Peter, 'Get behind me, Satan! You are a stumbling block to me; you do not have in mind the concerns of God, but merely human concerns' (Matthew 16:23).

6. With these things in mind, also remember that just because the text doesn't directly "say" it happened, we cannot automatically assume that it absolutely did not happen, especially if other biblical evidence clearly indicates the very real possibility of the phenomenon occurring. Such is the case with the contextual speculation on my part that I have employed in this narrative section.

71. 1 Corinthians 2:8: "None of the rulers of this age understood it, for if they had, they would not have crucified the Lord of glory."

72. See my book *Masquerade: Preparing for the Greatest Con Job in History* (Crane, MO: Defender Publishing, DATE), wherein I take several chapters to do an in-depth exploration of this biblical truth.

73. To use a football analogy to describe how Satan could be *defeated* at Calvary, yet we still see so much evil and devastation, consider the following. It's the fourth quarter. Your team has 45 points, the other team has 7 points. There's only two minutes left to play in the game. Technically, until the clock stops, a "winner" will not be officially declared. But anyone with any sense at all understands…your team has already won. You are now just "running out the clock." Satan knows his time is up. The clock is merely ticking down to the final buzzer. The game is over. He loses. (See Revelation 12:12)

74. The preincarnate Jesus Christ is the Creator; John 1:3; Colossians 1:16; 1 Corinthians 8:6; John 1:10; Hebrews 1:1–3.

75. Ezekiel 28:12–14.

76. *Elohim* is the second-most prolific name by which the Creator is known in the Bible; the most often used name for God is *Yahweh*. However, *Elohim* is

the first name of God we're introduced to in the Scriptures. Genesis 1:1: "In the beginning, Elohim created the heavens and the earth."

Elohim is often translated as "God" in the English translations. However, it can also be translated as "gods" or "angels," or "divine beings." This is a complex Hebrew word, as the same word can be either singular or plural, depending upon the qualifying words that surround it. In that way, the word is similar in nature to our words "deer," or "buffalo." However, when the word is used in the plural, its proper interpretation is: "divine beings," "angels," "rulers," "the demonic realm," or "gods"—as in "Thou shalt have no other *gods* before me." Please see my book *Gods and Thrones* (Crane, MO: Defender Publishing, 2017) for a detailed scholarly examination of this important Hebrew word and the significance of its proper contextual understanding.

77. Ezekiel 28:13–19.

78. The Divine Council: The biblical understanding of the heavenly "court" of angels that serve as God's witnesses and assistants in the administration of God's decrees throughout His Creation. See my book, *Gods and Thrones*, for an in-depth study of this biblical truth and its eternal ramifications.

"God has taken his place **in the divine council**; in the **midst of the gods** he holds judgment." (Psalm 82:1; emphasis added)

"In the **council of the holy ones** God is greatly feared; he is more awesome than all who surround him" (Psalm 89:7; emphasis added).

79. See my book, *Gods and Thrones*, for a detailed examination of the matter of the Divine Council.

Cherubim "great, mighty" See: OT:3742, *Kerub*. "Brown-Driver-Briggs" (Noun: masculine), https://biblehub.com/hebrew/3742.htm.

Also see: Abarim Publications. "Cherubim Meaning." (See especially the bottom of the page, subsection: "Cherubim Meaning"), Accessed on 11/12/18, http://www.abarim-publications.com/Meaning/Cherubim.html#. W8Jz0WhKhdg.

80. In my book, *Gods and Thrones* (Crane, MO: Defender Publishing, 2017), I undertake a detailed study of the concept of "becoming like us, or like God Himself."

81. In my book, *Masquerade* (Crane, MO: Defender Publishing, 2020), I do a detailed study of the literal musical nature in which Satan's very being was created—according to the truths of God's Word, and borne out through in-depth word studies and the declarations of renowned biblical scholars.

82. Adam and Eve were actually **together** during the temptation event. Eve was not alone in the affair, as some mistakenly interpret the account.
Genesis 3:6: "She also gave some to her husband, **who was with her**, and he ate it" (NIV).
Keil and Delitzsch Biblical Commentary on the Old Testament: "She took of its fruit and ate, and gave to her husband by her (who was present), and he did eat" (Parenthesis in original). https://biblehub.com/commentaries/genesis/3-6.htm.
Gill's Exposition of the Entire Bible: "The Jews infer from hence, that Adam was with her all the while, and heard the discourse between the serpent and her, yet did not interpose nor dissuade his wife from eating the fruit." https://biblehub.com/commentaries/genesis/3-6.htm.
Ellicott's Commentary for English Readers: "The demeanor of Adam throughout is extraordinary. It is the woman who is tempted—not as though Adam was not present…for she has not to seek him—but he shares with her at once the gathered fruit." https://biblehub.com/commentaries/genesis/3-6.htm.
See my book, *Gods of Ground Zero*, for an in-depth examination of the Garden temptation and sin.
83. See Proverbs 6:16–19.
84. A number of Bible students ask how long Adam and Eve were in the Garden before the Fall. Obviously, they were not there exceeding Adam's life span of 930 years. Genesis 4:25 tells us that Seth was born after Cain slew Abel. Since the biblical account is clear that Seth was born outside the Garden, and since Genesis 5:3 informs us that Adam was 130 years old when Seth was born, it is obvious that Adam and Eve could not have been in the Garden of Eden any longer than 130 years.
85. Dr. John McArthur says, regarding the third chapter of Genesis: "Here's what Satan is thinking: 'I failed to a degree in heaven and yet I succeeded. I was thrown out of heaven but I took a third of the angels with me so I have my kingdom.' He's trying to be a sovereign in his own right. And he is successful in capturing Adam and Eve. He's successful. And at this point Satan may well have felt that he had made a massive dent in the divine purpose, that God had gone to all of this wondrous effort to create a universe and place man and woman in His universe on the earth and it was so magnificent and it was a paradise like the original paradise of heaven before the angels were thrown out and Satan succeeded in wrecking paradise. He succeeded in gaining the devotion of Adam and Eve. And that is really essentially what happened." https://www.gty.org/library/sermons-library/90-241/the-curse-on-the-serpent-part-1.

86. See Job 38:4–7.

87. In Ezekiel 28:13,16, Yahweh declares that He cast Satan out of the Garden and off the Divine Council because of his "profanity" in the Garden:

> "You were in Eden, the garden of God.... Thou hast sinned: therefore I will **cast thee as profane out of the mountain of God**: and I will destroy thee, O covering cherub, from the midst of the stones of fire" (KJV; emphasis added).

The Hebrew word for "profane" is *chalal*. It is OT:2490. The word is particularly hideous, and, according to *Brown-Driver-Briggs* Hebrew lexicon and dictionary, it can sometimes be used to mean: "defile, pollute: sexually, Genesis 49:4 (poem) = 1 Chronicles 5:1 (the father's bed); a woman = הַנֵּ Leviticus 19:29; Leviticus 21:7, 9 (H); וְעָרֶ Leviticus 21:15 (H). See: OT:2490. "Brown-Driver-Briggs," (Verb form: Pollute, Defile, Profane), Biblehub.com, https://biblehub.com/hebrew/2490.htm.

Also see my book *Gods of Ground Zero* for an in-depth development of the full meaning of this word and its connections to the Garden of Eden.

88. See Hebrews 8:5.

89. See Isaiah 14:12–14.

90. Genesis 3:15.

91. See Genesis 6.

92. See two of my previous books, *Gods and Thrones* and *Gods of Ground Zero* (Defender Publishing) for thorough studies of each of these biblical truths.

93. 1 Peter 1:20: "He was chosen before the creation of the world, but was revealed in these last times for your sake."
Revelation 13:8: "All inhabitants of the earth will worship the beast—all whose names have not been written in the Lamb's book of life, the Lamb who was slain from the creation of the world."

94. Romans 8:21; Ephesians 1:4; 1 Peter 1:20; Revelation 13:8.

95. Ibid.

96. Luke 17:26–30.

97. Ezekiel 5:5: "This is what the Sovereign LORD says: This is Jerusalem, which I have set in the center of the nations, with countries all around her."

98. See my books *Gods and Thrones*, *Gods of Ground Zero*, and *Gods of the Final Kingdom* for a detailed study of this extremely important and otherwise mysterious passage of Scripture. (The sons of God, the Nephilim, etc.) Most translations have "sons of Gods" instead of divine beings. Yet, the exact term used in Genesis 6, in the original Hebrew, is *bene Elohim*. In every other place

in Scripture where these words are used, almost all the scholarly translations render those words as "angels" or "divine beings."

Dr. C. Fred Dickason: "*Bene elohim* is a technical term for angels and is…the sense in which 'the sons of God' in Genesis 6 is used. It refers to angels as a class of mighty ones or powers. Some say that this term is also used of God's own people; but close inspection of the passages usually listed will show that the exact term is not *bene elohim*."

See: C. Fred Dickason, ThD, "Sons of God," *Names of Angels* (Chicago: Moody Press, 1997).

Dr. Michael Heiser: "When it comes to Genesis 6:1–4…. The truth is that the writers of the New Testament know nothing of…any view that makes the sons of God in Genesis 6:1–4 humans."

See: Michael S. Heiser, PhD, *The Unseen Realm: Recovering the Supernatural World View of the Bible* (Bellingham, WA: Lexham Press, 2015) 101.

99. Wright, David. "Timeline for the Flood," Answers in Genesis, 3/9/12, https://answersingenesis.org/bible-timeline/timeline-for-the-flood.

100. Of course, the Bible does not actually tell us that Noah foresaw the cross of Jesus' agony. However, some scholars speculate that he did indeed have at least a shadowy vision of it. For instance, how could Moses not know at least something about Jesus and the cross, considering the lamb sacrifice he prescribed for the Passover in Exodus 12? How could Abraham not have had a vision of it when he was sacrificing his son, Isaac? Just like David in Psalm 22, Isaiah in Isiah 53, and Zechariah in Zechariah 12, surely they saw glimpses of this glory yet to come in Jesus on the cross? Accordingly, I have taken literary license here and biblically speculated that Yahweh may have revealed similar things to Noah, the one who would preach the salvation of God for all who would turn to Him, and then be "raptured" out to safety just as the flood waters began to rise.

101. See Genesis 6:20, 7:8, 15.

102. Revelation 12:9; 20:2.

103. The Seed that "blesses" all the families of the earth is Jesus Christ—Savior and Lord.

104. This fact is not lost on those who truly know and understand the contextual historical connections. In March 2019, Fox News personality Judge Jeanine Pirro summarized this truth on a Fox broadcast: "Jews have been persecuted almost from the beginning of time when they were forced out of Egypt to the six million killed in the Holocaust and now, we are witnessing

the rise of anti- Semitism in Europe where incidents are up 74% in the last year alone in France, where Jewish cemeteries are regularly desecrated with swastikas and people relay the common tropes of Jews with too much money and influence."

See: Mateus Kadesh. "Fox News Host Under Fire after Controversial Segment," IPatriot.com, March 13, 2019, https://ipatriot.com/ fox-news-host-under-fire-after-controversial-segment-watch-it-here.

105. Daniel 1–6.

106. *Barnes' Notes on the Bible*: "Now it so happens that [at the time of the church] the 'dragon' had become a common standard in the Roman armies, and had in some measure superseded the eagle. Revelation 12:4."

See: *Barnes' Notes on the Bible*, Biblehub.com, https://biblehub.com/ commentaries/revelation/12-4.htm.

107. The draco, the late Roman military standard: "The Draco ('dragon' or 'serpent', plural dracones) was a military standard of the Roman cavalry. Carried by the draconarius, the Draco was the standard of the cohort as the eagle (Aquila) was that of the legion."

See: Vermaat, Robert. "The Draco, The Late Roman Military Standard," Fectio.org, accessed 11/2/18, http://www.fectio.org.uk/articles/draco.htm.

Roman Military Standards: "The Draco was usually carried by the cavalry units. A Draco was created by shaping metal to form a hollow head that resembled a toothed dragon. A cloth tube tail was also attached to the neck of the head, so it would expand when the wind passed through it as the standard was being carried high in the air. If the Draco was carried at the correct speed, a subtle hissing noise would be created by the air-stream passing through the dragon's mouth."

Also see: Yust, Walter (1953). *Encyclopædia Britannica: A New Survey of Universal Knowledge*, p. 570.

108. Revelation 12:1–9.

109. The chapters of this entire section, as they are presented in narrative form, were inspired, in large part, by a similar description found in the following resource (but with my many added details, material, and creative license). See: Edersheim, Alfred. "Life and Times of Jesus," accessed 11/25/21, https:// www.ccel.org/ccel/edersheim/lifetimes.vii.vi.html#fna_vii.vi-p23.1.

110. Herod was born in 73 BCE as the son of a man from Idumea named Antipater and a woman named Cyprus, the daughter of an Arab sheik. Antipater was an adherent of Hyrcanus, one of two princes struggling to become king of Judaea.

See: "Herod the Great," accessed 3/12/21, https://www.livius.org/articles/person/herod-the-great.

111. Biblical lineage is traced through the father.
See Arnold Fruchtenbaum. "The Genealogy of Messiah," 4/20/18, https://jewsforjesus.org/publications/issues/issues-v05-n06/the-genealogy-of-the-messiah.

> **"When one examines all the genealogies in the Hebrew Scriptures**, several facts become quite obvious. Other than extremely infrequent exceptions, **only the male line is traced in those genealogies**. Usually, only men's names appear, again, with a few exceptions. However, the lineages of the women is not given. This is not an intentional slight against women in general, as some might suggest. Rather **it is simply a biblical fact that it was the lineage of the father** who determined both national and tribal identity."

112. *Expositor's Greek Testament*: "Luke 2:4–5. If Bethlehem was Joseph's home, he would have gone to Bethlehem sooner or later in any case. Because of the census he went just then (Hahn).—σὺν Μαριὰμ, coming after ἀπογράψ., naturally suggests that Mary had to be enrolled too. Was this necessary? Even if not, reasons might be suggested for her going with her husband: her condition, the intention to settle there as their real home, she an heiress, etc.—ἐγκύῳ (here only in N. T.), preparing for what follows." https://biblehub.com/commentaries/luke/2-4.htm.

113. Pope, Charles. "What Were the Villages Like in Jesus' Day?" 3/27/17, http://blog.adw.org/2017/03/villages-like-jesus-day.

114. Ibid.

115. *Ellicott's Commentary for English Readers*: "She went up with him, not necessarily because she too had to be registered at Bethlehem, but because her state, as "being great with child," made her, in a special sense, *dependent on Joseph's presence and protection*" (emphasis added). https://biblehub.com/commentaries/luke/2-5.htm.

116. *Cambridge Bible for Schools and Colleges*: "It is uncertain whether her presence was obligatory or voluntary; but it is obvious that at so trying a time, and after what she had suffered (Matthew 1:19), **she would cling to the presence and protection** of her husband. **Nor is it wholly impossible that she saw in the providential circumstances a fulfilment of prophecy** [Micah 5:2]" (emphasis added).
https://biblehub.com/commentaries/luke/2-5.htm.

117. *Expositor's Greek Testament*: "If Bethlehem was Joseph's home, he would have gone to Bethlehem sooner or later in any case. Because of the census he went just then.... **Reasons** might be **suggested for her going with her husband**: her condition, or **the intention to settle there as their real home**" (emphasis added).

118. There are only two reasonable routes they could have taken. One would have put them going through Samaria, then through Jerusalem, then arriving in Bethlehem. One of the most common alternative theories, however, is the one I've chosen for this narrative. It makes more sense that Joseph would not have submitted his wife to the possibility of attack during an obviously dangerous trip through Samaria. Thus, he would have chosen the very common Jordon River trail. At the following article, the reader can explore both of these possibilities: https://www.travelujah.com/stories/in-the-footsteps-of-mary-and-joseph-the-nativity-trail.

119. Sodom and Gomorrah: Two hundred square miles is about the same size as Chicago. See: http://demographia.com/db-uscity98.htm.

The following information is taken from an archeological research article titled: "Biblical Archeology: Sodom and Gomorra," by Leibel Reznickprint, https://www.aish.com/ci/sam/48931527.html.

"The area consisted of five cities, each with its own king. There was (1) Bera, king of Sodom, (2) Birsha, king of Gomorrah, (3) Shinab, king of Admad, (4) Shember, king of Zeboiim, and (5) the king of Bela, which is also called Zoar (Genesis 14:8). This thriving group of city-states is referred to in the Bible (Genesis 13:12) as the Cities of the Plain.

"[The latest archeological discoveries in that area have uncovered many amazing finds, remains, and artifacts.] The healthy diet, rich in fruits and vegetables of all kinds, manifested itself in the physique of the inhabitants: skeletal remains indicate that a height of 5'9"– 6'4" was quite normal.

The known number of burials (to date) in this area of the Dead Sea Desert—1,500,000 bodies—indicates that this was once a thriving, and heavily populated region...numbering in total into the many millions of residents during Abraham's day. To this day, exactly five cities (just as the Bible records) have been unearthed in the area."

The article's conclusion:

"To summarize, the archaeology evidence as to the destruction of the five Cities of the Plain is inconclusive. However the preponderance of other evidence with regards to the Torah's story of Sodom and Gomorrah is overwhelming."

120. Scientific evidence for the obliteration of Sodom and Gomorrah:
1) Mack, Eric. "New Science Suggests Biblical City of Sodom Was Smote by an Exploding Meteor," *Forbes*, 12/4/18, https://www.forbes.com/sites/ericmack/2018/12/04/new-science-suggests-biblical-city-of-sodom-was-smote-by-an-exploding-meteor/?sh=34692ea5c677.
2) Borschel-Dan, Amanda. "Evidence of Sodom? Meteor Blast Cause of Biblical Destruction, Say Scientists," *Times of Israel*, 11/22/18, https://www.timesofisrael.com/evidence-of-sodom-meteor-blast-cause-of-biblical-destruction-say-scientists.
3) Gough, Evan. "A Meteor May Have Exploded in the Air 3,700 Years Ago, Obliterating Communities Near the Dead Sea," Phys.org, 12/5/18, https://phys.org/news/2018-12-meteor-air-years-obliterating-dead.html.

121. Tanakh—Hebrew for the collection of Scriptures we now call the Old Testament.

122. See Messianic Rabbi Zev Porat's book, *Unmasking the Chaldean Spirit* (Defender Publishing), for the deep spiritual ramification of this great battle and its connection to the birth of Messiah in this valley village of Bethlehem.

123. Leviticus 12:1–5: "And the LORD spoke unto Moses, saying, Speak unto the children of Israel, saying, if a woman have conceived seed, and borne a male child: then shall she be unclean seven days, even as in the days of the separation for her infirmity shall she be unclean" (KJV).

124. Some of the incredible biblical truth that I have woven into these narrative portions is reproduced here, in this footnote. However, much more of the information is also found, profusely documented, in the book by Messianic Rabbi Zev Porat titled *Unmasking the Chaldean Spirit* (Crane, MO: Defender Publishing, publication date pending).

What is cited in this chapter of my book is from the work of renowned biblical scholar, teacher, and messianic author Alfred Edersheim in *The Life and Times of Jesus*. A portion of Edersheim's work is referenced next:

"That the Messiah was to be born in Bethlehem, was a settled conviction. Equally so was the belief, that **He was to be revealed** from **Migdal Eder**, 'the **tower of the flock**.' (Targum Pseudo-Jon. On Gen. 35:21). This Migdal Eder **was not the watchtower for the ordinary flock**s which pastured on the barren sheepground beyond Bethlehem, but lay close to the town, on the road to Jerusalem" (emphasis added).

"A passage in the Mishnah (Shek. vii. 4.) leads to the conclusion, that **the flocks, which pastured there, were destined for Temple-sacrifices,** and, accordingly, that **the shepherds**, who watched over them, **were not ordinary shepherds.** The latter were under the ban of Rabbinism, on account of their necessary isolation from religious ordinances, and their manner of life, which rendered strict legal observance unlikely, if not absolutely impossible." (Emphasis added)

"The same Mishnic passage also leads us to infer, that these flocks lay out all the year round, since they are spoken of as in the fields thirty days before the Passover - that is, in the month of February, when in Palestine the average rainfall is nearly greatest. Thus, Jewish tradition in some dim manner apprehended the first revelation of the Messiah from that Migdal Eder, where shepherds watched the Temple-flocks all the year round. Of the deep symbolic significance of such a coincidence, it is needless to speak."

See: Edersheim, Alfred. *Life and Times of Jesus*, Accessed2/25/21, https://www.ccel.org/ccel/edersheim/lifetimes.vii.vi.html#fna_vii.vi-p23.1.
125. Ibid.: "That the Messiah was to be born in Bethlehem, was a settled conviction. Equally so was the belief, that He was to be revealed from Migdal Eder, 'the tower of the flock.' (Targum Pseudo-Jon. On Gen. 35:21). This Migdal Eder was not the watchtower for the ordinary flocks which pastured on the barren sheepground beyond Bethlehem, but lay close to the town, on the road to Jerusalem.... Thus, Jewish tradition in some dim manner apprehended the first revelation of the Messiah from that Migdal Eder, where shepherds watched the Temple-flocks all the year round. Of the deep symbolic significance of such a coincidence, it is needless to speak" (emphasis added).
126. *Barnes' Notes on the Bible* (Micah 4:8 commentary): "And thou, O **tower of the flock—'Tower of Eder,'** which is interpreted 'tower of the flock,' about a mile from Bethlehem," says Jerome who lived there, "and fore-signifying (in its very name) by **a sort of prophecy the shepherds at the Birth of the Lord." There Jacob fed his sheep Genesis 35:21**, and there (since it was hard by Bethlehem) the shepherds, keeping watch over their flocks by night, saw and heard the Angels singing, "Glory to God in the highest, and on earth peace, good will toward men." **The Jews inferred from this place that the Messiah should be revealed there**"(emphasis added). https://biblehub.com/commentaries/micah/4-8.htm.
127. The Greek word for manger is Strong's #5336. Phatné. It is **also**

interpreted as *a* **"stall,"** [the actual room itself] or **sometimes**, as a feeding trough, **depending on the context**. (Emphasis added) https://biblehub.com/greek/5336.htm.

128. Sobell, Jason and Hallowell, Billy. "The Incredible Significance of Baby Jesus Being Wrapped in Swaddling Clothes after His Birth," Faithwire, 12/14/17, https://www.faithwire.com/2017/12/14/the-incredible-significance-of-baby-jesus-being-wrapped-in-swaddling-clothes-after-his-birth.

129. Micah 5:2; NIV.

130. Micah 4:8; KJV.

Barnes' Notes on the Bible: "And thou, O **tower of the flock—'Tower of Eder,'** which is interpreted 'tower of the flock,' **about a mile from Bethlehem**," says Jerome who lived there, "and fore-signifying (in its very name) by **a sort of prophecy the shepherds at the Birth of the Lord." There Jacob fed his sheep Genesis 35:21**, and there (since it was hard by Bethlehem) the shepherds, keeping watch over their flocks by night, saw and heard the Angels singing, "Glory to God in the highest, and on earth peace, good will toward men." **The Jews inferred from this place that the Messiah should be revealed there**" (emphasis added). https://biblehub.com/commentaries/micah/4-8.htm.

Jamieson-Fausset-Brown Bible Commentary: "Jerome takes the Hebrew for 'flock,' Eder or Edar, as **a proper name**, namely, **a village near Bethlehem**, for which it is put, Bethlehem being taken to represent the royal stock of David (Mic 5:2; compare Ge 35:21) (emphasis added). https://biblehub.com/commentaries/micah/4-8.htm.

Gill's Exposition of the Entire Bible: "And thou, O tower of the flock.... The words 'Migdal Eder' are left by some untranslated, and think that place to be intended so called, which was **near to Bethlehem**, Genesis 35:19; and perhaps is the same which Jerome calls the tower of Ader, about **a mile from Bethlehem**: this is supposed to be **the place where the shepherds** were watching over their flocks at the time **of Christ's birth, the tidings of which were first brought to them here;** and the Jewish doctors speak of it as near Jerusalem" (emphasis added). https://biblehub.com/commentaries/micah/4-8.htm.

131. Revelation 13:8 and 1 Peter 1:20.

132. "Shepherds and Swaddling Clothes": "The **newborn lamb was immediately wrapped in clean swaddling [bands]** to protect them and keep them from blemish and danger. Swaddling clothes described in the

Bible consisted of a cloth **tied together by bandage-like strips.** When the declaration was made to **these Levitical Shepherds** that watched their sheep in a special field full of sacrificial lambs, **they apparently knew exactly where to go to discover that Baby"** (emphasis added).
See: Littlefield, Linda. "Shepherds and Swaddling Clothes," *South Platte Sentinel*, 12/18/18, https://www.southplattesentinel.com/2018/12/18/shepherds-and-swaddling-clothes/#:~:text=Swaddling%20clothes%20described%20in%20the,go%20to%20discover%20that%20Baby.
133. *Pulpit Commentary*: "The troop of angels issues forth from the depths of that invisible world which surrounds us on every side" (emphasis added). https://biblehub.com/commentaries/luke/2-13.htm.
134. Luke 2:8–15.
135. Luke 2:8–15.
136. As to the host being the angelic armies of Heaven, as well as ten thousand times ten thousand of them, see the following:
Gill's Exposition of the Entire Bible: "These are styled a heavenly host, because they dwell in heaven; and to distinguish them from hosts **and armies** on earth; and said to be multitude, for **the angels are innumerable; there are thousands, ten thousands, and ten thousand times ten thousand of them**: it may be rendered "the multitude," and may intend the whole company of angels" (emphasis added). https://biblehub.com/commentaries/luke/2-13.htm.
Geneva Study Bible: "**Whole armies of angels**, who compass the majesty of God round about, **just as soldiers**, as it were" (emphasis added). https://biblehub.com/commentaries/luke/2-13.htm.
Pulpit Commentary: "The troop of angels issues forth from the depths of that invisible world which surrounds us on every side Ten thousand times ten thousand holy angels" (emphasis added). https://biblehub.com/commentaries/luke/2-13.htm.
Vincent's Word Studies: "A multitude of the heavenly host. Host (στρατιας) **is literally army.** '**Here the army** announces peace' (Bengel). Wyc., heavenly knighthood. Tynd., **heavenly soldiers**" (emphasis added). https://biblehub.com/commentaries/luke/2-13.htm.
137. As to the angels singing, see the following:
Matthew Poole's Commentary: "How they praised God is expressed Luke 2:14, **they sang**" (emphasis added). https://biblehub.com/commentaries/luke/2-13.htm.
Meyer's New Testament Commentary: "**The hymn** would also consist of only

two parts" (emphasis added). https://biblehub.com/commentaries/luke/2-13.htm.

Gill's Exposition of the Entire Bible: "The whole company of angels, who were **all of them together to sing the praises of God,** and glorify him at the birth of the incarnate Saviour, as well as to adore him" (emphasis added). https://biblehub.com/commentaries/luke/2-13.htm.

Good News Translation of the Bible: "Suddenly a great army of heaven's angels appeared with the angel, **singing praises** to God" (emphasis added). https://biblehub.com/luke/2-13.htm.

138. Luke 2:8–15.

139. Luke 2:8–15.

140. Littlefield, "Shepherds and Swaddling Clothes": "When the declaration was made to these Levitical Shepherds that watched their sheep in a special field full of sacrificial lambs, they apparently knew exactly where to go to discover that Baby."

141. Malachi 3:1: "Then suddenly the Lord you are seeking will come to his temple; the messenger of the covenant, whom you desire, will come," says the Lord Almighty."

142. Isaiah 52:14: "As many were astounded at thee; his visage was so marred more than any man, and his form more than the sons of men" (KJV).

143. See Matthew 2:11. This passage states that by the visit of the magi, they were in a house in Bethlehem.

144. Ross, Allen. "3. The Visit of the Wise Men (Matthew 2:1–12)," Bible.org, accessed 4/22/21, https://bible.org/seriespage/3-visit-wise-men-matthew-21-12.

145. See the narrative of Matthew 2:1–12.

146. Five planets—Mercury, Venus, Mars, Jupiter, and Saturn—were known to the ancients. To the unaided eye, these planets appear star-like. However, the planets moved relative to the stars. For this reason, they were called "wandering stars." Our word "planet" comes from the Greek word *planetes*, meaning "wanderer."
See: https://airandspace.si.edu/exhibitions/exploring-the-planets/online/discovery/greeks.cfm#:~:text=Five%20planets%20%E2%80%94%20Mercury%2C%20Venus%2C,were%20known%20to%20the%20ancients.&text=However%2C%20the%20planets%20moved%20relative,planetes%2C%20meaning%20%22wanderer.%22.

147. The Star of the Magi: "Did such a Star, then, really appear in the East seven years before the Christian era? Astronomically speaking, and without

any reference to controversy, there can be no doubt that the most remarkable conjunction of planets—that of Jupiter and Saturn in the constellation of Pices, which occurs only once in 800 years—did take place no less than three times in the year 747 a.u.c., or two years before the birth of Christ (in May, October and December). This conjunction is admitted by all astronomers. It was not only extraordinary, but presented the most brilliant spectacle in the night-sky, such as could not but attract the attention of all who watched the sidereal heavens, but especially of those who busied themselves with astrology." See: Edersheim, Albert. *The Life and Times of Jesus*, https://ccel.org/ccel/edersheim/lifetimes/ lifetimes.vii.viii.html. (I urge the reader to go to this website and read this fascinating work. The few paragraphs I've entered here are merely a reference point to the rest of the study of this topic).

See also: Martin, E. L. "The Star That Astonished the World." Martin makes the case that the Star of Bethlehem was more likely a series of conjunctions in 3 BC that culminated on September 11 of that year when Jupiter and Regulus came together, representing the king of the Roman pantheon and the "king star" in Leo. Martin's work is available to read free online at http://www. askelm.com/star/index.asp. Retrieved 12/28/20.

148. *Expositor's Greek Testament*: "Anything is credible of the man who murdered his own wife and sons. This deed shocks Christians; but it was a small affair in Herod's career, and in contemporary history."

See: Matthew 2:16, *Expositor's Greek Testament*, Biblehub.com, https:// biblehub.com/commentaries/matthew/2-16.htm.

149. "The sacred trees that produce Frankincense and Myrrh are almost impossible to grow outside of the Arabian Peninsula, which meant they were constantly in short supply and high demand. According to a famous Roman historian, the sap made the Arabians the richest people on earth by Jesus's time, more valuable than gold. Frankincense alone is responsible for creating the trade routes linking southern Arabia to India, the Mediterranean, and the Silk Road in China."

Herb and Root. "The Classic Tale of Three Gifts," Accessed 9/12/21, https:// herbandroot.com/pages/frankincense-myrrh-more-valuable-than-gold.

150. Matthew 2:19–23.

151. Towns, Elmer. "How Old Was Jesus When He Returned from Egypt? The Early Days of Jesus," Bible Sprout, accessed 3/12/21, https://www.biblesprout. com/articles/jesus-christ/old-jesus-returned-egypt.

152. Luke 2:25–40.

153. Matthew 11:13–15: "[Jesus said to them] For all the Prophets and the Law prophesied until John. And if you are willing to accept it, **he is the Elijah** who was to come. Whoever has ears, let them hear" (emphasis added).

Barnes' Notes on the Bible: "**If ye will receive it**—This is a mode of speaking implying that the doctrine which he was about to state was **different from their common views**; that he was about to state something which varied from the common expectation, and which therefore they might be disposed to reject. "The prophet Malachi Mal 4:5–6 predicted that 'Elijah' would be sent before the coming of the Messiah to prepare the way for him. **By this was evidently meant, not that he should appear 'in person,' but that one should appear with a striking resemblance to him**; or, as Luke 1:17 expresses it, 'in the spirit and power of Elijah.' **But the Jews understood it differently.** They supposed that Elijah would appear in person…. **This prevalent belief was the reason** why he used the words 'if ye will receive it,' implying that the affirmation that 'John' was the promised Elijah was a doctrine contrary to their expectation" (emphasis added).

154. Towns, "How Old Was Jesus When He Returned from Egypt?"

155. **The Divine Son of God**—*Divi Augusti filius.* His official tile was Tiberius Caesar Augustus Divi Augusti filius. Tiberius was Roman emperor from AD 14 to AD 37, succeeding the first emperor, Augustus.

156. The prince of this world; see John 12:31 and 14:30.

157. Luke 3:10–14.

158. Jesus would also call these religious leaders a "brood of vipers." Each time He does it, the context of His charge is the accusation of their direct alliance with Satan (Matthew 12:34; 23:33; John 8:44; Matthew 23:13).

159. *Gill's Exposition of the Entire Bible*: "Expresses their craft and subtlety, their inward poison, and venomous nature; their fair outside, and specious pretenses; their hypocrisy, malice, and wickedness; **in which they were like to the old serpent, their father the devil**" (emphasis added). https://biblehub. com/commentaries/matthew/23-33.htm.

Pulpit Commentary: "They were of devilish nature, inherited from their very birth the disposition and character of Satan. So Christ said on another occasion, 'Ye are of your father the devil, and the lusts of your father it is your will to do. He was a murderer from the beginning, and stood not in the truth' (emphasis added). https://biblehub.com/commentaries/matthew/23-33.htm.

160. Isaiah 40:3.

161. See: John 1:23. *Ellicott's Commentary for English Readers*, Biblehub. com, https://biblehub.com/commentaries/john/1-23.htm.

Pulpit Commentary: "A portion of this very oracle is quoted by Malachi when he exclaims, 'Behold, I send my messenger before my face, who shall prepare the way before me.' This 'messenger before the face of the Lord' is no other than he who should come in the spirit and power of Elijah. John, therefore, gathered up the significance of both prophecies, when he spoke of himself as 'a voice crying in the wilderness [actual and symbolic], Make straight the way of the Lord.' The Hebrew text, as we have translated it above, associates the words, 'in the wilderness,' with 'make straight' rather than with 'the voice crying.' The quotation by the evangelist from the LXX will suffer either arrangement of the words. John 1:23." https://biblehub.com/commentaries/john/1-23.htm.

162. Isaiah 53:2–3.

163. See my book, *The Rabbi, the Secret Message, and the Identity of Messiah* (Crane, MO: Defender Publishing, 2019), for an in-depth look at this orthodox Jewish belief.

164. See John 1:35–36.

Meyer's New Testament Commentary: "One was Andrew, John 1:41. The other? Certainly John himself, partly on account of that peculiarity of his which leads him to refrain from naming himself, and partly on account of the special vividness of the details in the following account, which had remained indelibly impressed upon his memory ever since this first and decisive meeting with his Lord." https://biblehub.com/commentaries/john/1-35.htm.

165. The potentialities of the narration of this section are attested to, at least in foundation, by numerous and reputable scholarly sources. Observe the following examples:

Expositor's Greek Testament: "[This event] **does not necessarily involve that an actual dove was visible. It was not the dove which was to be the sign**; what he saw **was the Spirit** descending…. It was the possession of this spirit by Jesus that convinced John that He could baptize with the Holy Spirit. That this conviction came to him at the baptism of Christ with a clearness and firmness which authenticated it as divine is guaranteed by the words of this verse. It was as plain to him that Jesus was **possessed by the Spirit** as if **he had seen the Spirit in a visible shape alighting upon Him**" (emphasis added). https://biblehub.com/commentaries/john/1-32.htm.

Ellicott's Commentary for English Readers: "The narrative implies (1) that our Lord and the Baptist were either alone, or that **they alone saw what is recorded**. 'The **heavens were opened** to **him**' as they were to Stephen (Acts

7:56). The Baptist bears record that he too beheld the Spirit descending (John 1:33–34), but there is **not the slightest ground for supposing that there was any manifestation to others.** The [overshadowing of the Holy Spirit upon Jesus "in bodily form" is here pictured in the] perfection of the tenderness, the purity, the gentleness of which **the dove was the acknowledged symbol**" (emphasis added). https://biblehub.com/commentaries/matthew/3-16.htm.
166. In John 1:30–4, we hear John the Baptizer explain this truth, in detail: "This is the one I meant when I said, 'A man who comes after me has surpassed me because he was before me.' **I myself did not know him**, but the reason I came baptizing with water was that he might be revealed to Israel." Then John gave this testimony: "**I saw the Spirit come down from heaven** as a dove and remain on him. And I myself did not know him, but the one who sent me [God Himself; John 1:6] to baptize with water told me, 'The man on whom you see the Spirit come down and remain is the one who will baptize with the Holy Spirit.' I have seen and I testify that this is God's Chosen One" (emphasis added).
Jamieson-Fausset-Brown Bible Commentary gives further clarification to John the Baptist's claim: "**Knew him not**—Living mostly apart, the one at Nazareth, the other in the Judean desert—to prevent all appearance of collusion, John only knew that at a definite time after his own call, his Master would show Himself…. **But the sign which he was told to expect was the visible descent of the Spirit** upon Him as He emerged out of the baptismal water. Then, catching up the voice from heaven, 'he saw and bare record that this is the Son of God'" (emphasis added). https://biblehub.com/commentaries/john/1-31.htm.
167. The gospel of John (1:29) records: "The **next day** John saw Jesus coming toward him and said, 'Behold, the Lamb of God, who takes away the sin of the world!'" (emphasis added).
There is some disparity among highly renowned scholars as to exactly *when* this "next day" was. At first glance, one would assume that it was the *very next day—the* one after John had confronted the Sanhedrin representatives at the Jordan River. This is the position that most commentators take. However, the uncertainty comes into play because of the fact that John, the writer of the Gospel, has Jesus returning to the river, on the "next day" yet again—for two "next days" in a row. On this particular second "next day," the declaration of the "Lamb of God" is again declared to the crowds. Furthermore, it is on this second "next day" event that we are told that some in the crowd began to follow Jesus as His disciples. We are also told that it was at this specific

point when Jesus began His earthly ministry. Oddly, John never mentions the wilderness temptation. John's account was the last one to be written, of the four Gospel accounts. However, Matthew, Mark, and Luke all record the fact of Jesus' temptation experience and the selection of His disciples *after* that temptation.

See an example of thirteen scholarly commentary speculations on this matter at https://biblehub.com/commentaries/john/1-29.htm.

Of the thirteen, five conclude that John's declaration of Jesus being the Lamb of God was made *after* the wilderness temptation. Eight agree that it was made *at the baptism* event and *before* the temptation in the wilderness—as I have represented in my narrative.

168. *Cambridge Bible for Schools and Colleges*: "The desert unpeopled by men was thought to be the abode of demons. So Jesus meets the evil spirit in his own domains, the Stronger One coming upon the strong man who keepeth his palace (Luke 11:21–22)." https://biblehub.com/commentaries/matthew/4-1.htm.

169. Matthew 12:29.

170. Mark's mention (1:13) of the wild animals in the wilderness temptation event is yet another connection to the Garden of Eden. This fact has not escaped the attention of numerous scholars.

Cambridge Bible for Schools and Colleges: "The Saviour was 'with the wild beasts,' unhurt by them, as Adam was in Paradise."

Bengel's Gnomen: "He even now, in the very height of His humiliation (self-emptying), exercised over the beasts the dominion which Adam had so soon suffered himself to lose."

Pulpit Commentary: "He dwelt amongst them as Adam lived with them in his state of innocence in Paradise."

Gill's Exposition of the Entire Bible: "[Jesus] was with the wild beasts...as Adam in Eden's garden."

171. For forty days, the floodwaters of Noah's day had deluged the earth. Moses had fasted forty days on Sinai, only to descend and find the people of God dancing around the graven image of a golden calf.

For forty days, the spies sent out by Moses had wandered into the Land of Promise only to bring back a bad report. Yahweh's punishment upon them? One year of wilderness wandering for every day they had trod in faithlessness upon the soil of Canaan—forty years.

Then, years later, when the Israelites continuously did evil in the sight of the Lord, He gave them into the hands of the Philistines—their most hated enemies. They were subservient to the Philistines for forty years (Judges 13:1). Also, it was for a period of forty days that that the Philistine, Goliath, came forth and taunted the armies of God's people. On the fortieth day, Goliath lost his head for his misplaced derisions.

Periods of forty were also used to mark God's hand of divine appointment. Deborah, the faithful judge of Israel, brought forty years of peace to her domain because of her fidelity and bravery in the service of the Lord (Judges 5:31)—the same for Gideon's days as judge (Judges 8:28).

It was King David who would bring the Tabernacle and the Ark of the Covenant back to the heart of Israel, in the city of Jerusalem, to reestablish a sacrificial worship of Yahweh. Thus David would be given the divine appointment of reigning forty years (2 Samuel 5:4). It was the same with his son, Solomon, the one who built the Temple of the Lord; he, too, was given forty years of divinely appointed rule (1 Kings 11:42).

172. Matthew 12:28–29.

173. See my book, *Gods of Ground Zero*, (Crane, MO: Defender Publishing, 2018) for a thorough study of this biblical truth.

In Ezekiel 28:16, Yahweh calls what Satan did in the Garden a "profane" thing: "Therefore I will cast thee as profane [Hebrew: *chalal*] out of the mountain of God: and I will destroy thee" (KJV).

The Hebrew word for "profane" is *chalal*. It is OT: 2490. The word is particularly hideous in nature, and, according to *Brown-Driver-Briggs* Hebrew lexicon and dictionary, it can sometimes be used to express: "to defile or **pollute sexually**, Genesis 49:4 (poem) = 1 Chronicles 5:1 (the father's bed); a woman Leviticus 19:29; Leviticus 21:7, 9 (H); Leviticus 21:15" (emphasis added).

OT: 2490. *Brown-Driver-Briggs*, (Verb form: Pollute, Defile, Profane), Biblehub.com, https://biblehub.com/hebrew/2490.htm.

174. 1 Corinthians 15:22–45. (Jesus as the Second Adam)

John Lightfoot's Commentary on the Gospels: "Jesus was led up by the Spirit into the wilderness to be tempted. The war, proclaimed of old in Eden between the serpent, and the seed of the serpent, and the seed of the woman, Genesis 3:15, now takes place; when that promised seed of the woman comes forth into the field (being initiated by baptism, and anointed by the Holy Ghost, unto the public office of his ministry) to fight with that old serpent, and at last to bruise his head" (emphasis added).

See: Matthew 4. *John Lightfoot's Commentary on the Gospels*, Studylight.org, https://www.studylight.org/commentaries/jlc/matthew-4.html#1.

175. *Barnes' Notes on the Bible*: "**When the first Adam** was created he was subjected to the temptation of the devil, and he fell and involved the race in ruin: it was not improper that **the second Adam**—the Redeemer of the race— should be subjected to temptation, in order that it might be seen that there was no power that could alienate him from God; that there was a kind and a degree of holiness which no art or power could estrange from allegiance" (emphasis added). https://biblehub.com/commentaries/matthew/4-1.htm.

176. *Nehushtan*—"the brazen one": "*Nehushtan* is the disparaging name tagged to the bronze serpent on a pole. It was first described in the Book of Numbers. (Numbers 21:4–9).

"In the book of 2 Kings, King Hezekiah institutes a reform of an existing heresy among the Israelites. Hezekiah insisted upon the destruction of 'the brazen serpent that Moses had made; for unto those days the children of Israel did burn incense to it; and it was called *Nehushtan.*'" The term means 'a brazen thing' (2 Kings 18:4). *Nehushtan* comes from OT: 5174, 5178, and 5180." See: *New Exhaustive Strong's Numbers and Concordance with Expanded Greek-Hebrew Dictionary*.

177. Mark 1:13.

178   *Matthew Henry's Concise Commentary*: "Mark notices his being in the wilderness and that he was with the wild beasts…The serpent tempted the first Adam in the garden, the Second Adam in the wilderness; with different success indeed."

Reference for all of the above commentaries: https://biblehub.com/commentaries/mark/1-13.htm.

 Matthew 4:2 clarifies this point: "**After** fasting forty days and forty nights, he was hungry. The tempter **came to him** and said…" (emphasis added).

Pulpit Commentary: "**It was only after** his six weeks meditation that he felt the need of food… It was the moment the tempter had waited for to make his decisive assault" (emphasis added). https://biblehub.com/commentaries/matthew/4-2.htm.

Barnes' Notes on the Bible: "The temptations, however, which are recorded by Matthew and Luke **did not take place until the forty days were finished**" (emphasis added). https://biblehub.com/commentaries/luke/4-5.htm.

179. 2 Corinthians 4:4.

180. *Pulpit Commentary*: "Had he been observed by any spectator whilst the

temptation was going on, he would have appeared all through it motionless upon the soil of the desert. But though the conflict did not pass out of the spiritual sphere, it was none the less real."
See: Luke 4:1, *Pulpit Commentary*, Biblehub.com, http://biblehub.com/commentaries/Luke/4-1.htm.
181. Ephesians 2:2.
182. See Job 1:6–7 (and the following commentary entries for this passage). *Jamieson-Fausset-Brown Bible Commentary*: "Sons of God—angels (Job 38:7; 1Ki 22:19). They **present themselves to render account** of their 'ministry' in other parts of the universe (Heb. 1:14). [In other words, they had been "summonsed" by Yahweh—they didn't merely enter His presence at will] … Satan had been the agent in Adam's temptation. Hence his name is given without comment. The feeling with which he looks on Job is similar to that with which he looked on Adam in Paradise (emphasis added). https://biblehub.com/commentaries/job/1-6.htm.
The *Pulpit Commentary* also agrees with my assessment: "We may gather, perhaps, from this place and Job 2:1 that **there are fixed times** at which the angelic host, often sent out by the Almighty on distant errands, **has to gather together**, [they are summoned] one and all, before the great white throne, to pay homage to their Lord, and probably **to give an account** of their doings (emphasis added). https://biblehub.com/commentaries/job/1-6.htm.
183. James 1:14–15.
184. See Matthew 7:15–19, Ezekiel 31, and Song of Solomon 2:3.
185. Did Satan know at this point the "whole" truth that Jesus was the genuine Messiah—God in the flesh? No. He did not. From this point forth in Jesus' ministry, Satan would attempt to discern whether He really was the genuine thing…the Seed who had come to destroy him. Satan had seen many "false messiahs" come and go through the ages. While Satan is supernaturally smart, he is not God. There's much he doesn't know.
Paul emphatically declares this truth as well: "None of the rulers of this age understood it, for if they had, they would not have crucified the Lord of glory" (1 Corinthians 2:8).
Additionally, the Apostle Peter declares, "Concerning this salvation, the prophets, who spoke of the grace that was to come to you, searched intently and with the greatest care, trying to find out the time and circumstances to which the Spirit of Christ in them was pointing when he predicted the sufferings of the Messiah and the glories that would follow. It was revealed to

them that they were not serving themselves but you, when they spoke of the things that have now been told you by those who have preached the gospel to you by the Holy Spirit sent from heaven. Even angels long to look into these things" (1 Peter 1:10–12).

If the prophets of Messiah's coming, and even the angels around the throne of God did not understand everything about what God was doing in the person of Jesus Christ - how could Satan have known? The answer is that he didn't. Not until after the resurrection. Then he knew. But by then, it was too late.

See a representative sampling of the scholarly attestation of this biblical truth:

Clarke's Commentary on the Bible: "It is certain, whatever Satan might suspect, he did not fully know that the person he tempted was the true Messiah. Perhaps one grand object of his temptation was to find this out."

See: Matthew 4:3. *Clarke's Commentary on the Whole Bible*, Bible Study Tools, https://www.bibletools.org/index.cfm/fuseaction/Bible.show/ sVerseID/23213/eVerseID/23213/RTD/clarke/version/nasb.

186. The Masquerade—The majority of scholars agree that, at this point, Satan's manifestation was in the realm of the physical and had moved far beyond any "mental" and "emotional" temptations that Jesus had thus far encountered.

187. Lucifer—"the shining one." Not his "name," but a pejorative description of Satan by Yahweh Himself. See Isaiah 14:12 (KJV). See my book *Masquerade: Preparing for the Greatest Con Job in History* (Crane, MO: Defender Publishing, 2020). God is calling Satan a braggart, and con artist by calling him the "shining one."

188. Stewart, Don. "What Do We Know about Jesus' Earthly Parents: Joseph and Mary?" Blue Letter Bible, https://www.blueletterbible.org/faq/don_stewart/ don_stewart_198.cfm.

189. "The village seems to have been held in some contempt in 1st century Palestine. It was a nondescript dot on the map with not much to offer, overshadowed by nearby Sepphoris, the luxurious Greek-style capital of Herod Antipas."

Fletcher, Elizabeth. "Basic facts about Nazareth," accessed 10/22/18, http://www.jesus-story.net/nazareth_about.htm.

John 1:46: "And Nathanael said to him, can there any good thing come out of Nazareth? Philip said to him, Come and see."

Barnes' Notes on the Bible: "The character of Nazareth was proverbially bad.

To be a Galilean or a Nazarene was an expression of decided contempt."
https://biblehub.com/commentaries/john/1-46.htm.
For an in-depth Hebrew study of the word "Nazareth," see http://www.abarim-publications.com/Meaning/Nazareth.html#.XGhu1uhKjIU.
190. Since you are the son of God…or "If" you are the son of God.
Clarke's Commentary on the Bible: "If thou be *the Son of God*—Or, *a son of God*, is here, and in Luke 4:3, written without the article; and therefore should not be translated The Son, *as if it were*, which is a phrase that is applicable to Christ as the Messiah: but *it is certain*, whatever Satan might suspect, *he did not fully know that the person he tempted* was the true Messiah. Perhaps one grand object of his temptation was to find this out" (emphasis added).
See:https://www.bibletools.org/index.cfm/fuseaction/Bible.show/sVerseID/23213/eVerseID/23213/RTD/clarke/version/nasb.
People's Bible Commentary: "**If thou be** the Son of God. 'If' suggests **a doubt**, and, perhaps, a taunt" (emphasis added).
See:https://www.bibletools.org/index.cfm/fuseaction/Bible.show/sVerseID/23213/eVerseID/23213/RTD/pcnt/version/nasb.
Jamieson-Fausset-Brown: Commentary Critical and Explanatory on the Whole Bible: "What was the high design of this?… That the tempter, too, might get a taste, at the very outset, of **the new kind of material** in man which he would find he had here to deal with" (emphasis added).
See:https://www.biblestudytools.com/commentaries/jamieson-fausset-brown/matthew/matthew-4.html.
The Cambridge Bible for Schools and Colleges: "*If thou art*…The same words were tauntingly addressed to our Lord on the Cross (Matthew 27:40). The Greek strictly means "*Assuming* that Thou art" (emphasis added).
See: https://biblehub.com/commentaries/luke/4-3.htm.
191. *Elohim* is the first name by which the Bible addresses our Creator. It is often translated in the English from the Hebrew as "God." The very first verse of Genesis says, "In the beginning, Elohim created the heavens and the earth."
192. See Genesis 3:15; 22:18; Galatians 3:19.
A Commentary on the New Testament from the Talmud and Hebraica by John Lightfoot: "The war, proclaimed of old in Eden between the serpent, and the seed of the serpent, and the seed of the woman, Genesis 3:15, now takes place; when that promised seed of the woman comes forth into the field (being initiated by baptism, and anointed by the Holy Ghost, unto the public office of his ministry) to fight with that old serpent, and at last to bruise his head."

See: https://www.biblestudytools.com/commentaries/lightfoot-new-testament/matthew/4.html.

193. What was it that Satan did not know about Jesus?
The Biblical Illustrator: "It does not follow that Satan 'knew the whole truth' respecting Him. If Satan had no just view of the person of Christ, of His true divinity, he would necessarily have imperfect views of His perfect holiness." Matthew 4, *Biblical Illustrator*, ("What Satan Knew of Christ"), Biblehub.com, https://biblehub.com/commentaries/illustrator/matthew/4.htm.

194. **Two places at once?** Is this really what the biblical language is asserting?
Pulpit Commentary: "Had Jesus been observed by any spectator whilst the temptation was going on, **he would have appeared all through it motionless upon the soil of the desert**. But though the conflict did not pass out of the *spiritual sphere*, it was *none the less real*" (emphasis added).
Luke 4:1, *Pulpit Commentary*, Biblehub.com, http://biblehub.com/commentaries/Luke/4-1.htm.

"As far as the science of the matter goes, today's field of quantum mechanics has certainly shown—at least at the subatomic level—that a single atomic particle can be in two places at one time.

"Physicists in New Zealand have devised an experiment which could **demonstrate once and for all** that quantum theory correctly predicts the weird nature of the subatomic world.... **The experiment will show that a single photon—a particle of light—can be in two places at once**" (emphasis added).
See: Brown, William. "Science: How a Photon Can Be in Two Places at Once," *New Scientist*, 3/30/1991, https://www.newscientist.com/article/mg12917624-000-science-how-a-photon-can-be-in-two-places-at-once.

"Objects of the quantum world...can simultaneously take different paths and **end up at different places at once**. Physicists [call this phenomena] *quantum superposition* of different paths" (emphasis added).
See: "Atoms Can Be in Two Places at the Same Time," PHYS.org, January 20, 2015, https://phys.org/news/2015-01-atoms.html.

195. How did Satan get Jesus to the Temple in Jerusalem? The classical scholars of ages past understood the clear context of the New Testament language in this extraordinary instance. Note the commentaries of the following renowned classical scholars:
    1) *Pulpit Commentary*: "Had Jesus been observed by any spectator whilst the temptation was going on, **he would have appeared all through it**

motionless upon the soil of the desert. But though the conflict did not pass out of the **spiritual sphere**, it was **none the less real**" (emphasis added). Luke 4:1, *Pulpit Commentary*, Biblehub.com, http://biblehub.com/commentaries/Luke/4-1.htm.

2) *Pulpit Commentary*: "Some think that, as at the end of the temptation Christ is in the wilderness, this removal to Jerusalem is solely mental, without any motion of his body. **Improbable**; for to make such a temptation real, our **Lord's mind must have suffered complete illusion**" (emphasis added). Matthew 4:5, *The Pulpit Commentary*, Biblehub.com, https://biblehub.com/commentaries/matthew/4-5.htm.

3) *Gill's Exposition of the Entire Bible*: "Satan, by **divine permission**, and with the consent of Christ, which shows his great humiliation and condescension, **had power over his body**, to **move it from place to place**; in some **such like manner** as the Spirit of the Lord **caught away Philip**, Acts 8:39" (emphasis added). Matthew 4:5, *Gill's Exposition of the Entire Bible*, Biblehub.com, https://biblehub.com/commentaries/matthew/4-5.htm.

4) *Meyer's NT Commentary*: "[Satan] places Him, which implies the involuntary nature of the act on the part of Jesus, and the power on the part of the devil. A more precise determination of what is certainly a miraculous occurrence is not given in the text, which, however, does not permit us to think of it as something [merely] internal taking place [as in] the condition of a trance." Matthew 4:5, *Meyer's New Testament Commentary*, Biblehub.com, https://biblehub.com/commentaries/matthew/4-5.htm.

5) *Bengel's Gnomen*: "**A marvelous power was granted to the tempter**, until our Lord says to him, in Matthew 4:10, 'Depart'" (emphasis added). Matthew 4:5, "Bengel's Gnomen," Biblehub.com, https://biblehub.com/commentaries/matthew/4-5.htm.

6) *Vincent's Word Studies*: "The preposition παρά (with, by the side of), implies **taketh along with himself, or conducted**. It is **the same word** which all three evangelists use of **our Lord's taking his chosen apostles** to the Mount of Transfiguration (Matthew 17:1; Mark 9:9; Luke 9:28)" (emphasis added). Matthew 4:5, *Vincent's Word Studies*, Biblehub.com, https://biblehub.com/commentaries/matthew/4-5.htm.

7) *Ellicott's Commentary for English Readers*: "**Taketh him up into**

the holy city—The analogy of Ezekiel 37:1; Ezekiel 40:2, where the prophet is **carried from place to place** in the vision of God, leads us to think of **this "taking"** as **outside the conditions of local motion**" (emphasis added). Matthew 4:5, *Ellicott's Commentary for English Readers*, Biblehub.com, https://biblehub.com/commentaries/matthew/4-5.htm.

196.

8) *Ellicott's Commentary* also presents this enlightening observation. He is addressing the Apostle Paul having been "caught up" to Paradise, and then describing his "out of body experience" in 2 Corinthians 12:2: "No words can describe more accurately the phenomena of consciousness in the state of trance or ecstasy. It is dead to the outer world. **The body remains**, sometimes standing, sometimes recumbent, but, in either case, motionless. **The man may well doubt, on his return to the normal condition of his life, whether his spirit has actually passed into unknown regions in a separate and disembodied condition**, or whether the body itself has been also a sharer in its experiences of the unseen" (emphasis added). 2 Corinthians 12:2, *Ellicott's Commentary for English Readers*, Biblehub.com, https://biblehub.com/commentaries/2_corinthians/12-2.htm.

9) Likewise, the *Benson Commentary* ventures into the same arena of "quantum science" concerning Paul's supernatural "transport" experience: "It is equally possible with God…as seems to have been the case with Ezekiel in the visions mentioned Ezekiel 11:24, and Ezekiel 37:1; and with John in those recorded Revelation 17:3; Revelation 21:10; or, as the Spirit caught away Philip, (Acts 8:39) **to transport both soul and body for what time he pleases to heaven; or to transport the soul only thither for a season, and in the meantime to preserve the body fit for its re-entrance**" (emphasis added). 2 Corinthians 12:2, *Benson's Commentary*, Biblehub.com, https://biblehub.com/commentaries/2_corinthians/12-2.htm.

See Psalm 91.

197. See 1 Peter 5:8.

198. Ibid. "How did Satan get Jesus to the Temple in Jerusalem?" Also, I deal with this topic in great detail, quoting a number of renowned scholars, in my

book *Gods of the Final Kingdom* (Crane, MO: Defender Publishing, 2017).

199. Some translations of this verse render "Away from me Satan!" with an exclamation point at the end. Others do not. It is a matter of choice on the part of the translators.

In the New Testament era, when Koine Greek was used as the everyday common language, Greek was most often written with no punctuation. The words ran together, with no spacing or markup. With very few exceptions, accents, breathing marks, spaces, and other punctuation were not added until a much later time.

I prefer to think that Yeshua had no need to raise His voice to Satan at this point. Yeshua's mere words alone were enough to silence and tame the evil one. Also note the most important point: Satan *obeyed* Jesus—and it wasn't because Jesus had raised His voice.

200. Isaiah 14:13–14.

201. This narrative is based upon the accounts of Matthew 12–13 and their counterparts found in Mark 2–3 and Luke 6. Names of characters that are not specifically mentioned in Scripture are fictional names assigned by the author.

202. Malkiel is not named in the Scriptures. I have given this fictitious name for the sake of the narrative. Throughout this section, I have given names to other biblically unnamed characters as well in order to assist in the narrative having a more personal feel.

203. "Matthew 12:4," *Ellicott's Commentary for English Readers*, Biblehub. com.

"In the position in which the narrative stands in the other two Gospels, the Pharisees would appear as belonging to the company that had come down from Jerusalem to watch and accuse the new Teacher (Luke 5:17)." https://biblehub. com/commentaries/matthew/12-4.htm.

204. John 2:12.

205. See Matthew 4 and Luke 4.

206. Matthew 4.

207. "Kinneret," in Hebrew, means "a harp." The lake is so named because of its harp-like shape. It is also called "the Sea" and "Lake Galilee."

208. Matthew 4.

209. Matthew 4.

210. Isaiah 9:1–2.

211. "Matthew 12:2," *Cambridge Bible for Schools and Colleges*, Biblehub. com.

"This prohibition is a Pharisaic rule not found in the Mosaic Law. It was a principle with the Pharisees to extend the provisions of the Law and make minute regulations over and beyond what Moses commanded in order to avoid the possibility of transgression." https://biblehub.com/commentaries/matthew/12-2.htm.

212. Luke 4:16–30.

213. "Matthew 12:2," *Benson Commentary*, Biblehub.com. "It was into the house or chamber of the high-priest that he entered, situated beside the tabernacle, and called the house of God on that account. See note on 1 Samuel 21:3–6. Thus the apartment in which the High-priest Eli and his servant Samuel slept, is called the house of the Lord, 1 Samuel 3:15." https://biblehub.com/commentaries/matthew/12-2.htm.

214. With this declaration, Jesus declared that from now on, His "body"—and the "church" that would come from it—would be the true and greatest earthly "temple" of God. Within two decades of Jesus speaking these words, the Temple was destroyed. As of this date, it has not been rebuilt. Yet, Paul wrote profusely about the Church itself as being the new and "rebuilt" Temple of God in the last days. The vast majority of the scholars all the way back to the first several centuries understood that this is exactly what Jesus and Paul meant. This topic will be explored more fully in later chapters of this book.

215. Hosea 6:6.

216. Matthew 12:9, *Ellicott's Commentary for English Readers*, Biblehub.com. "He went into their synagogue—i.e., that of the Pharisees whom He had just reproved, probably, therefore, the synagogue of Capernaum. **The narratives in St. Matthew and St. Mark convey the impression that it was on the same Sabbath. St. Luke, however, as if he had made more careful inquiry, states definitely that it was on another**, and this the others do not directly contradict." https://biblehub.com/commentaries/matthew/12-9.htm.

217. *Gill's Exposition of the Entire Bible*: "Luke says, it was his **right hand**, which was so much the worse; and **means not only his hand, but the whole arm. Such a case is mentioned in the Talmud**, 'it happened to one,' that his arm was dry, or withered. Jerome says, in the Gospel which the Nazarenes and Hebionites used, this man is **said to be a plasterer**, and so might possibly come by his misfortune through his business; and being a man that got his bread by his hand labor, the case was the more affecting" (emphasis added). https://biblehub.com/commentaries/matthew/12-10.htm.

218. *Shaliach Tzibbur*—a Jewish prayer leader in the synagogue; also known as a cantor.

219. The full prayer consists of Deuteronomy 6:4; 11:13–21; Numbers 15:37–41.

220. Torah (or the Law)—is the first five books of the Old Testament, Genesis through Deuteronomy. The Nevi'im—is the biblical collection of the Prophets.

221. Concerning Jesus' challenging question to the Pharisee:
Meyer's New Testament Commentary: "There must have been no doubt as to whether such a thing was allowable, for Jesus argues ex concesso. [An argument based on a prior admission or confession of one's opponent.] The Talmud (Gemara) contains no such concession, but answers the question partly in a negative way, and partly by making casuistical stipulations."
See: https//biblehub.com/commentaries/matthew/12-11.htm.

222. Phylactery: A small leather box containing Hebrew texts, worn by Jewish men, especially the orthodox Jewish leaders, as a reminder to keep the law.

223. Herodians: "The Herodians derived their name as followers of King Herod. The Herodians were a political party that wanted to restore a Herod to the throne in Judea as well as other areas ruled by Herod the Great. They were political foes of the Pharisees who wished to restore the kingdom of David."
https://www.blueletterbible.org/faq/don_stewart/don_stewart.

224. Matthew 12:14: "But the Pharisees went out and plotted how they might kill Jesus."

225. Trees, Fruit, Vipers:
Dictionary of Scripture and Ethics: "Biblical metaphors highlight the personal and social degradation associated with vice. One image involves the tree and its fruit, which calls to mind the story in which Adam and Eve eat of the forbidden fruit in the Garden of Eden. [In the same way] Jesus warns that bad trees can be expected to bear bad fruit (Matthew 12:33)."
See Joel Green, *Dictionary of Scripture and Ethics* (Baker Academic; 11/1/11) 807. (Joel B. Green is professor of New Testament interpretation and associate dean for the Center for Advanced Theological Studies, Fuller Theological Seminary.)
MacLaren's Expositions: "'Take the bitter tree,' as I remember an old Jewish saying has it, 'take the bitter tree and plant it in Eden, and water it with the rivers there; and let the angel Gabriel be the gardener, and the tree will still bear bitter fruit.'" https://biblehub.com/commentaries/matthew/12-33.htm.
Lange's Commentary on the Holy Scriptures: Critical, Doctrinal, and Homiletical: "Poisonous plants, and a generation of vipers, were the noxious remnants of pre-Adamic times, and hence served as allegorical figures of

satanic evil. Hence the first symbol of coming salvation was, that the seed of the woman should bruise the head of the serpent.—How can ye? etc.— The physical impossibility that a generation of vipers could give forth what was salutary, served as an emblem of the moral impossibility of this moral generation of vipers speaking good things. https://www.studylight.org/commentaries/lcc/matthew-12.html.

226. Ibid.

227. Matthew 12:14. "But the Pharisees went out and plotted how they might kill Jesus." (Also see Mark 3:6. Here, the Pharisees join forces with the Herodians to kill Jesus).

228. See Matthew 12:36 and Matthew 13:1. The "house" was most likely that of Peter.

Pulpit Commentary: "Went Jesus out of the house. Where he had been when his mother came (Matthew 12:46, note), and presumably the one to which he returned in ver. 36. Possibly it was St. Peter's house at Capernaum (Matthew 8:14)." https://biblehub.com/commentaries/matthew/13-1.htm.

229. *Gill's Exposition of the Entire Bible*: "This parable fitly suited them, the Scribes and Pharisees, and the men of that generation, from whom in some measure the unclean spirit might be said to depart through the doctrine, and miracles of Christ, to go into the Gentile world; but being followed there with the preaching of the Gospel by the apostles, returns to the Jews, and fills them with more malice, blasphemy, and blindness, than ever, which issued in their utter ruin and destruction; of which this parable may be justly thought to be prophetical." https://biblehub.com/commentaries/matthew/12-45.htm.

230. See Mark 3:20–21. *MacLaren's Expositions*: "Members of His own family—sad to say, as would appear from the context, including His mother—came with a kindly design to rescue their misguided kinsman from danger, and laying hands upon Him, to carry Him off to some safe restraint in Nazareth, where He might indulge His delusions without doing any harm to Himself. https://biblehub.com/commentaries/mark/3-21.htm.

231. The word "brothers" was often used in the ancient Hebrew culture to speak of the larger family group as a whole, including uncles, cousins, and other relatives even more distant.

232. John 7:4–5: "For no one who wants to be known publicly acts in secret. Since you are doing these things, show yourself to the world. For even His own brothers did not believe in Him" (Berean Study Bible).

233. Mark 3:8: "When they heard about all [Jesus] was doing, many people

came to him from Judea, Jerusalem, Idumea, and the regions across the Jordan and around Tyre and Sidon."

234. See my previous book, *Gods of the Final Kingdom* (Crane, MO: Defender Publishing, 2019), for the biblical and scientific understanding of this certain spiritual truth.

235. See examples of first-century Pharisee garments at Bible History Online: https://www.bible-history.com/pharisees/PHARISEESDress.htm. Watch Tower Online: https://wol.jw.org/en/wol/d/r1/lp-e/1001072005.

236. Tallit—The Jewish prayer shawl, often worn to this day by the very Orthodox. Rabbi Abraham Millgram, "The Tallit: Spiritual Significance," My Jewish Learning, accessed 7/12/19, https://www.myjewishlearning.com/article/the-tallit-spiritual-significance.

237. Ephesians 6:10–13: "Finally, be strong in the Lord and in his mighty power. Put on the full armor of God, so that you can take your stand against the devil's schemes. For our struggle is not against flesh and blood, but against the rulers, against the authorities, against the powers of this dark world and against the spiritual forces of evil in the heavenly realms. Therefore put on the full armor of God, so that when the day of evil comes, you may be able to stand your ground, and after you have done everything, to stand."

238. John 9:39–41: "Jesus said, 'For judgment I have come into this world, so that the blind will see and those who see will become blind.' Some Pharisees who were with him heard him say this and asked, 'What? Are we blind too?' Jesus said, 'If you were blind, you would not be guilty of sin; but now that you claim you can see, your guilt remains.'"

239. The next narrative chapters are a fictionalized account of Jesus' journey from the region of Galilee on down toward Jericho, by way of the Jordan Valley. From there, Jesus and the disciples made their way up to Jerusalem, on the way to the cross. Based upon Matthew 22–24 and Luke 17.

240. **Baruch**. A Hebrew name for a male meaning "blessing." This is a fictional name inserted here to make the narrative more personal. Baruch was the name of Jeremiah's scribe, mentioned numerous times in that book.

241. *Hashem* is a Hebrew title used in Judaism to refer to God, and literally means "the Name."

242. Zechariah 12:10: "And I will pour out on the house of David and the inhabitants of Jerusalem a spirit of grace and supplication. They will look on me, the one they have pierced, and they will mourn for him as one mourns for an only child, and grieve bitterly for him as one grieves for a firstborn son."

Isaiah 53:5: "But he was pierced for our transgressions, he was crushed for our iniquities; the punishment that brought us peace was on him, and by his wounds we are healed."

Psalm 22:1, 16: 8 (A Psalm of David): "My God, my God, why have you forsaken me? Dogs surround me, a pack of villains encircles me; they pierce my hands and my feet. All my bones are on display; people stare and gloat over me. They divide my clothes among them and cast lots for my garment."

243. *Bengel's Gnomen*: "You ought not to look to times that are future, or places that are remote: for the kingdom of God is **within** you; **even as the King Messiah is in the midst of you: John 1:26** ["There standeth one among you whom ye know not"] (emphasis added; brackets in original).

Pulpit Commentary: "The kingdom of God **could not be said to be in the hearts of those Pharisees** to whom the Master was especially directing his words of reply here. It should be **rather understood in the midst of your ranks** [in the person of Jesus]" (emphasis added).

Matthew Poole's Commentary: "The kingdom of God is **now in the midst among you**, though you **observe it not**" (emphasis added).

All three commentary entries are found at: https://biblehub.com/commentaries/luke/17-21.htm.

244. For an example as to where in the Scriptures the Orthodox might have pinned this belief, see Malachi 3:1: "Behold, I will send my messenger, and he shall prepare the way before me: and **the Lord, whom ye seek, shall suddenly come to his temple**, even the messenger of the covenant, whom ye delight in: behold, **he shall come**, saith the LORD of hosts." (KJV)

Benson Commentary: "All the Jews, before the birth of Christ, firmly believed that the Messiah was to come into that very temple." See: https://biblehub.com/commentaries/malachi/3-1.htm.

To this very day, the Orthodox rabbis of Israel seem almost obsessed with the notion that they themselves will be the one to first "meet with" and finally "announce" to the world the arrival of Messiah.

See examples:

Jones, Ryan. "Israeli Rabbi Says He's Already Holding Meetings with Messiah," *Israel Today*, 10/15/20, https://www.israeltoday.co.il/read/israeli-rabbi-says-hes-already-holding-meetings-with-messiah.

Israel Today staff. "Top Rabbi: Messiah's Name Will Soon Be Revealed," *Israel Today*, 11/15/20, https://www.israeltoday.co.il/read/top-rabbi-messiah-name-will-soon-be-revealed.

245. Luke 19:11.

246. John 12:1.

247. He was quoting Zechariah 13:7.

248. *Meyer's New Testament Commentary*: "[This prophecy] must not be limited to the Roman Empire (Luke 2:1), but should be taken quite generally: over the whole habitable globe, a sense which is alone in keeping with Jesus' consciousness of His Messianic mission." https://biblehub.com/commentaries/matthew/24-14.htm.

Pulpit Commentary: "In all the world = in all the inhabited earth. We are not to expect more than that Christian missions shall reach the uttermost parts of the earth, and that all nations shall have the offer of salvation, before the final appearance of Christ." https://biblehub.com/commentaries/matthew/24-14.htm.

249. Matthew 21:18–22.

250. The fig tree parable as the returned Israel of 1948.

Matthew 24:32–35. For an in-depth study of Jesus' parable—a prophecy of the return of Israel in the last days—see the chapter entitled "A Certain Tree" in my book *The Summoning*, (Crane, MO: Defender Publishing, 2021).

Arno Gaebelein's Annotated Bible: "In Matthew 21:1–46, we see in *the withered fig tree* a *type of Israel's* spiritual and *national death*. That withered tree *is to be vitalized*. The fig tree *will bud again*" (emphasis added). Matthew 24. *Arno Gaebelein's Annotated Bible*, Studylight.org, https://www.studylight.org/commentaries/gab/matthew-24.html.

Also, it is a biblical fact that the fig tree is frequently used in both the Old and New Testaments to describe the nation of Israel itself, either in a physical/geographical sense or in a spiritual one.

A study of Judges 9:10–11; Jeremiah 8:13; Jeremiah 24:10; Jeremiah 29:17; Hosea 9:10; Habakkuk 3:17; Haggai 2:19; as well as the books of Matthew 21:19; Mark 11:13, 20–1; and Luke 13:6–7 bear out this biblical truth.

Jesus did not mean by "this generation" that He was speaking of the very generation in which the disciples were living.

Lange's Commentary on the Holy Scriptures: Critical, Doctrinal, and Homiletical: "This generation means the generation of those who know and discern these signs…. The continued use of (elapse or pass away) in Matthew 24:34–35, *should have saved the commentators from the blunder of imagining that the then living generation was meant*, seeing that the prophecy is by the next verse carried on to the end of all things; and that, as matter of fact, the Apostles and ancient Christians did continue to expect the Lord's coming, *after that generation* had passed away" (emphasis added). Matthew 24. *Lange's Commentary on the Holy Scriptures: Critical, Doctrinal, and Homiletical*, Studylight.org, https://www.studylight.org/commentaries/lcc/matthew-24.html. *John Trapp Complete Commentary*: "**That generation that immediately precedes the end of the world**. That **this is the sense**, appears by the antithesis, Matthew 24:36; 'But of that day and hour knoweth no man'… the generation and age wherein Christ shall come ye may know by the signs that foreshow it" (emphasis added). Matthew 24. *John Trapp Complete Commentary*, Studylight.com, https://www.studylight.org/commentaries/lcc/matthew-24.html.

Expository Notes of Dr. Thomas Constable: "The demonstrative pronoun 'this' (Gr. aute)…could refer *to the end times rather than to that generation*…. Jesus meant that *the generation of disciples that saw the future signs* would also witness His return…. The earliest signs then would correspond to the branches of the fig tree becoming tender" (emphasis added). Matthew 24. *Expository Notes of Dr. Thomas Constable*, Studylight.org, https://www.studylight.org/commentaries/lcc/matthew-24.html.

251. Stewart, Don. "Did Jesus Receive a Fair Trial?" Blue Letter Bible, https://www.blueletterbible.org/faq/don_stewart/don_stewart_250.cfm.

252. See John 10:18 and Matthew 26:57–67.

253. Isaiah 53:7.

254. John 10:18.

255. Revelation 13:8.

256. *Pulpit Commentary*: "This is **a strong affirmative asseveration**, and on Christ's lips carries with it **the full meaning of the words** used by Caiaphas, '**I am** the Messiah, the Son of the Blessed One, **God of God, of one substance with the Father**.' From this moment, beginning from now, from my Passion, my triumph and my reign are inaugurated…you shall see the events about to be consummated, the preludes of the great assize, and the coming of Messiah's kingdom. This was the plainest and most specific declaration of his real nature, power, and attributes, made with calm majesty, though he knew it was to seal his condemnation, and open the immediate way to his death." https://biblehub.com/commentaries/matthew/26-64.htm.

257. Clouds of Heaven as "clouds of witnesses"…or as redeemed "people" as opposed to *literal clouds in the sky*.
"The comparison of a multitude of persons to a cloud is common in the classic writers."

(From *Barnes' Notes*, Electronic Database Copyright © 1997, 2003, 2005, 2006 by Biblesoft, Inc. All rights reserved.)

Cambridge Bible for Schools and Colleges: "In the Greek order: together with them will be caught up in the clouds, emphasis being thrown on the precedence of the dead: 'we the living shall join their company, who are already with the Lord.' Together with implies full association." https://biblehub.com/commentaries/1_thessalonians/4-17.htm.

Gill's Exposition of the Entire Bible: "In the clouds; the same clouds perhaps in which Christ will come, will be let down to take them up; these will be the chariots, in which they will be carried up to him; and thus, as at our Lord's ascension a cloud received him, and in it he was carried up out of the sight of men." https://biblehub.com/commentaries/1_thessalonians/4-17.htm.

Ellicott's Commentary for English Readers: "In the "clouds" St. Augustine sees the emblem of the saints of the Church, which is His body, who spread as a vast fertilizing cloud over the whole world." https://biblehub.com/commentaries/ellicott/revelation/1.htm

Pulpit Commentary: "Aquinas and other writers make the clouds symbolize the saints." https://biblehub.com/commentaries/1_thessalonians/4-17.htm.

Hebrews 12:1: "Therefore, since we are surrounded by such a great cloud of witnesses, let us throw off everything that hinders and the sin that so easily entangles. And let us run with perseverance the race marked out for us."

Isaiah 60:8 (KJV): "Who are these that fly as a cloud, and as the doves to their windows?"

Expositor's Greek New Testament: "Used frequently in Homer and elsewhere, as 'nubes' in Latin and 'cloud' in English to suggest a vast multitude. 'Witnesses,' persons who by their actions have testified to the worth of faith." https://biblehub.com/commentaries/hebrews/12-1.htm.

258. Yet again, I have taken the liberty to insert into the narrative something that the Scriptures do not specifically declare, but I believe to be a very distinct biblical possibility for all of the many reasons I have previously stated regarding similar narratives.

259. As with all Roman flogs, the straps were impaled with shards of jagged bone and sharpened stones. The instrument had been designed in this fashion so as to inflict the absolute maximum damage and pain upon its victim. *Especially the pain.* The Roman practice of meting out the devastating punishment knew no limits. Only that of the cruelty of the executioner, or the physical endurance of the sufferer. But Yeshua had been spared death, the end

result that was normally brought on by the murderous blows of the straps. On this day, the unusual "mercy" was given to Him not because of pity. It was given because the Jews were demanding more…they wanted a crucifixion, the most hideous form of death. Their bloodlust now knew no boundaries when it came to this "teacher" from Nazareth.

260. The Scourge

Benson Commentary: "The priests and multitude required the governor to scourge him openly in their sight; and that he, to pacify them, consented, contrary to his inclination, hoping, as some suppose, that this previous punishment would excite the pity of the Jews and prevent Christ's crucifixion. That, however, was not the case. Nothing short of that ignominious and torturing death would satisfy them." https://biblehub.com/commentaries/matthew/27-26.htm.

261. Isaiah 50:6: "I gave **my back to the smiters**" (emphasis added).

Psalm 129:3: "The ploughers **ploughed on my back**: they made **long their furrows**" (emphasis added).

Isaiah 53:5: "By his stripes we are healed."

Matthew 20:18–19: "[And Jesus told them,] 'We are going up to Jerusalem, and the Son of Man will be delivered over to the chief priests and the teachers of the law. They will condemn him to death and **will hand him over to the Gentiles to be mocked and flogged and crucified**'" (emphasis added).

262. **Beelzebub.** Little is known about this god and his worship, and the name itself appears to be a Hebrew variation designed to denigrate the deity as the "Lord of the Flies."

See: https://www.newworldencyclopedia.org/entry/Beelzebub.

See also: Compelling Truth. "Who Was the Beelzebub/Beelzebul That the Pharisees Attributed Christ's Work To?," accessed 3/21/21, https://www.compellingtruth.org/beelzebub.html.

263. Of course there is no direct mention in the Scriptures of Satan being present at the cross. It is however depicted in this manner in some cinemagraphic portrayals, as well as various literary ones. This is because, it is practically unimaginable that in a dimension seen only by Jesus, Satan would not have been standing by in order to observe, and even manipulate, the spectacle that he thought they he had actually orchestrated. The crucifixion of Jesus was what Satan would have thought to have been his great "plan" to rid the heavens and earth of this man who might very well be the one sent from Heaven to destroy his kingdom of darkness. For this reason, I have taken the

liberty to express the possibilities of such an "appearance" by the adversary of
Heaven's throne.

264. See Isaiah 14:12–15 for Satan's declaration of this plot.

Jamieson-Fausset-Brown Bible Commentary (Revelation 20:3): "**Satan
imagined that he had overcome Christ on Golgotha**, and **that his power
was secure forever**, but the Lord in death overcame him by His ascension as
our righteous advocate cast out Satan, the accuser from heaven" (emphasis
added). Revelation 20:3, *Jamieson-Fausset-Brown Bible Commentary*,
Biblehub.com, https://biblehub.com/commentaries/revelation/20-3.htm.

1 Corinthians 2:6–8: "None of the rulers of this age understood it, for if they
had, they would not have crucified the Lord of glory."

Thayer's Greek Lexicon says of the "rulers of this age" in the 1 Corinthians
2 passage: "[The rulers of this age] The **rulers of nations**, universally, of
magistrates; especially judges, members of the Jewish Sanhedrin, **and perhaps
also, [that] one who has great influence among the Pharisees** [and those
other earthly powers]…**the devil, the prince of evil spirits**" (emphasis added).
NT: 758. Archón (rulers). *Thayer's Greek Lexicon*, Biblehub.com, https://
biblehub.com/greek/758.htm.

265. See Psalm 22, especially verse 6 and following.

266. Psalm 22:1, 7–8, 15–18.

267. After the crucifixion and resurrection (and even before), there were
believers among the Pharisees, priests, and teachers of the Law, as well as
among rabbis, leaders in the synagogues, and even Roman centurions. See:
Acts 6:7; 15:5; 18:8; John 19:38–39; Acts 10.

268. John 19:38–39: "Later, Joseph of Arimathea asked Pilate for the body
of Jesus. Now Joseph was a disciple of Jesus, but secretly, because he feared
the Jews. With Pilate's permission, he came and took the body away. He was
accompanied by Nicodemus, the man who earlier had visited Jesus at night.
Nicodemus brought a mixture of myrrh and aloes, about seventy-five pounds."

269. Mark 15:43 and Luke 23:50–56. Apparently they were not a part of the
Sanhedrin's consensus vote for Jesus' death. These men had absolutely nothing
to gain and everything to lose by publicly associating themselves with Jesus.
Indeed, unbeknownst to them they were fulfilling Jesus' earlier prophecy that
"When I am lifted up from the earth, [I] will draw all men to myself." (John
12:32) There could not have been a starker and more immediate fulfillment of
Jesus' words than the actions of these two courageous men. More than likely
these two important men, at this early point in the gospel explosion, were at

least nascent believers in Jesus as Messiah and Lord. We can only assume that after the resurrection event, three days later, they became true and outspoken believers. However, the Scriptures do not make this claim in a direct manner using their actual names. Nevertheless, we know for a biblical certainty that after the resurrection (and even before) there were believers among the Pharisees, priests, and teachers of the law, as well as among rabbis, leaders in the synagogues, and even among several Roman centurions. See Acts 6:7, 15:5, 18:8; John 19:38–39; and Acts 10.

270. Matthew 27:62–66.

271. Excerpt from the *Zondervan Handbook of Biblical Archaeology*. "Sealing the Tomb of Jesus," Olivetree.com, accessed 3/21/21, https://www.olivetree.com/blog/sealing-tomb-jesus.

"The body of the deceased was laid out on a stone bench and a heavy stone was set into the small entrance door and sealed to thwart the unwanted entrance of animals and grave robbers. **Matthew reports that a 'big' (Greek *megan*) stone was rolled against (Greek *proskulisas*) the door of Jesus' tomb.** Later, **Matthew recounts how an angel 'rolled back' (Greek *apekulisen*) this sealing stone from the door** (Matt 28:2; cf. Mark 16:3–4; Luke 24:2). … These had a carved out slotted groove to one side of the entrance of the tomb made to receive a disk-shaped stone. The family could roll the stone forward in the track to cover the entryway of the tomb or roll it back to open it, allowing for new burials. **These rolling stones weighed tons and could not have been moved by a single person**" (emphasis added).

272. Matthew 28:2–4: "There was a violent earthquake, for **an angel of the Lord** came down from heaven and, **going to the tomb, rolled back the stone and sat on it**. His appearance was like lightning, and his clothes were white as snow. **The guards were so afraid of him that they shook and became like dead men**" (emphasis added).

Mark 16:2–8: "Very early on the first day of the week, they came to the tomb when the sun had risen. They were saying to one another, '**Who will roll away the stone** for us from the entrance of the tomb?' Looking up, they saw that **the stone had been rolled away, although it was extremely large**. Entering the tomb, they saw a young man sitting at the right, wearing a white robe; and they were amazed. And he said to them, 'Do not be amazed; you are looking for Jesus the Nazarene, who has been crucified. **He has risen; He is not here**; behold, here is the place where they laid Him'" (emphasis added)

273. See my book *Gods and Thrones* (Defender Publishing, 2017) 255–264,

for a detailed biblical examination of why Jesus was on the earth for exactly forty days after His resurrection.

274. See the entirety of Revelation 12, especially the last four verses.

275. 1 Corinthians 3:16–17 and 6:19; 2 Corinthians 6:16; Ephesians 2:21. Also see my book *Masquerade* (Crane, MO: Defender, 2020) for a detailed study of this truth and what it means to our own prophetic times.

276. For a full unveiling of this fact, see *Gods of Ground Zero* (Crane, MO: Defender, 2018).

277. Luke 16:19–31.

278. *Ellicott's Commentary for English Readers*: "In the figurative language in which the current Jewish belief clothed its thoughts of the unseen world, the Garden of Eden took its place side by side with 'Abraham's bosom,' as a synonym for the eternal blessedness of the righteous."
See: Luke 23:43, *Ellicott's Commentary for English Readers*, Biblehub.com, http://biblehub.com/commentaries/luke/23-43.htm.
Vincent's Word Studies: "In the Septuagint, Genesis 2:8, of the Garden of Eden. In the Jewish theology, the department of Hades where the blessed souls await the resurrection; and therefore equivalent to Abraham's bosom (Luke 16:22, Luke 16:23)."
See: Luke 23:43, *Vincent's Word Studies*, Biblehub.com, http://biblehub.com/commentaries/luke/23-43.htm.
Pulpit Commentary: "The place whither the blest Lazarus went is termed 'Abraham's bosom.' This term was used by the Jews indifferently, with 'the garden of Eden.'"
See: Luke 16:22, Pulpit Commentary, Biblehub.com, http://biblehub.com/commentaries/luke/16-22.htm.

279. Hebrews 9:27.

280. Psalm 22; Isaiah 53; Zechariah 12; John 10:18.

281. John 1:1–12; Colossians 1:15–20; Hebrews 1:1–3.

282. 1 Corinthians 15:6.

283. John 21:6.

284. Ephesians 4:8–10; 1 Corinthians 2:7–8; Colossians 2:15.

285. Hebrews 9–10.

286. Hebrews 1:3–4.

287. Hebrews 4:14–16.

288. Hebrews 8–10.

289. 2 Corinthians 12:2–4

290. The *Benson Commentary* gives elucidation upon Paul's visit to the Third Heaven: The Third Heaven is the seat of God, and of the holy angels, into which Christ ascended after his resurrection.
See: 2 Corinthians 12:2, *Benson Commentary*, Biblehub.com, http://biblehub.com/commentaries/2_corinthians/12-2.htm.
Barnes' Notes on the Bible offers a similar assessment: "It was this upper heaven, the dwelling-place of God, to which Paul was taken, and whose wonders he was permitted to behold—this region where God dwelt; where Christ was seated at the right hand of the Father."
See: 2 Corinthians 12:2, *Barnes' Notes on the Bible*, Biblehub.com, http://biblehub.com/commentaries/2_corinthians/12-2.htm.
291. 2 Corinthians 5:8.
292. Revelation 4:1.
293. The *Expositor's Greek New Testament* affirms: "[John] is **no longer in the island** but up at the gates of heaven.… A heavenly voice comes after he has seen…**a door set open** (ready, opened) in **the vault of the mysterious upper world** which formed God's house" (emphasis added).
See: Revelation 4:1, *Expositor's Greek Testament*, Biblehub.com, http://biblehub.com/commentaries/revelation/4-1.htm.
294. **Melito of Sardis** (Died c. 180) was the bishop of Sardis near Smyrna in western Anatolia, and a great authority in early Christianity. Melito held a foremost place in terms of bishops in Asia due to his personal influence and his literary works, most of which have been lost. What has been recovered, however, has provided great insight into Christianity during the second century. See: https://en.wikipedia.org/wiki/Melito_of_Sardis.
Melito of Sardis: "From that hour the holy mother of God remained especially in the care of John, as long as she had her habitation in this life. And when the apostles had divided the world by lot for preaching, **she settled in the house of his parents near Mount Olivet.**…Then Mary, undressing herself, put on better garments. And, taking the palm which she had received from the hands of the angel, **she went out to the mount of Olivet**, and began to pray" (emphasis added).http://www.rosarychurch.net/answers/ap082000.html.
295. Dr. Tabor, James. "Locating Golgotha," Jamestabor.org, 2/6/16, https://jamestabor.com/locating-golgotha.
296. Wikipedia. "John the Apostle (Other References to John)," accessed 3/15/21, https://en.wikipedia.org/wiki/John_the_Apostle#cite_note-zahn-57.
297. Ibid.

298. Ibid.
299. "John, the Apostle," Biblestudytools.org., https://www.biblestudytools.
com/encyclopedias/isbe/john-the-apostle.html.
300. Tertullian (/tər'tʌliən/; Latin: *Quintus Septimius Florens Tertullianus*; c.
AD 155–c. 240) was a prolific early Christian author from Carthage in the
Roman province of Africa.
See: Barnes, Timothy (1971). *Tertullian: A Literary and Historical Study*
(Reprinted with appendix of revisions 1985 ed.). Oxford. p. 58.
301. Wikipedia. "John the Apostle (Extra-Biblical Traditions),"
accessed 3/15/21, https://en.wikipedia.org/wiki/John_the_
Apostle#:~:text=According%20to%20Tertullian%20(in%20The,and%20
suffering%20nothing%20from%20it.&text=It%20is%20traditionally%20
believed%20that,the%20apostles%20and%20survived%20them.
302. While certain literary liberties were necessary to employ, it was my
intention to present a highly accurate historical and biblical description of
what may have taken place at John's trial and his subsequent Patmos vision.
I heavily researched these matters before putting pen to paper. The historical
facts and statements made within this narrative were gleaned from numerous
and reliable sources of the study of Roman and biblical history during the time
of John.
Admittedly, there are some scholars who reject the authorship of Revelation as
being that of John the Apostle, the same one who was one of the Twelve, and
wrote the Gospel of John and the three letters of 1 John, 2 John, and 3 John; I
hold with the majority of scholars on this view. John the Apostle was the same
one who ascended to Heaven's throne and was shown the events in what we
now know as the book of Revelation.
See: Wagner, Richard; Helyer, Larry R. *The Book of Revelation for Dummies*.
(John Wiley & Sons, 2011) 26. "Other contemporary scholars have vigorously
defended the traditional view of apostolic authorship."
303. Pliny: "Early tradition says that John was banished to Patmos by the
Roman authorities. This tradition is credible because banishment was a
common punishment used during the Imperial period for a number of offenses.
Among such offenses were the practices of magic and astrology. Prophecy
was viewed by the Romans as belonging to the same category, whether Pagan,
Jewish, or Christian. Prophecy with political implications, like that expressed
by John in the book of Revelation, would have been perceived as a threat to
Roman political power and order. Three of the islands in the Sporades were

places where political offenders were banished. (Pliny Natural History 4.69–70; Tacitus Annals 4.30)"

See: Adela Collins. (1985). "Patmos" [In] Paul J. Achtemeier [Ed.]. *Harper's Bible Dictionary*. (San Francisco, CA: Harper & Row, 1985) 755.

304. "According to church tradition, the book *Travels of St. John in Patmos* was written by Prochorus (Acts 6:5), secretary to John."

See: https://biblearchaeology.org/research/new-testament-era/3099-the-king-and-i-exiled-to-patmos-part-2.

"Tradition says that John received the vision of Revelation from heaven verbatim and dictated it to his assistant Prochorus, who wrote it down [therefore, he was on the island with John]. Prochorus is mentioned in Acts 6:5 as one of the seven original deacons. Many other traditions on the island are associated with miraculous works of John and are found in the Acts of John by Prochorus, a pseudipigraphal work that was written in the 5th century and attributed to John's scribe (cf. Acts 6:5)."

See: https://www.bibleplaces.com/patmos.

305. "First-century Patmos, with its natural protective harbor, was a strategic island on the sea lane from Ephesus to Rome. A large administrative center, outlying villages, a hippodrome (for horse racing), and at least three pagan temples made Patmos hardly an isolated and desolate place... The proconsul of Asia Minor wanted John out of Ephesus so he sent him to Patmos, also within his jurisdiction.

Franz, Gordon. "The King and I (Part 2): Exiled to Patmos," (Journal: *Bible and Spade* (Second Run), Volume: BSPADE 012:4 (Fall 1999) Galaxie.com, https://www.galaxie.com/article/bspade012-4-004?highlight=1%20samuel.

306. As for the significance of the symbolism of the seven churches of Revelation, in the context of overall eschatology, I hold with the following position. It is a course held by numerous reputable scholars, from the first century to modern times:

Ellicott's Commentary for English Readers: "Seven churches. It has been maintained by some (notably by Vitringa) that the epistles to the seven churches are prophetic, and set forth the condition of the Church in the successive epochs of its after-history. The growth of error, the development of schisms, the gloom of superstition, the darkness of medieval times, the dawn of the Reformation, the convulsions of after-revolutions, have been discovered in these brief and forcible epistles. Such a view needs no formal refutation. The anxiety for circumstantial and limited fulfilments of prophecy has been at the root of such attempts.

"When we read God's words **as wider than our thoughts** we stand in no need of such desperate efforts at symmetrical interpretations; **for the truth then is seen to be that words addressed to one age have their fitness for all; and that these epistles are the heritage of the Church in every epoch. In this sense the churches are types and representatives of the whole family of God.** Every community may find its likeness here. **This much is admitted by the best commentators of all schools.**

> The seven churches, says St. Chrysostom, are all churches by reason of the seven Spirits. By the seven, writes St. Augustine, **is signified the perfection of the Church universal, and by writing to the seven he shows the fullness of one.**
> And the words, **He that hath an ear,** let him hear what the Spirit saith unto the churches, are, as has been well observed, **a direct intimation that some universal application of their teaching was intended** (emphasis added). https://biblehub.com/commentaries/revelation/1-4.htm.

Pulpit Commentary: "To the seven Churches. **From the earliest times** it has been pointed out that the number seven here is not exact, but **symbolical; it does exclude other Churches, but symbolizes all.** Thus the **Muratorian Fragment**: 'John in the Apocalypse, though he wrote to the seven Churches, **yet speaks to all.**' Augustine: **'By the seven is signified the perfection of the universal Church,** and by writing to seven he shows **the fullness of the one'"** (emphasis added). https://biblehub.com/commentaries/revelation/1-4.htm.
307. Paraphrased from the NIV translation of Revelation 5:2–11.
308. Ibid.
309. Wikipedia. "Nerva", Wikipedia.com, https://en.wikipedia.org/wiki/Nerva.
310. "The Shiloh Excavations" (first published in the Fall 1999
issue of *Bible and Spade*), https://biblearchaeology.org/research/new-testament-era/3099-the-king-and-i-exiled-to-patmos-part-2.
"The length of John's exile on Patmos differs from tradition to tradition. Most likely it lasted only 18 months, and upon Domitian's death John was free to return to Ephesus. Dio Cassius wrote, [Emperor] Nerva also released all who were on trial for maiestas (high treason) and restored the exile (Cary 1995:361). Eusebius adds: the sentences of Domitian were annulled, and the Roman Senate decreed the return of those who had been unjustly banished and the restoration of their property...the Apostle John, after his banishment to the island, took up his abode at Ephesus (Lake 1980:241)."

311. *International Standard Bible Encyclopedia.* "John, the Apostle," Bible Study Tools. Accessed 3/15/21, https://www.biblestudytools.com/encyclopedias/isbe/john-the-apostle.html.

312. Procopius of Caesarea, *On Buildings.* General Index, trans. H. B. Dewing and Glanville Downey, vol. 7, Loeb Classical Library 343 (Cambridge, MA: Harvard University Press, 1940) 319.

313. Thomas Alfred Gurney. *The Church of the First Three Centuries* (Sagwan Press, 2018) 40.

314. John. *Fox's Book of Martyrs*, Bible Study Tools, https://www.biblestudytools.com/history/foxs-book-of-martyrs/john.html.

315. 2 Corinthians 12:2–3.

316. The region of the seven churches to which the book of Revelation was addressed was a province of the Roman Empire called Asia Minor. Today it is called Turkey. Turkey is where the headwaters of the Euphrates River form. It is also the place where Noah's ark came to rest, and from where the world began again. It later became the central starting point of the Ottoman Empire, an Islamic controlled empire that was spread over three continents and two million square miles. Today Turkey is a vital part of the OIC (Organization of Islamic Cooperation). The OIC was founded in 1969, consisting of fifty-seven member states, with a collective population of over 1.8 billion.
A number of biblical scholars and prophecy watchers consider modern Turkey to be a central player in end-time prophecy culmination. They see it as a resurrecting Ottoman Empire and a direct threat to the prophetically returned nation of Israel, as well as the overall stability of the Middle East. In 2018, after the return of Jerusalem as the official and legal capital of Israel, the OIC immediately breathed out threats of war against Israel. Turkey's capitol, Ankara, is exactly due north of Jerusalem. The prophecies of Ezekiel 38 speak of the end-times coalition attack against Jerusalem originating from the "north." This is the area to whom the book of Revelation was originally addressed.
Edroos, Faisal. "Erdogan Calls on Muslim Countries to Unite and Confront Israel," *Al Jazeera*, May 18, 2018, https://www.aljazeera.com/news/2018/05/erdogan-calls-muslim-countries-unite-confront-israel-180518185258629.html.
YeniSafak: "What if a Muslim army was established against Israel? If the member states of the OIC unite militarily, they will form the world's largest and most comprehensive army." https://www.yenisafak.com/en/world/what-if-a-muslim-army-was-established-against-israel-2890448, 12/12/17. (Yeni Şafak

is a conservative Turkish daily newspaper known for its hardline support of President Recep Tayyip Erdoğan and the AK Parti).

317. Revelation 21:10.

318. Revelation 6:12–17.

319. Revelation 20.

320. Ezekiel 28:18–19; Isaiah 14:12–17; Revelation 20:10–15.

321. For example, Daniel 10:8–12.

322. Nelson, Ryan. "How Did the Apostles Die? What We Actually Know." Overviewbible.com, 12/17/19, https://overviewbible.com/how-did-the-apostles-die.

323. John 21:22.

324. Siegfried, Tom. "A Two-Time Universe? Physicist Explores How Second Dimension of Time Could Unify Physics Laws," Phys.org, May, 2007, https://phys.org/news/2007-05-two-time-universe-physicist-explores-dimension.html. Also note that both Psalm 90:4 and 2 Peter 3:8 emphatically declare: A day with the Lord is like a thousand years, and a thousand years are like a day. *Meyer's New Testament Commentary* on 2 Peter 3:8: "**The words lay stress on the difference between the divine and the human reckoning of time.** It does not designate God as being absolutely without limitations of time, for it is not the nature of God that is here in question, but **God's reckoning of time which He created** along with the world, and the words only bring out that **it is different from that of man.**"

325. Job 38:7.

326. **Eden Restored.** These exact words are used as a subsection title for Revelation 22 in the NIV version. There are several other versions of the Bible that also directly identify as Revelation 22 as the final restitution of all things as being the original Garden of Eden restored to saved humanity's existence, like it was in the beginning.

327. John 14:6.

328. In this sense, I am speaking of a generation as being close to one hundred years in total length, in that after one hundred years, practically everyone who was born at the beginning of that time period is now gone, and a brand new "generation" is on the earth. However, so many of the prophetic last-days' events of the Bible have not only happened in the last hundred years, but the majority have happened only in the last several decades.

329. Petersen, Jonathan. "Extremely Low Percentage of Americans Hold Biblical Worldview: An Interview with George Barna," Bible Gateway,

5/28/20, https://www.biblegateway.com/blog/2020/05/extremely-low-percentage-of-americans-hold-biblical-worldview-an-interview-with-george-barna.

330. 1 Timothy 4:1: "The Spirit clearly says that in later times some will abandon the faith and follow deceiving spirits and things taught by demons."
2 Timothy 3:1–5: "But mark this: **There will be terrible times in the last days**. People will be lovers of themselves, lovers of money, boastful, proud, abusive, disobedient to their parents, ungrateful, unholy, without love, unforgiving, slanderous, without self-control, brutal, not lovers of the good, treacherous, rash, conceited, **lovers of pleasure rather than lovers of God— having a form of godliness but denying its power. Have nothing to do with such people**."
2 Thessalonians 2:1–3: "Now, brethren, **concerning the coming of our Lord Jesus Christ** and our gathering together to Him, we ask you, not to be soon shaken in mind or troubled, either by spirit or by word or by letter, as if from us, as though the day of Christ had come. **Let no one deceive you** by any means; for that Day will not come **unless the falling away comes first**."
331. Rachel E. Menzies, and Ross G. Menzies. "Death Anxiety in the Time of COVID-19: Theoretical Explanations and Clinical Implications," 6/11/20, https://www.ncbi.nlm.nih.gov/pmc/articles/PMC7308596/#:~:text=Fear%20 of%20death%20has%20recently,target%20the%20dread%20of%20death.
"The recent COVID-19 pandemic has triggered a surge in anxiety across the globe. Much of the public's behavioural and emotional response to the virus can be understood through the framework of terror management theory, which proposes that fear of death drives much of human behaviour. In the context of the current pandemic, death anxiety, a recently proposed transdiagnostic construct, appears especially relevant. Fear of death has recently been shown to predict not only anxiety related to COVID-19, but also to play a causal role in various mental health conditions. Given this, it is argued that treatment programmes in mental health may need to broaden their focus to directly target the dread of death."
332. Matthew 7:24–27 and 1 Corinthians 10:4.
333. If a string of falling dominoes could be arranged to circumnavigate the globe at the equator, it would take approximately an entire year, give or take, for the last domino to topple. Dominoes fall in a line at the rate of equatorial circumference of the earth (40,075,000 miles) divided by rate of travel of the domino wave at 4/3 m/s—meters per second. That calculation would result

in 347 days, 21 hours, or just under a year. This process would take about 1.8 billion dominoes to complete.

See: https://science.madison.k12.wi.us/files/Dominoes.pdf

Prophecy works in a similar manner. From first to last, there are probably billions of parts to its final fulfilment. Year after year, with each solar orbit of the globe, the dominoes fall until they reach the point of their decreed completion. Yet, those dominoes fall in the midst of every one of humanity's generations. This is why some generations miss the prophetic nature of their day, entirely. This is a truly astonishing fact to consider.

334. Matthew 24:14.

335. *Meyer's New Testament Commentary*: "[This prophecy] must not be limited to the Roman Empire (Luke 2:1), but should be taken quite generally: over the whole habitable globe, a sense which is alone in keeping with Jesus' consciousness of His Messianic mission." https://biblehub.com/commentaries/matthew/24-14.htm.

Pulpit Commentary: "In all the world = in all the inhabited earth. We are not to expect more than that Christian missions shall reach the uttermost parts of the earth, and that all nations shall have the offer of salvation, before the final appearance of Christ." https://biblehub.com/commentaries/matthew/24-14.htm.

336. See my books, *The Rabbi, The Secret Message, and the Coming of Messiah* as well as *Masquerade*. Both books are published by Defender Publishing, and both lay out the prophecies of Israel's return and how they match every single element of the *Israel* that now stands in the Middle East. They both dismantle every cogent argument that has been leveled against the current day nation of Israel as not being "the real Israel."

337. For examples, see Ezekiel 38—the entire chapter, with special note of verses 16 and 33. See also 39:7, 21–29.

338. See my book, *The Summoning: Preparing for the Coming Days of Noah*, (Crane, MO: Defender Publishing, 2021). Several chapters are dedicated to the scholarly evidence for this prophetic phenomenon and historical fact. Especially see the chapters on the fig tree prophecy. This book also has several chapters pertaining to the "objections" of our day, claiming that the current Israel is not the "real Israel." The Word of God answers every single objection to that false notion.

339. Israel is a top international leader in science and technology.

See: Michelle Jamrisko, Lee J Miller, and Wei Lu. "These Are the World's Most Innovative Countries." Bloomberg.com. 1/21/-

19, https://www.bloomberg.com/news/articles/2019-01-22/
germany-nearly-catches-korea-as-innovation-champ-u-s-rebounds.
See: Skop, Yarden. "Israel's Scientific Fall from
Grace." *Haaretz*, 9/2/13, https://www.haaretz.com/.
premium-israeli-scientific-studies-declining-1.5328140.
340. See Zechariah 12:1–9 and Luke 21:20–33.
341. See my book, *Masquerade: Preparing for the Greatest Con Job in History*
(Crane, MO: Defender Publishing, 2020), for lists of these unprecedented
technologies. All of them were revealed in God's Word over two thousand
years ago.
342. I expand upon and document this fact in my international bestseller, *The
Summoning: Preparing for the Coming Days of Noah* (Crane, MO: Defender
Publishing, 2021).
343. Menzies, Rachel E. and Ross, G. "Death Anxiety in the Time of COVID-
19: Theoretical Explanations and Clinical Implications," National Institutes
of Health (NIH), 6/11/20, https://www.ncbi.nlm.nih.gov/pmc/articles/
PMC7308596/.
344. "European estimates (i.e. estimates in countries with similar age profiles
and healthcare quality as the UK) put the fatality rate at somewhere between
0.5% and 1%, meaning the 'survival rate' could be somewhere between 99%
and 99.5%, but not as high as 99.8%.... However, we can be almost certain that
the survival rate here is not as high as 99.8%, because of the sheer number of
people who have already died."
See: Fullfact.org. "Covid-19 Survival Rate is Less than 99.8%," 2/19/21,
accessed 5/22/21, https://fullfact.org/online/covid-19-survival-rate-less-998/.
345. Sherwood, Harriet. "Christian Persecution Rises as People
Refused Aid in COVID Crisis"—Report: "Advocacy Group Open
Doors Says Hardline Regimes across World Exploit Pandemic,"
1/12/21. https://www.theguardian.com/world/2021/jan/13/
christian-persecution-rises-as-people-refused-aid-in-covid-crisis-report.
346. Acts 17:26. *Gill's Exposition of the Entire Bible*, Biblehub.com, https://
biblehub.com/commentaries/acts/17-26.htm.
Gill's explores the wondrous depths of the revelation about which Paul was
speaking in Acts 17:26: "All [human beings] belong to one family.... And
[Yahweh] hath determined the times before appointed; how long the world he
has made shall continue; and the several distinct periods, ages, and generations,
in which such and such men should live, such and such nations should exist,
and such monarchies should be in being...."

"Which are so bounded, and kept so distinct in their revolutions, as not to interfere with, and encroach upon each other; and *likewise the several years, months, and days of every man's life*...and how long they shall continue there the age or *distinct period of time, in which every man was*, *or is to come* into the world, *is fixed and determined by God*;

"Nor can, nor does anyone come into the world sooner or later than that time; and also the particular country, city, town, and spot of ground where he shall dwell; and the term of time how long he shall dwell there, and then remove to another place, or be removed by death....

"**To which may be added**, the times of the law and Gospel; the time of Christ's birth and death...the time of antichrist's reign and ruin, Revelation 13:5, and of Christ's personal coming, and the day of judgment, 1 Timothy 6:15, and of his reign on earth for a thousand years, Revelation 20:4. **All these are appointed times, and determined by the Creator and Governor of the world.**

347. Ibid.
348. 1 Corinthians 2:6–10: "We do, however, speak a message of wisdom among the mature, but not the wisdom of this age or of the rulers of this age, who are coming to nothing. No, we declare God's wisdom, **a mystery that has been hidden** and that God destined for our glory **before time began**. None of the rulers of this age understood it, for if they had, they would not have crucified the Lord of glory. However, as it is written: "What no eye has seen, what no ear has heard, and what no human mind has conceived"—the **things God has prepared for those who love him**—these are the things God **has revealed to us** by his Spirit" (emphasis added).
Matthew 28:20: "[Jesus said to them] And surely I am with you always, to the very end of the age."